English-Medium Instruction and Pronunciation

SECOND LANGUAGE ACQUISITION
Series Editors: **Professor David Singleton**, *University of Pannonia, Hungary* and Fellow Emeritus, *Trinity College, Dublin, Ireland* and **Associate Professor Simone E. Pfenninger**, *University of Salzburg, Austria*

This series brings together titles dealing with a variety of aspects of language acquisition and processing in situations where a language or languages other than the native language is involved. Second language is thus interpreted in its broadest possible sense. The volumes included in the series all offer in their different ways, on the one hand, exposition and discussion of empirical findings and, on the other, some degree of theoretical reflection. In this latter connection, no particular theoretical stance is privileged in the series; nor is any relevant perspective – sociolinguistic, psycholinguistic, neurolinguistic, etc. – deemed out of place. The intended readership of the series includes final-year undergraduates working on second language acquisition projects, postgraduate students involved in second language acquisition research, and researchers, teachers and policymakers in general whose interests include a second language acquisition component.

All books in this series are externally peer-reviewed.

Full details of all the books in this series and of all our other publications can be found on http://www.multilingual-matters.com, or by writing to Multilingual Matters, St Nicholas House, 31-34 High Street, Bristol, BS1 2AW, UK.

SECOND LANGUAGE ACQUISITION: 131

English-Medium Instruction and Pronunciation

Exposure and Skills Development

Karin Richter

MULTILINGUAL MATTERS
Bristol • Blue Ridge Summit

For Alexander and Jakob

DOI https://doi.org/10.21832/RICHTE2456
Library of Congress Cataloging in Publication Data
A catalog record for this book is available from the Library of Congress.
Names: Richter, Karin - author.
Title: English-Medium Instruction and Pronunciation: Exposure and Skills Development/Karin Richter.
Description: Blue Ridge Summit, PA: Multilingual Matters, [2019] | Series: Second Language Acquisition: 131 | Includes bibliographical references and index.
Identifiers: LCCN 2018038738| ISBN 9781788922456 (hbk : alk. paper) | ISBN 9781788922470 (epub) | ISBN 9781788922487 (kindle)
Subjects: LCSH: English language—Pronunciation—Study and teaching. | English language—Study and teaching—Foreign speakers.
Classification: LCC PE1137 .R495 2019 | DDC 428.1/3071—dc23 LC record available at https://lccn.loc.gov/2018038738

British Library Cataloguing in Publication Data
A catalogue entry for this book is available from the British Library.

ISBN-13: 978-1-78892-245-6 (hbk)
ISBN-13: 978-1-80041-331-3 (pbk)

Multilingual Matters
UK: St Nicholas House, 31-34 High Street, Bristol BS1 2AW, UK.
USA: NBN, Blue Ridge Summit, PA, USA.

Website: www.multilingual-matters.com
Twitter: Multi_Ling_Mat
Facebook: https://www.facebook.com/multilingualmatters
Blog: www.channelviewpublications.wordpress.com

Copyright © 2019 Karin Richter.

All rights reserved. No part of this work may be reproduced in any form or by any means without permission in writing from the publisher.

The policy of Multilingual Matters/Channel View Publications is to use papers that are natural, renewable and recyclable products, made from wood grown in sustainable forests. In the manufacturing process of our books, and to further support our policy, preference is given to printers that have FSC and PEFC Chain of Custody certification. The FSC and/or PEFC logos will appear on those books where full certification has been granted to the printer concerned.

Typeset by Deanta Global Publishing Services Limited.

The complexities of second language acquisition, like those of first language acquisition, represent puzzles that scientists will continue to work on for a long time

Lightbown and Spada (2006: 50)

Source: Clker

Contents

Tables and Figures	xi
Abbreviations and Acronyms	xiii
Acknowledgements	xv

1	Introduction		1
	1.1	Research Background	2
	1.2	Aims and Objectives	5
		1.2.1 Specification 1: Universities of Applied Sciences	7
		1.2.2 Specification 2: L1 teachers of English	8
		1.2.3 Specification 3: The Austrian accent in English	10
	1.3	Outline of the Book	12
2	English-Medium Instruction in European Higher Education		14
	2.1	Defining EMI: A Jungle of Acronyms	14
	2.2	The Internationalisation of Higher Education in Europe	18
	2.3	The Spread of EMI in European Higher Education	21
	2.4	The Case of the UAS Vienna	24
	2.5	Conclusion	26
3	Language Learning in the English-Medium Classroom		27
	3.1	EMI and Language Learning Theories	27
		3.1.1 The Input Hypothesis	28
		3.1.2 The Output and the Interaction Hypothesis	32
		3.1.3 Sociocultural Theory	36
		3.1.4 Conclusion	40
	3.2	Language Learning and L2 Phonology	41
		3.2.1 Defining foreign accent	42
		3.2.2 Explaining the development of foreign accent	42
		3.2.3 Conclusion	59
	3.3	Language Learning Outcomes in the English-Medium Classroom	60

		3.3.1	Linguistic gains	60
		3.3.2	Phonological gains	62
	3.4	Insights from the UAS Vienna		65
		3.4.1	Measuring the development of the degree of foreign accent of the learners: The challenges	65
		3.4.2	Analysing the development of the degree of foreign accent: The results	73
		3.4.3	Conclusion	81
4	Factors Influencing L2 Pronunciation Mastery			82
	4.1	Individual Variables		84
		4.1.1	Attitude and identity	84
		4.1.2	Motivation	86
		4.1.3	Anxiety	92
		4.1.4	Formal pronunciation instruction	96
		4.1.5	Gender differences	99
		4.1.6	Musicality	102
		4.1.7	Exposure to the target language	104
		4.1.8	Conclusion	109
	4.2	Insights from the UAS Vienna		109
		4.2.1	Individual factors	111
		4.2.2	The factor 'exposure to the target language'	122
		4.2.3	Conclusion	129
5	The Development of the Austrian Accent in the EMI Classroom			130
	5.1	Contrasting German and English Phonology		131
		5.1.1	Segmentals in RP	131
		5.1.2	Segmentals in GA	134
		5.1.3	Suprasegmentals	134
		5.1.4	The specifics of Austrian German	136
	5.2	Empirical Research into the Austrian Accent in English		137
		5.2.1	Wieden and Nemser (1991)	137
		5.2.2	Grosser	141
		5.2.3	Hrubes	142
		5.2.4	Mende	142
		5.2.5	Tatzl	143
		5.2.6	Conclusion	143
	5.3	Insights from the UAS Vienna		144
		5.3.1	Segmental features of the Austrian accent in English	145
		5.3.2	Suprasegmental features of the Austrian accent in English	152

6	Conclusion	154
	6.1 Synopsis	154
	6.2 Limitations of the Study	156
	6.3 Suggestions for Further Research	158
	6.4 Implications	159

Appendix	162
References	175
Index	199

Tables and Figures

Tables

Table 2.1	Overview of English-taught courses in HE (adapted from Unterberger, 2014: 46–47)	16
Table 3.1	Descriptive statistics of the scores obtained for the two groups at T1 and T2 by skill (cf. Richter, 2017)	74
Table 3.2	Descriptive statistics of the development of FA	76
Table 3.3	Differences between groups according to tasks (Richter, 2017)	77
Table 4.1	Factors influencing pronunciation development (Adapted from Richter, 2017)	111
Table 4.2	Anna: FA rating scores	113
Table 4.3	Anna: Attitude	114
Table 4.4	Anna: Motivation	114
Table 4.5	Anna: Self-assessment of English language skills at T1	115
Table 4.6	Anna: Self-assessment of English language skills at T1 as reported in Q2	115
Table 4.7	Anna: Self-assessment of English language skills at T2	115
Table 4.8	Scores obtained for informant #49	118
Table 4.9	David: Attitude	118
Table 4.10	David: Motivation	119
Table 4.11	David: Self-assessment of English language skills at T1	119
Table 4.12	David: Self-assessment of English language skills at T1 as reported in Q2	120
Table 4.13	David: Self-assessment of English language skills at T2	120
Table 4.14	ID variables according to groups	122
Table 4.15	Media exposure: Focus group	126
Table 4.16	Media exposure: Control group	127
Table 4.17	Exposure according to groups	128
Table 5.1	Difficult English vowels for German learners	132
Table 5.2	Difficult English consonants for German learners	133
Table 5.3	Segmental features likely to cause problems for ALs of English	144

Table 5.4 Suprasegmental features likely to cause problems for
          ALs of English   145
Table 5.5 Overview of informants for phonetic analysis   146
Table 5.6 Segmental features of the Austrian accent in
           English at T1   147
Table 5.7 Segmental features of the Austrian accent in
           English at T2   148
Table 5.8 Frequencies of vowels and diphthongs ranked   149
Table 5.9 Frequencies of consonants ranked   150
Table 5.10 Development of GA phonemes   150
Table 5.11 How would you rate your own accent?   151
Table 5.12 Suprasegmental features of Austrian-accented
           English at T1 and T2   152

Figures

Figure 3.1 Screenshot of the rating bar   68
Figure 3.2 Screenshot of instructions for using the rating bar   69
Figure 3.3 Distribution of average difference   78
Figure 3.4 FA – self-report   79
Figure 3.5 FA – rating   80
Figure 4.1 Exchange semester abroad   123
Figure 4.2 Exchange semester – comparison   124
Figure 4.3 Internship abroad   125
Figure 4.4 Internship abroad – comparison   125
Figure 5.1 Learning stages (adapted from Wieden & Nemser,
            1991: 230)   139

Abbreviations and Acronyms

AH	At home
AL	Austrian learner
AOL	Age of onset of learning
BA	Bachelor's
CAH	Contrastive analysis hypothesis
CBL	Content-based learning
CLIL	Content and Language Integrated Learning
CPH	Critical Period Hypothesis
DST	Dynamic Systems Theory
EAP	English for academic purposes
EE	Extramural English
EHEA	European higher education area
ELF	English as a lingua franca
ELT	English language teaching
EMI	English-medium instruction
EMP	English-medium programmes
ESP	English for specific purposes
FA	Foreign accent
GA	General American
HE	Higher education
HEI	Higher education institutions
HR	Human resources
ICLHE	Integrating Content and Language in Higher Education
ID	Individual differences
L1	First language
L2	Second language
LAD	Language acquisition devise
LOR	Length of residence
MA	Master's
NLM	Native language magnet
NS	Native speaker
NNS	Non-native speaker
NEST	Native English-speaking teacher

NNEST	Non-native English-speaking teacher
PAM	Perceptual Assimilation Model
Q	Questionnaire
RQ	Research question
RP	Received pronunciation
SA	Stay abroad
SCT	Sociocultural theory
SLA	Second language acquisition
SLM	Speech Learning Model
T	Time
UAS	University of Applied Sciences
ZPD	Zone of proximal development

Acknowledgements

During the process of researching and writing, I received great inspiration and immensely helpful guidance from many people who have travelled this journey with me.

First and foremost, I would like to express my sincere gratitude to my dear colleagues from the University of Vienna, most notably Ute Smit and Christiane Dalton-Puffer, Gunther Kaltenböck, Susanne Reiterer, Pia Resnik, Angelika Rieder-Bünemann and Gabrielle Smith-Dluha. As for the University of Applied Sciences Vienna, my heartfelt appreciation goes to Cath Prewett-Schrempf and Murray Barkema.

I am also deeply grateful to all the raters and all the students who agreed to participate in this project. Without you, this would not have been possible!

Special thanks are also due to the anonymous reviewer for the constructive feedback and Laura Longworth, Sarah Williams and the whole team at Multilingual Matters for their encouraging guidance.

Last but not least, I would also like to thank my family and friends for their endless patience and emotional support!

1 Introduction

In the 21st century, the internationalisation of education and the wish to compete globally have triggered a dramatic increase in the number of English-medium instruction (EMI) programmes offered by universities all over the world. This current call for EMI is deeply rooted in the common belief that language learning takes place incidentally when content is delivered in a foreign language, which – in most cases – is English. And indeed, empirical research in the field of language learning and teaching at secondary school level seems to support the assumption that a second language (L2) is learned most effectively when it is used to convey content that is both interesting and relevant to the learner. However, to date, tertiary education has seen little empirical evidence that this is in fact the case. In particular, the field of pronunciation learning appears to be characterised by a dearth of scientific data to confirm or reject the view that EMI can have a positive effect on learners. As a consequence, many EMI students, teachers and programme designers alike wonder if and to what extent learners benefit from this approach. Can EMI keep its promises?

In exploring a very specific EMI context at an Austrian university of applied sciences (UAS), I seek to shed light on these highly pertinent questions by zooming in on the development of the pronunciation skills of a group of Austrian business students. As such, this book provides fresh insights into both the method as well as the language learning process in a very specific tertiary EMI classroom. Tracking and analysing the phonological development of 55 adult students over the entire duration of their bachelor (BA) studies, this research contributes to our understanding of pronunciation learning in a promising teaching approach that currently seems to be sweeping the world at remarkable speed. Thus, I hope that the findings presented in this book combine to create a single piece that fits into the much larger jigsaw puzzle of L2 acquisition.

A crucial point that needs to be addressed before I introduce the research background concerns considerations of anonymity. Of course, all the subjects involved in this study were promised anonymity and confidentiality. In order to avoid the cues that would reveal the participants' identities, I have decided to discuss all the details that are relevant to the present project but to keep the study-external identifiers (such as the precise name of the UAS, the names of the participants and the exact time of data collection) as vague as possible. For this reason, the university is only referred to as the UAS or the UAS Vienna and I have used pseudonyms for those students whose individual variables are discussed in more detail (i.e. Anna and David). Instead of exact dates, reference to time is given by the respective semester. The data were collected in the second decade of the 21st century.

This chapter sets out to describe the background to the research and my own motivation for the study. Following this, the purpose of the study will be detailed and finally, the structure of the book will be outlined.

1.1 Research Background

The study presented in this book is based on a research project that developed out of my personal interest and involvement in two core areas of educational linguistics, namely the current spread of EMI at European universities and the development of L2 pronunciation skills in adult learners.

In the early years of the 21st century, the UAS Vienna where I was teaching English for specific purposes (ESP) courses at the time, pioneered a bilingual BA programme (German/English) as a novelty in the field of business education. This move was triggered not only by the demand of the management to pay tribute to a number of policies introduced by the European Union that aimed to promote multilingualism, but also by their wish to attract excellent local as well as international students. In those early days of EMI, institutional decision-makers hoped that the use of English to teach content courses would enhance both content and language competence, at the same time assuming that learners benefit from 'two for the price of one' (Bonnet, 2012: 66). This idea was further reinforced by the fact that the truly global society of the 21st century makes it more important than ever for business people working with colleagues, customers and partners across borders to understand each other and thus to form effective and productive working relationships. Business students today are expected to speak more than one language in order to occupy a favourable position in society and also in the labour market where the 'war for talent' (Michaels *et al.*, 2001) is still said to be raging around the globe. In other words, the UAS Vienna identified a clear need for graduates who have the necessary skills to operate in culturally and linguistically diverse environments and to this end, content courses in English were introduced.

Given its status as a global language or lingua franca, it comes as little surprise that English is often the first choice when selecting an L2 to be learned and taught. As a result, more and more educational institutions, particularly in Europe, are now jumping on the bandwagon by promoting the learning of English to pay tribute to the changing demands of the labour market. This also ties in neatly with the fact that English is already the most dominant language of research in higher education (Ament & Perez-Vidal, 2015). Of course, caution has to be exercised as the concentration on one single language, i.e. English, may be counterproductive in that one language is monopolised, thereby severely restricting the use of others. As a consequence, some researchers already see English as the 'killer language' (Price, 1984: 170) fostering linguistic hegemony, whereas for others it is still the key that may open the door to the global marketplace.

Regardless of the perspective from which these undeniable changes are viewed, internationalisation has become a hard and fast reality. To keep up with this trend, schools and universities all over the world have introduced strategies for internationalising their programmes. In Europe, raising international awareness, teaching intercultural communication skills and increasing foreign language competence are often considered central educational concerns. A closer look at regional practices to achieve these goals brings forth a multifaceted and multilayered picture of how educational institutions cope with the changing demands of professional bodies and the labour market. This becomes evident in the plethora of measures and strategies employed, such as cross-border study programmes and research projects, the recruitment of international staff and students and the introduction of internationalised curricula (Knight, 2008: ix–xi). Recognising the need to respond swiftly and effectively to those global changes, the UAS Vienna took up this challenge and responded by offering one of three parallel classes of the Entrepreneurship BA programme as a bilingual degree programme with the intention of attracting both international students as well as international lecturers.

One of the major challenges with the UAS' introduction of this programme was the task of hiring suitable teachers for their English-taught courses. As it turned out, first and foremost, native speakers (NSs) of English were recruited. In hindsight, this circumstance can only be seen as a mere coincidence rather than a strategic choice. As far as I know, there was never an official commitment from the institute head or the chief executive officer, neither oral nor in writing, stating that preference should be given to first language (L1) speakers of English. At a time when recruitment was not centralised in the form of an established human resources (HR) department, the programme designers relied heavily on existing or newly formed partnerships with other universities mainly located in the United States and Australia to recruit guest lecturers for their EMI courses. Slowly, a network of L1 teachers of English unfolded and gave the UAS the chance to set itself apart from other business degree programmes by offering a bilingual (German/English) programme that was, to a large extent, taught by NSs of English.

Having witnessed the various stages of this newly created programme since its very beginning and having the knowledge gained in the course of this research project about the various implications of the successful implementation of EMI, one can now only marvel at the courage it took the programme designers to implement an approach for which they did not even have a name let alone a conceptual framework. Initially, it was strongly believed that this transition would not entail any major changes to the curriculum. The only challenge appeared to be to find lecturers who could teach the subject matter – as described in detail in the German curriculum – in English. In fact, the international office of the UAS, which was installed around the same time and established partnerships with universities abroad, proved to be of great help in this respect. Although the programme has undergone a number of significant changes since then, it still enjoys a unique position in the Viennese educational landscape today with high numbers of applicants and overwhelmingly satisfied graduates confirming its popularity.

What particularly spurred my interest in this context, however, was how these L1 teachers' accents impacted the students' pronunciation skills. As I also taught pronunciation classes to future English teachers in an entirely different setting at the University of Vienna, I felt inclined to investigate the implications of implicit pronunciation learning in the bilingual programme. In particular, the questions I asked myself were: Do the students simply pick up the teacher's accent without consciously engaging in the matter or is it irrelevant what accent (foreign or native) the teacher speaks as adult learners at this level have already passed the critical period for acquiring a native-like accent?

As English-medium teaching is still a fairly new field, it comes as little surprise that studies into the linguistic gains of tertiary EMI students are still scarce (cf. Macaro et al., 2018). Yet, it has to be noted that in the last few years, growing scholarly interest in the teaching of content courses in English can be observed as demonstrated by the number of specialised conferences (e.g. the Integrating Content and Language in Higher Education [ICLHE] conference in Maastricht in 2013, in Brussels in 2015 and in Copenhagen in 2017) as well as several publications (e.g. Dearden, 2014; Fortanet-Gomez & Räisänen, 2008; Smit, 2010; Valcke & Wilkinson, 2017; Wilkinson & Walsh, 2015). Nonetheless, there are numerous related fields which require further investigation to shed light on the significance of EMI in the university context, with the development of the students' language competence being one of them.

Owing to a general dearth of reliable data on the language outcomes of EMI in tertiary education, it seems useful to draw on results reported in the secondary school context always bearing in mind that the learners differ considerably regarding a number of factors, most notably age and motivation. Generally speaking, a considerable body of research carried out in primary and secondary schools suggests that Content and Language Integrated Learning (CLIL) is an effective way of increasing students' foreign language competence (e.g. Dalton-Puffer & Nikula, 2006; Lasagabaster, 2008; Nikula *et al.*, 2013; Ruiz de Zarobe, 2008). Indeed, one of the most frequently given arguments in favour of CLIL is the assumption that increased exposure to and active use of an L2 in the classroom enhances language proficiency. However, certain aspects of language competence are said to develop more than others. According to Dalton-Puffer (2008), receptive skills, vocabulary, morphology, creativity, risk-taking, fluency, quantity and affective outcomes benefit most, whereas syntax, writing, informal language, pragmatics and pronunciation appear to remain unaffected. In fact, pronunciation seems to be the least affected of the speaking dimensions (Dalton-Puffer, 2011). So far, there has been little empirical evidence to support this claim.

By and large, research seems to suggest that the main reasons why English-medium teaching has so little impact on students' pronunciation skills are related to three central issues: firstly, the quantity of input (only a few courses are taught in English); secondly, the quality of input (teachers are often L2 speakers of English); and lastly, a clear lack of long-term observation. This is precisely where my research project comes into play since it provides the ideal context and setting to answer questions that have not been addressed in empirical studies so far.

1.2 Aims and Objectives

The main objective of the present study is to investigate a specific EMI setting at an Austrian UAS with regard to the development of the students' pronunciation skills. In order to find out if and how the EMI students' pronunciation changed over a longer period of time, two cohorts were tracked over a period of roughly three years (the entire duration of their BA studies); namely, a group of students in the bilingual (English/German) programme (focus group) and a group of students in the German programme (control group). The curriculum was the same for both groups but the EMI group had up to 50% of their content courses taught in English mostly by L1 speakers of the language.

Owing to the fact that there is generally very little to no language teaching in EMI courses, it must be assumed that what the learners learn or do not learn relates – to a large extent – to the conditions of language use that are given during content teaching. In other words, the quality of classroom discourse is crucial when investigating learning outcomes. Thus, the question arises as to whether and to what extent increased exposure to the target language in English-medium classrooms can lead to incidental learning of L2 pronunciation. To address a gap in the existing research, this research project set out to explore how pronunciation skills develop when learners are exposed to increased NS input in the EMI classroom.

Broadly speaking, the study is situated in the context of foreign language acquisition and aims to contribute to the international literature and theory building concerning the effects of English-medium teaching on learners' language competence. As Macaro *et al.* (2018) in their state-of-the art article on EMI in higher education note, there is a clear need for research employing objective tests rather than relying on self-reports of the learners. In addition, they point out that the studies conducted to date generally lack control or comparison. The present study is in fact the first of its kind to take account of both: an objective measurement of the long-term linguistic gains of an EMI group and the comparison of the results with a control group. Hence, it will be interesting to see how the findings of linguistic research on language learning in an EMI context tie in with the data obtained in this study. The interpretation of the final results is meant to contribute to and extend long-standing scientific debates on whether or not EMI promotes language learning.

More specifically, this study is meant to promote further investigations into the development of foreign-accented speech in adult learners. It is hoped that approaching this issue from a longitudinal perspective can expand the discussion of whether or to what extent the Critical Period Hypothesis (CPH) may hold true for adult learners' foreign accent. A number of authors (e.g. Long, 1990) have suggested that there are in fact several critical periods for the various linguistic abilities. Accordingly, the first ability that appears to be lost would be the one required to develop a native-like pronunciation of an L2. However, so far no study has succeeded in providing convincing evidence for the claim that L2 speech will automatically be free of any traces of the learner's L1 if learned before the end of the critical period and that it will definitely be foreign-accented if learned after puberty. In tertiary education, the CPH has far-reaching implications impinging on the linguistic gains to be obtained not only in the foreign language classroom but also during exchange semesters or internships abroad.

For the present study, this means that if the CPH indeed holds water, it does not matter what accent the lecturer speaks or how much English the learners are exposed to (both inside and outside school) because the window for acquisition for tertiary-level students has already been closed and they are not likely to benefit in this respect. Hence, the context of the UAS Vienna seems ideal to bolster our understanding of age effects in L2 learning by providing insight into the pronunciation learning process of adult learners over a period of almost three years.

From an applied linguistic point of view, it is hoped that the research findings will sensitise designers of EMI programmes to the impact of the language competence of their teaching staff on the students' language skills within the field of foreign language acquisition. For instance, in many secondary schools in Austria, school heads themselves can decide if a teacher can teach his/her subject in a foreign language. The same is also true for most private tertiary educational institutions, such as the UAS, where staff selection is often based on grounds other than language competence. In fact, most EMI teachers at university level are non-native speakers (NNSs) of the target language and do not have a professional background in language pedagogy either (cf. Hellekjær & Westergaard, 2003: 73; Tatzl, 2011: 256). As Wilkinson and Walsh (2015: 11) note, 'it is understandable that content teachers are rather surprised when presented with the theory and methodology behind teaching a course in English'. For the university management, this may also play a role when addressing quality assurance questions. In their study on students' attitudes to lecturers' English at the University of Copenhagen, Jensen *et al.* (2011), for example, found that the students' perception of the teacher's general lecturing competence was greatly influenced by their perception of his/her English language skills and vice versa. This means that those lecturers whose English language skills are perceived as problematic risk also being downgraded in terms of their general lecturing competence. Hence, it may be difficult to determine whether comprehension problems reported by the students can be attributed to the lecturer's language competence or his/her general lecturing competence.

Before discussing the reasons for the rise of EMI in European higher education, three decisive specifications relevant for the present study are outlined, namely the type of educational institution (i.e. the UAS), the concept of the L1 teacher and finally the Austrian accent in English. These are of crucial importance for the interpretation of the research findings.

1.2.1 Specification 1: Universities of Applied Sciences

The first specification refers to the type of tertiary education focused on in this project, which is, as already indicated above, a UAS.

In Austria, as in many other European countries, the tertiary sector essentially comprises two main types of higher education institutions: universities and UAS. The term 'Fachhochschule' or its commonly used abbreviation 'FH' (which was later translated as UAS) was originally coined in Germany as a type of tertiary education specialising in professional fields such as engineering, business or health. In Austria, the first UAS degree programmes started in the winter semester 1994/1995 and since then this sector has been expanding rapidly (www.fachhochschulen.at).

The practice-oriented focus of UAS is often reflected in their curricula, which include obligatory career-based practical training or internships. In many cases, the students are also required to undertake projects involving real companies with the idea that the knowledge gained can be beneficial for both the students and the world of business. Additionally, the lecturers usually work full-time in the area of their specialisation. For them, teaching tends to be a side job, which implies that they bring their practical experience directly into the classroom. This also means that for many UAS, pedagogical training is a desirable yet not mandatory requirement for lecturers.

In stark contrast to regular universities, UAS guarantee that their learners can finish their studies within the minimum period (i.e. BA degree: six semesters; master's degree: two, three or four semesters). In order to gain a degree within this carefully planned time frame, studying at a UAS requires a tight organisational structure resulting in students having a fixed timetable each semester and groups staying together for the entire duration of their studies. At a UAS, not only the course length but also the number of places available is predetermined. On the one hand, this results in university management often taking great pride in providing small groups of learners with an interactive and more individual learning and teaching environment. On the other hand, UAS also tend to have fairly rigid admission procedures in order to select the best and most suitable students. These might involve IQ tests, personal interviews, presentations, subject-specific competence tests, the evaluation of social skills or even assessment-centre procedures lasting several days.

From the point of view of the student, studying at an Austrian UAS typically involves challenging admission schemes, working in small groups on practice-oriented topics, more interaction in the classroom, clear time frames and structures, a high percentage of lecturers coming from the private sector, an obligatory internship, an optional or obligatory semester abroad and being able to complete the study programme within the minimum study period.

From the point of view of the teacher and researcher, UAS are generally organised in a school-like manner with fixed groups, making it easier to keep track of the students' progress than at an Austrian state university where students have considerably more freedom in choosing what courses to take and when, and where dropout rates are frequently much higher.

1.2.2 Specification 2: L1 teachers of English

The second specification relates to the fact that in this study the majority of the lecturers teaching in English are NSs of the language, which has to be seen as a striking contrast to most European EMI programmes that are taught predominately by L2 speakers of English (e.g. Hellekjær & Westergaard, 2003: 73).

The rise of EMI programmes across Europe has increased the need for many programme designers to recruit suitable teachers who are ideally proficient in both the content and the language. Interestingly, the majority of EMI teachers seem to be discipline-area specialists, yet NNSs of English (e.g. Dalton-Puffer, 2008; Smit & Dafouz, 2012). It comes as little surprise that many EMI lecturers appear to be selected on the basis of their theoretical or practical knowledge of the content rather than their English language competence in general or their accent in particular.

In recent years, the very sensitive issue of a lecturer's language proficiency has attracted the attention of a number of applied linguists and EMI programme designers alike. Surveys conducted in countries such as Sweden (Bolton & Kuteeva, 2012), Norway and Germany (Hellekjær, 2010) and Austria (Tatzl, 2011) have brought to the fore a growing concern about the lack of sufficient English language competence of some lecturers. In the same vein, various language-related problems were reported by a group of non-native English lecturers in Klaassen and Graaff's (2001) study, which mainly addressed problems related to oral language production, including pronunciation, accent, fluency and intonation. Similarly, Ball and Lindsay (2013) found that EMI lecturers encountered major problems in pronunciation in the course of teaching content classes.

Recently, Valcke and Pavon (2015: 324) have pointed out that while a number of Spanish university teachers can follow lectures at international conferences and both read and write academic papers, they still find it challenging to teach in English. In their study, which was carried out collaboratively at the universities of Cordoba and Brussels, they investigated the relationship between teacher pronunciation and student comprehension. Their results show that providing pronunciation training to non-native EMI teachers can significantly improve comprehensibility and is also highly appreciated by the students.

As a consequence of this growing concern among all stakeholders, universities are now reconsidering language policies for quality assurance. In a number of European countries, universities have started to develop language certification schemes and assessment tools for their EMI teaching staff. Accordingly, countries like Spain (Ball & Lindsay, 2013), the Netherlands (Klaassen & Bos, 2010) and Denmark (Dimova & Kling, 2015) have pioneered introducing language policies including target levels (Klaassen & Bos, 2010) and installing courses to support the teaching staff (Valcke & Pavon, 2015). However, as Dimova and Kling (2015) note, this assessment process itself does not necessarily influence lecturers' motivation to improve their English skills. Despite the fact that they receive feedback on their strengths and weaknesses, they rarely seem to take measures to enhance their English language competence (Dimova & Kling, 2015: 71).

Interestingly, Dimova and Kling (2015: 71) also observe that lecturers with strong accents were viewed as less competent by their students. This notion of credibility, or image, is consistent with a general finding in the literature on the social psychology of language. Studies have demonstrated that listeners tend to judge speakers negatively based merely on variation in accent (e.g. McKenzie, 2008). Similarly, the same mechanisms can be expected to exert an influence on how teachers are perceived in the classroom, not only linguistically but also academically and pedagogically.

In the present study, the majority of the EMI teachers are L1 speakers of English. Obviously, language learning is a creative, cognitive as well as social process that does not only depend on the teacher, much less on the teacher's accent. Without doubt, contextually significant variables have to be considered too. It goes without saying that NSs are not automatically assumed to be better teachers. Neither can it be taken for granted that an L1 accent is easier for learners to understand than a foreign accent they are perhaps accustomed to. In other words, L1 pronunciation and grammar, two value-ridden concepts that are highly disputed, do not automatically make a successful English language teacher.

It also needs to be mentioned that in this study the pronunciation skills of the teaching staff are neither tested nor evaluated. The mere fact that these teachers perceive themselves as L1 speakers of English is taken as sufficient proof of their English language proficiency and the lack of a foreign accent in their pronunciation.

1.2.3 Specification 3: The Austrian accent in English

The third specification of the study is related to the development of Austrian learners' foreign accent. The issue of foreign accent as such, one of the most salient traces of foreign language acquisition, has been highly debated in the literature since the advent of the Audio-Lingual Method, which set NS fluency as a goal for language learners. As Munro *et al.* (2006a) note, there is now a growing awareness among L2 researchers, teachers and teacher trainers of the crucial role of pronunciation in communication.

In this study, the decision to focus on foreign accent in general and the Austrian accent in particular, has largely been motivated by the insights I have gained in teaching speaking skills to Austrian students at a number of different tertiary-level institutions for more than a decade. Through this experience, the investigation and implementation of effective learning methods to enhance pronunciation skills has become one of my major concerns.

At the University of Vienna, where I teach courses in practical phonetics, all students majoring in English and American studies have to take compulsory classes to improve their pronunciation. It is believed that pronunciation needs to be an inherent part of language teaching at tertiary level as good pronunciation skills are an indispensable qualification for future language experts (Dalton-Puffer *et al.*, 1997: 115) and of particular importance for future language teachers. One part of this pronunciation module within their study programme is a class called 'Practical Phonetics and Oral Communication Skills 1', which elaborates on the main aspects of English pronunciation and reinforces the students' theoretical and practical knowledge of phonetics. For this course, the students either choose American or British English as a model depending on what they can identify with most. The final examination is oral and consists of reading a text, a short presentation on a topic of their choice and a casual conversation between examiners and students. For the oral exam, two examiners are present and both need to agree on the final grade. For me, one of the specifically interesting aspects of teaching this class is related to the questions: Who improves to what extent and why? Why would a student who has lived in London for a year or even longer retain such an undeniable and clearly noticeable Austrian accent? And why would a student who has never set foot in an English-speaking country be easily mistaken for an NS? As a teacher, of course, it is crucial to know how to foster the learning process. In other words, a pronunciation teacher needs to know what to focus on when teaching segmental and suprasegmental aspects of a particular language variety. Which features of English pose special difficulties and when does learning take place? How do the characteristics of Austrian English vary in the course of acquisition? These are precisely the questions I aimed to explore in the course of my research.

Clearly, this book touches upon two very sensitive and highly disputed issues in relation to teaching and learning in the foreign language classroom; namely, the notion of the NS norm and the role of foreign-accented speech in communication. Therefore, it is of paramount importance to me to clarify upfront what this book cannot and does not want to be in order to disqualify false assumptions and inferences that might be created here.

As far as norms are concerned, the highly controversial dichotomy involving the two concepts 'native speaker' versus 'non-native speaker' has triggered a wide-ranging discussion on the implications stemming from internationalisation and the diversification of English as a lingua franca. As a consequence, probing questions about ownership (Widdowson, 1994), standards or norms (Ellis, 1997) and models (Kirkpatrick, 2006) have found their way into the English as a foreign language (EFL) classroom. A key concern that has been hotly debated in this context pertains to the question: should learners aim at NS norms of English when in fact English is increasingly used in NNS contexts? Apart from the notion that an NS accent does not seem to be an attainable target for many language learners, it has also been argued that NS norms do not reflect linguistic realities where NNS developments in English often do not adhere to NS norms (Walker, 2010: 5).

Firstly, for this project a case study employing a mixed-method approach was deemed most suitable to tackle the questions that I was interested in. As this design allows for an in-depth exploration of the given EMI setting, it is of course meant to be descriptive in nature and certainly not prescriptive. In no way has it been my intention to raise my voice in favour of native English-speaking teachers (NESTs) setting the norm. Far from that, my intention has been to put the students' language competence to the test. It is therefore the learners who are in the limelight and not the teachers.

Secondly, I am not suggesting that language learners need to aim at NS pronunciation. By attempting to describe a certain phenomenon in a real-life setting, I looked at the development of the learners' foreign-accented speech and not at their ultimate attainment. Hence, it was not my aim to identify those learners whose pronunciation most closely resembled that of an L1 speaker of English. If I had intended to measure overall achievement and to identify the highest performers, the design and methodology of the study would have been different.

Lastly, I was also interested in eliciting typical features of the Austrian learners' foreign accent in English. In its design, this study is not an investigation of the implications of this particular accent such as perception by interlocutors, comprehensibility or intelligibility. In other words, I was looking at the form of foreign accent and not the function. A number of empirical studies, however, have done exactly that. For example, in Bent and Bradlow's (2003) listening comprehension experiment, NS and NNS participants were confronted with text passages read aloud by NS and NNS of English. Interestingly, the results reveal that NS understand other NS better than NNS. Yet, NNS also understand other NNS equally well as NS provided that they share the same L1 (Bent & Bradlow, 2003: 1607). To date, there is no sound empirical basis for the default assumption that native speech is by nature more intelligible than non-native speech.

1.3 Outline of the Book

Overall, each main chapter of this book is structured in a similar way by moving from the broader macro perspective of a certain aspect of educational linguistics to the micro cosmos of a very specific EMI setting and the insights I gained in the course of my research project.

Having established the research background and the aims of this book in this chapter, Chapter 2 aims to describe the rise of EMI in European higher education. First, it is essential to define what I understand by EMI because this acronym is only one among many to denote similar concepts. Then, powerful political changes within the realm of the European Union are discussed, which are claimed to have prompted the internationalisation of higher education institutions, a development that is largely responsible for the rise of EMI teaching. Starting with the broader European perspective, this chapter then zooms in on the situation in

Austria and the UAS in Vienna. Crucial background information about this particular educational institution is provided which sets the scene for the analysis of the data obtained in the described study.

Chapter 3 endeavours to answer the question of how languages are learned in the English-medium classroom. Here, a number of language learning theories and their purported benefits for learners are critically viewed and the controversies surrounding these models and frameworks are addressed. This chapter then turns to language learning and L2 phonology in general and the development of foreign accent in particular. The theoretical underpinnings of the notion of foreign accent are given and related to the participants in the present project. Among these theories, the CPH is of central concern. Next, an overview of empirical studies into the language learning outcomes in the English-medium classroom is given. These theoretical considerations are then further elucidated and brought together in the context of the data derived from the participants of this study at the UAS Vienna.

Drawing on the latest research in the field, Chapter 4 goes beyond the EMI classroom and considers other individual learner variables that may be influential in the language learning process. In this chapter, a comprehensive overview of the most recent and most influential studies into individual learner differences (i.e. attitude and identity, motivation, language learning anxiety, etc.) is given. The core part of this chapter is devoted to a discussion of the results obtained in the present study and the question how these findings tie in with previous studies.

Chapter 5 centres on the specifics of the Austrian accent in English and its development in the EMI classroom. By contrasting (Austrian) German and English phonology, typical problem areas for Austrian learners of English are first identified on the basis of the existing literature and then explored further by means of a detailed analysis of a few selected participants. This chapter closes with practical implications for the EFL classroom.

Finally, the conclusion (Chapter 6) summarises the main findings of the study reported in the book and the ways in which this study can contribute to the discussion about the effects of EMI on students' language learning outcomes.

2 English-Medium Instruction in European Higher Education

This chapter has two main objectives. First, the term 'English-medium instruction' (EMI) will be defined more closely and secondly, EMI will be contextualised in the field of European tertiary education in the 21st century. To begin with, a myriad of acronyms that have been used to denote the different types of English-taught courses are compared and contrasted. In an attempt to disentangle a web of intersecting, conflicting and sometimes overlapping terms, I seek to establish a common understanding of these terms which is necessary to facilitate a profound and comprehensive discussion of these concepts. Then, some of the most recent political and economic changes that have greatly shaped the European higher education (HE) scene will be discussed. Most notably, the growing pressure on academic institutions stemming from the reconsideration of the economic role or marketisation of HE will be outlined, as this is often claimed to have triggered the rise of EMI. Next, an overview of current themes and findings related to research into the spread of EMI programmes in Europe will be provided. The focus will be on the situation in Austria.

2.1 Defining EMI: A Jungle of Acronyms

The scientific discourse on the use of English in HE has given rise to the creation of several terms and concepts to describe practices and approaches, very often synonymously and thus highly ambiguous for the inexperienced reader (cf. Ament & Perez Vidal, 2015; Gustafsson & Jacobs, 2013; Unterberger, 2014). Hence, acronyms such as EMI, Content and Language Integrated Learning (CLIL), Integrating Content and Language in Higher Education (ICLHE), content-based learning (CBL), English for specific purposes (ESP), English for academic purposes (EAP), English as a lingua franca (ELF) and many more have greatly shaped the educational landscape and left their mark in many foreign language classrooms. It has been argued that this lack of consensus as to what term is appropriate for what context and the many varied understandings should be seen as a reflection of the wide range of contexts in which

English-medium practice and research have evolved (e.g. Gustafsson & Jacobs, 2013: v). Even if the abundance of acronyms is used to illustrate the richness and diversity of the different settings and contexts involved, it can at the same time be utterly confusing and far from ideal for a novice in the field to be confronted with all these different labels. Therefore, this chapter aims to elaborate on the most relevant concepts and the corresponding terminology. In addition, I will clarify which label I consider the most appropriate for the context of the present study.

As has already been indicated in Chapter 1, the use of English to teach content courses (such as geography or biology) is becoming increasingly popular in many European educational institutions. In fact, the extent to which this phenomenon seems to have reached in primary and secondary schools in Europe has already been described as 'exponentially exploding' (Smit, 2003: 3), the pace of which 'has surprised even the most ardent advocates' (Maljers et al., 2007: 7). At this educational level, the acronym CLIL (Dalton-Puffer & Smit, 2007: 7) has become the most popular label to be used. Indeed, it is this dual focus which CLIL teachers and researchers alike believe to be beneficial to learning (Mehisto et al., 2008: 30). That is, in the teaching and learning process, there is a focus not only on content, and not only on language. Each is interwoven, even if the emphasis is greater on one or the other at a given time (Coyle et al., 2010: 1).

However, the tertiary sector is different from its secondary counterpart in many respects (cf. Smit & Dafouz, 2012) and the findings obtained from research into secondary CLIL cannot be directly transferred to the university context, as Unterberger and Wilhelmer (2011: 94–95) point out: 'Higher education is a completely different setting, especially regarding the role that the language of instruction occupies and the way language learning objectives are set'. In this respect, the most crucial difference between primary and secondary schools on the one hand and tertiary educational institutions on the other hand can be seen in the fact that English at university predominantly takes on a 'vehicular function' (Järvinen, 2008: 78). In other words, English is regarded as the language of instruction, the tool with which content matters are communicated 'rather than a subject in itself' (Järvinen, 2008: 78). Clearly, the '[w]idely advertised dual focus' (Dalton-Puffer, 2011: 183) of CLIL is only rarely realised in tertiary education. Instead, in English-taught degree programmes at the tertiary level the focus is mainly on the acquisition of subject knowledge with the language relegated to the sides. Unterberger and Wilhelmer (2011) have found that in tertiary education, EMI courses tend to have implicit language learning aims but explicitly formulated content learning objectives. This lack of explicitly defined language learning aims does not, however, mean that these universities do not seek to enhance their students' English language competence but that they 'simply perceive it as an implicit aim because it is assumed that English skills will be honed incidentally and, at this educational stage, are often considered to be sufficient' (Unterberger & Wilhelmer, 2011: 95). Therefore, it comes as little surprise that the labels CLIL or ICLHE – its counterpart for tertiary education – are only rarely appropriate for university settings. According to Smit and Dafouz (2012: 4), 'the specific conceptual take' of the individual researcher seems to determine whether English-medium education is viewed through an ICL or EMI lens.

More recently, Unterberger (2014) has provided an updated paradigm that seeks to capture the diverse realities of English-medium education at the tertiary level. Inspired by Greere and Räisänen's (2008: 6–8) CLIL continuum, she argues that English-medium teaching in HE can be divided into five distinct categories, namely Pre-sessional ESP/EAP, Embedded ESP/EAP, Adjunct ESP, EMI and ICLHE, as Table 2.1 shows.

As can be seen in Table 2.1, the types of courses are largely defined by three parameters; namely, programme design, learning objectives and teaching staff. Unterberger argues that the main difference between ICLHE and EMI lies in their focus. Whereas ICLHE propagates the highly acclaimed dual focus language and content (with explicit aims in both and teaching staff from both domains cooperating), EMI merely uses the language to convey content knowledge (language learning aims are implicit and the teachers are subject experts rather than language experts). In this respect, Wilkinson (2011: 115) points out that programme developers and teachers alike expect incidental language

Table 2.1 Overview of English-taught courses in HE

Type of class	Programme design	Learning objectives	Teaching staff
Pre-sessional ESP/EAP	Voluntary or obligatory course before the start of an EMI programme	To introduce students to diciplne-specific language and genres	Language specialists
Embedded ESP/EAP	ESP/EAP course included in the EMI programme	To develop discipline-specific and general academic skills	Language specialists
Adjunct ESP	Tailor-made ESP class for a specific content course	To aid students' understanding of language and genres for a specific course	Language specialists
EMI	English used as medium of instruction for a specific content course or for a full programme	To acquire and master content and knowledge (mostly implicit language learning aims)	Subject specialists
ICLHE	English used as medium of instruction for a specific content course or for a full programme	To acquire and master content and knowledge and language	Subject and language specialists

Source: Adapted from Unterberger (2014: 46–47).

improvement to take place based on the assumption that the increased exposure to the foreign language leads to increased language competence.

A decisive feature of the ICLHE concept is the formulation of explicit language learning aims in the curriculum. Essentially, an ICLHE course aims at enhancing both the learners' content knowledge as well as their foreign language skills. Subsequently, any university pursuing this approach needs to involve language experts not only when it comes to designing the curriculum but also in the teaching of the content courses. As Gustafsson and Jacobs (2013) point out, integrating both content and language essentially means

> [...] dovetailing the structure and sequence of subjects and curricula; joint lessons, team-teaching and shared classroom materials; the design and marking of joint assessment tasks; collaborative partnerships between language and content lecturers; as well as collaboration across disciplines and contexts. (Gustafsson & Jacobs, 2013: iv)

This shows that implementing a full ICLHE programme would present an enormous challenge for most institutions of higher education. Considerable effort and commitment of everyone involved would be indispensable prerequisites as well as the necessary financial means to cover the extra costs for teaching staff and organisational matters. As these fairly far-reaching conditions are hardly ever met at European universities, the most appropriate term for many programmes of this type appears to be EMI (with English being the medium but not necessarily the target) rather than ICLHE.

In a nutshell, the distinguishing factor that defines these acronyms lies in the focus, i.e. the lens through which a course is viewed. Whereas in **ESP** or **EAP** courses the acquisition of discipline-specific language is of central concern, in EMI the language element is relegated to the sides by taking on a vehicular role through which the mastering of content knowledge is facilitated. A dual focus on both language and content is then realised in the form of **ICLHE**. The successful implementation of such a course, however, calls for the collaborative effort of both language and content specialists in programme design, teaching and assessment. For universities, this essential prerequisite often represents a laborious and costly endeavour that many programme designers find an enormous, if not impossible, challenge (Unterberger, 2014: 52).

In this book, I will draw on the definitions detailed above. Therefore, the bilingual programme at the University of Applied Sciences (UAS) Vienna can be considered EMI by nature as the focus is clearly on the learners acquiring content knowledge through the medium of English. In this particular case, no explicit language learning goals are formulated in the curriculum; the teachers are all subject specialists and the university management assumes that the students improve their English language skills implicitly, which is generally considered to be sufficient at this stage.

2.2 The Internationalisation of Higher Education in Europe

In the last decade, powerful changes have affected all levels of the European educational landscape, leaving their imprint on an environment that used to be characterised by great disparity. This gradual reorganisation process has been triggered by a series of political and strategic reforms to make educational practices more transparent, more uniform and also more effective.

Above all, it was the Bologna Declaration of 1999 (European Ministers of Education, 1999) and its aim to create a common European Higher Education Area (EHEA) which has fundamentally transformed the face of European HE, thereby paving the way for new ideas that serve the needs of a changing society. Against the backdrop of regional requirements, a number of strategies have been introduced to modify and unify basic HE structures and to advance quality assurance systems in order to promote cross-border student and staff mobility (Eurodyce Report, 2015).

As far as HE in Austria is concerned, the aftermath of the Bologna Declaration precipitated a number of fundamental and far-reaching changes. Austrian universities were faced with the adoption of the three-cycle system (bachelor [BA]/master/doctoral) and the development of a European Credit Transfer and Accumulation System (ECTS). This switch not only found supporters but also met with harsh criticism from influential people, mostly from the fields of law, medicine and teacher education. For instance, the president of the Austrian Bar Association argued that the Bologna Process was inapplicable to the education of jurists, claiming that the BA diploma was insufficient and a master's programme unnecessarily long. This, he added, would only lead to additional costs for Austrian universities that had long been suffering from financial problems (cf. Maier, 2010). Also, the curriculum of medicine seemed to be difficult to convert into a two-cycle system. In fact, the very last degree programme in Austria to adopt the BA–master system was teacher education when the go-ahead was finally given in October 2014 (Figl, 2013).

In their attempt to establish a coherent and cohesive HEA, European universities have generated new opportunities for the increased mobility of students and faculty, encouraging cooperation among institutions. However, this has also meant that universities entered into a European-wide competition with critical voices lamenting this 'marketisation' (Molesworth *et al.*, 2011) or 'commercialisation' (Knight, 2008: 13) of formal education, which seems to have reached a point at which instruction has become 'an internationally tradable service' (Knight,

2008: 13). Clearly, research thrives on the exchange of expertise and resources, and networking across cultures and countries is becoming increasingly important, not only among research institutions but also between research and industry. Therefore, higher education institutions (HEIs) can no longer afford to stay local if they want to acquire external research funds and attract excellent students and lecturers. In order to remain competitive, they seem to strive for an international profile which is often a decisive criterion on which global university rankings are based. Along these lines, Hultgren (2017) observes a clear correlation between the rank of a university (in lists such as the Academic Ranking of World Universities [ARWU]) and its use of EMI. This finding prompts her to assert that EMI seems to be 'intrinsically embedded in neoliberal ideologies and time characteristic battles for excellence' (Hultgren, 2017: 4).

This is the precise context in which the current orientation of the tertiary sector towards internationalisation and globalisation has to be seen. Student and teacher mobility and close cooperation in teaching and research across national borders are essential instruments to enhance the status and profile of a university as a competitive player in the global education market (Wächter & Maiworm, 2008: 15). Being internationally attractive or 'marketable' (Molesworth et al., 2009) is generally seen as an indicator of the quality of the study programmes on offer and thus linked directly to the employability of their graduates. In other words, owing to this marketisation of educational institutions, international university rankings (Egron-Polak & Hudson, 2010: 6) have come to play a decisive role these days.

In addition to the immediate consequences linked to the restructuring of their curricula, universities have also been faced with an increasing demand for didactic innovation such as learner autonomy, the promotion of foreign languages, multidisciplinary thinking and intercultural awareness. These driving forces are increasingly met by implementing English-medium teaching both at course as well as programme level. Accordingly, Jenkins (2014: 5) sees EMI as a strategic response to the globalisation of HEIs, implying that if universities want to stay competitive, they need to offer content courses taught in English. As a consequence, English-medium education has become an important strategic management tool (Maiworm & Wächter, 2003; Wilkinson, 2008a: 178).

A number of studies have explored the more specific reasons that have prompted universities to introduce English-taught courses (e.g. Ammon & McConnell, 2002; Marsh, 2002; Marsh & Laitinen, 2005; Räisänen, 2000). In this respect, Coleman (2006: 4) has identified seven different categories of reasons why universities adopt EMI: CLIL, internationalisation, student exchanges, teaching and research materials, staff mobility, graduate employability and the market in international students. Clearly, this rainbow of motives has ethical, pedagogical, pragmatic and commercial implications for all stakeholders.

A logical consequence of the rapid implementation of EMI programmes in tertiary education is the reinforcement of English as the language of HE. Hence, it comes as little surprise that the point of criticism which has frequently been raised concerns the assumption that although the Bologna Process originally aimed to preserve linguistic diversity, it in fact seems to support an English-only policy (e.g. Fortanet-Gomez & Räsänen, 2008; Ruiz-Garrido & Fortanet-Gomez, 2009). In this respect, an international conference in Segovia, Spain, in 2013 on 'The Role of English in Higher Education: Issues, Policy and Practice', triggered a debate on the rising prominence of ELF at university level. There, the director of the British Council in Spain, Rod Pryde (quoted in Rigg, 2013), pointed out that EMI is clearly on the rise across Europe, with a 30% increase in the number of degrees taught entirely in English. Particularly in countries where the national language is little spoken or taught elsewhere, staff mobility and student exchanges across borders are often only possible if courses are taught in an international language, which is most frequently English. Brumfit (2004: 166) goes even further and claims that from a global perspective, English is already the most dominant L2 medium of instruction and Marsh and Laitinen (2005: 2) expect it to gain further momentum.

This thorny issue of perilous English hegemony has prompted researchers to bemoan the death of languages today with the real culprits identified as brutal market forces (Skutnabb-Kangas, 2001: 201) or – more specifically – English as the 'killer language' (Price, 1984) or even the 'Tyrannosaurus Rex' (Swales, 1997: 374). Critics fear that this trend could foster inequality between those students who can speak English, who are often from wealthier backgrounds, and those who cannot (De Cillia & Schweiger, 2001). From a more pragmatic view, English acts as a lingua franca in the academic world in order to promote student and staff mobility. English can thus be seen as a means to facilitate academic discourse, the shared language of teachers and students in internationalised programmes which have a culturally and linguistically diverse faculty and student body (Smit, 2010: 379).

Leaving aside the perspective from which the spread of English as the language of instruction in HE is seen, it is clear that the implementation of EMI is a reality in European HE that cannot be ignored. Van Leeuwen (2007: 7), for instance, asserts that teaching content courses in English is now 'more than just a fashion; it is a new reality in hundreds of higher education institutions, which changes the life of thousands of staff and the new generations of students'. This, however, bears the great risk of external factors (such as university rankings) prompting a speedy and ill-considered introduction of EMI (Räisänen & Fortanet-Gómez, 2008b: 20). As a consequence, a great number of organisational and pedagogical implications tend to be ignored (Dearden, 2014; Unterberger & Wilhelmer, 2011). Without doubt, policymakers' aims to rapidly internationalise educational institutions by introducing EMI may have a harmful effect on the quality of the respective programmes.

As has been shown, significant global challenges in the field of HE have reinforced the implementation of EMI programmes as a commonly considered end to meet the requirements posed by political, economic and social realities in the 21st century. Phillipson (2009: 37) puts it in a nutshell: 'What emerges is that in the Bologna Process, internationalization means English-medium higher education'.

2.3 The Spread of EMI in European Higher Education

To date, a number of large-scale studies documenting the spread of English-medium degree programmes in Europe have been carried out. In their survey at the beginning of the 21st century, Ammon and McConnell (2002) claimed that from 22 European countries that they analysed, the Netherlands and Finland, followed by Germany, took the lead in offering EMI courses in HE. The most comprehensive account of the exponential rise of English-medium programmes (EMPs) in Europe can be found in a series of three studies published by Maiworm and Wächter (2002) and Wächter and Maiworm (2008, 2014).

In the academic year 2001/2002, Maiworm and Wächter (2002) embarked on a large-scale survey analysing 1558 institutions of HE in 19 different European countries. Interestingly, they placed Austria at the bottom of the league with only six EMPs reported by the 47 participating Austrian institutions (Maiworm & Wächter, 2002: 26–28). This finding was also confirmed by De Cillia and Schweiger (2001) in their article titled 'English as a Language of Instruction in Austrian Universities'. The authors claimed that while English was on the brink of replacing German as the most influential scientific language, very few Austrian universities offered content courses in English and public interest in the matter was negligible. They see Austria's EU membership, the opening of Eastern Europe resulting in increased cultural and business activities in Central and Eastern Europe, as well as globalisation processes per se, as the main reasons that led to a loosening of the law stating that only German could be used as the language of instruction in Austrian schools. As a consequence, the amended School Organisation Act of 1997 allowed schools to introduce a foreign language of instruction 'if this appears useful in view of the number of foreigners speaking foreign languages and living in Austria' (SchuG Schulunterrichtsgesetz article 3 § 16). However, the actual implementation thereof took time.

Maiworm and Wächter's (2007) follow-up study five years later included 2381 HEIs in 27 European countries. Again, they listed the Netherlands at the top of the table with 774 EMI programmes reported from 30 institutions. Comparing the data from 2001/2002 with the findings in 2006/2007, the total number of EMPs in Europe increased six-fold between 2002 and 2007. As far as Austria is concerned, the authors identified 23 programmes at 36 participating Austrian universities. This indicated that in Austria the number of courses quadrupled in as little as five years.

In addition, Maiworm and Wächter found that the average percentage of international students who were enrolled in the universities surveyed was 8.4% (up from 6.8% in 2002). In Switzerland, the percentage was highest at 19.6%, followed by Germany (15.5%) and Austria (13.9%). The high percentage values for Switzerland and Austria were in line with the Organisation for Economic and Cultural Development (OECD) data for the HE systems of these countries (Switzerland: 18.4% and Austria: 14.1%). This means that for a small European country like Austria, student mobility was a particularly important issue.

Two further findings by Maiworm and Wächter concerned the content subjects and the level of the degree programme. Across Europe, the subject area in which English-taught programmes (ETPs) seemed to be most frequently offered was engineering (27%), followed by business studies (24%) and the social sciences (21%). These three subject areas together constituted 72% of all programmes offered. As regards academic degrees, English-medium education appeared to be mainly offered at the master's level, with a share of almost four-fifths of all programmes. In some countries (e.g. Sweden, Belgium, Switzerland and Germany), the postgraduate share exceeded 90%. Apparently, since 2002 (when the postgraduate share stood at 68%), the trend towards master's programmes has thus been further enforced.

The third and most recent study conducted by Maiworm and Wächter in 2014 aimed at mapping and analysing the latest trends in the provision of ETPs in Europe. With a few exceptions, the design and methodology were kept similar to the two previous studies. This time, their survey addressed a total of 2637 HEIs in 28 member states. Most importantly, they found that the number of identified ETPs increased from 725 programmes in 2001 to 2389 in 2007 and to 8089 in 2014. These numbers clearly illustrate the exponential growth since the beginning of the 21st century. The authors therefore conclude that 'there is now little doubt that a critical mass of ETPs is on offer across non-English-speaking Europe' (Wächter & Maiworm, 2014: 16).

As far as the distribution of ETPs within Europe is concerned, the Nordic countries take the lead with Finland (83%) and Sweden (81%). Austria has a share of 46%, which means that from the 73 HEIs surveyed in Austria almost half of them provided an EMP. When looking at the ranking of the 28 EU member states according to the number of ETPs offered and the number of students enrolled in those programmes, Austria scores in the top third taking ninth place. The Netherlands is still in the lead. The overall ranking presented in the study again confirms what the authors call the 'north–south divide', which was already observed in earlier studies. Accordingly, the growth rates are highest in South West Europe whereas most Southern European countries lag behind and can still be found at the bottom of the list.

Furthermore, Maiworm and Wächter classified the subject areas in which ETPs were offered. In contrast to the findings seven years previously, the category 'social sciences, business and law' showed the highest proportion with 35% (particularly in undergraduate programmes), followed by sciences with 23% (more prominently in master's programmes) and engineering with 18%.

Unterberger (2014), who investigated the status quo at English-taught economics and business degree programmes offered by Austrian state universities in the academic year 2012/13, provided a more detailed look at the situation in Austria. In her database search, she identified 29 EMPs (out of 95 in total). Given the result of the 2007 survey discussed above, which disclosed 23 EMPs across all disciplines, this number seems to indicate a remarkable increase within the last few years. Compared with the overall number of programmes, English is hence the language of instruction for over 30% of all master's programmes implemented in 2012 at Austrian business universities. Unterberger points out that this observation largely corresponds with a general trend that can be observed in many European countries, as the surveys conducted by Maiworm and Wächter also listed the discipline area of business and economics as number one in 2002 and number two (behind engineering) in 2007. This focus seems to be particularly pronounced in Austria, as the 2008 survey detailed above also corroborates the notion that business studies are attributed the biggest share (Wächter & Maiworm, 2008: 45–48). It has to be noted, however, that Unterberger's study centres on master's programmes at Austrian state universities, and does not include BA or PhD programmes or UAS.

Further information on EMPs available in Austria can be obtained from the database of the Österreichischer Austauschdienst (ÖAD), the Austrian agency for international mobility and cooperation in education, science and research. The latest list surveying international programmes offered by Austrian HEIs includes universities as well as their more vocation-oriented counterparts, UAS and all three tiers: BA, master's and PhD programmes (ÖAD, 2017). Interestingly, at BA level the number of bilingual programmes (English/German) is three times higher than the number of English-only programmes. In contrast, at master's level twice as many English-only programmes as bilingual ones are offered. The prevalence of bilingual tertiary education at undergraduate level appears to undermine the frequently expressed assumption that the introduction of English-only courses is the key to solving multilingual matters.

The UAS Vienna, where the present study is set, seems to have been a pioneer by introducing a bilingual (German/English) programme at BA level at the very beginning of the 21st century. Whereas there were initial intentions to offer an English-only BA programme, the organisers soon had to admit that although this concept seemed a promising method to attract more and better students, the actual realisation of the programme (especially the provision of financial and human resources) turned out to be unfeasible. Most notably, it seemed to be difficult to hire lecturers with both the necessary content knowledge and language skills to guarantee high-quality teaching. For this reason, the management decided that it was sufficient to offer up to 50% of the content courses in English, a decision that has not been revised so far.

Clearly, the figures presented in the studies discussed above reveal that English-medium teaching is still gaining momentum in HE and may not have reached its peak yet. Spreading fast across the vast majority of European countries, all academic levels as well as disciplines, the emerging trend to 'go English' is a reality that cannot be denied. Austria seems to be no exception in this respect.

2.4 The Case of the UAS Vienna

For the present study, the UAS Vienna was chosen as a research site as it offers unique conditions to study the differences between an EMI and an ESP classroom setting. This is also the place where I was working as a lecturer and research associate when I decided to turn a strong interest into a research project. For me, it was the ideal context that promised to provide answers to two questions that had been burning in me since the beginning of my teaching career: do adult students pick up the accent of the teacher without realising it and why are some students more successful than others in acquiring a native-like accent?

The UAS Vienna, a private but state-subsidised university, launched its first degree programme in tourism management in the early 1990s and since then has established a number of additional programmes in the field of management and communication. Today, more than 15 bachelor's and master's degree programmes covering a broad spectrum of specialisations from real estate management to entrepreneurship, corporate communications and tourism management are offered. The student body is approximately 2500, which corresponds to roughly 6% of all UAS students in Austria.

Regarding student numbers, the largest of the degree programmes on offer is the BA programme in entrepreneurship which provides a three-year general education in business administration. The topics covered in the courses range from management and law to controlling, marketing and social skills. As far as the students' foreign language competence is concerned, applicants have to prove – among other qualifications – a level of English proficiency comparable to the Common European Framework of Reference for Languages: Learning, Teaching, Assessment (CEFR)-B2. In the current curriculum, English is the only foreign language taught – other foreign languages are optional and are subject to an additional fee. In the third semester, students are given the opportunity to do a voluntary semester abroad at one of the partner universities all over the world. Between the fourth and sixth (and last) semester, students are required to do a 12-week internship in a company of their choice, either in Austria or abroad.

What clearly sets this programme apart from others, however, is the fact that one group comprising 36 students each academic year is run as a 'bilingual programme'. This means that in one of five parallel groups up to 50% of the content courses are held in English, the other four groups have content courses in German only. Furthermore, the majority of the lecturers teaching in English are native speakers of the language who either fly in from one of the partner universities or are expatriates living and working in Vienna. This has to be seen in striking contrast to the majority of EMI courses taught at European HEIs where the teachers of the content courses are predominantly L2 speakers of the language (cf. Hellekjær & Westergaard, 2003: 73; Tatzl, 2011: 256).

In the EMI courses, the focus is above all on content knowledge with English taking on a vehicular role, the medium through which business concepts are conveyed and discussed. In the curriculum and in the course descriptions, explicit language learning goals are not formulated and language skills are neither discussed in the classroom nor assessed. It is clearly taken for granted that the students' foreign language skills are enhanced incidentally, which the institution considers to be adequate at this stage. All applicants interested in this bilingual programme go through the same entrance procedure as the other applicants, with one exception: the application interview with a member of staff is held in English and points are awarded for spoken language competence.

This study focuses on the performance of two parallel groups or cohorts: the EMI group (focus group) from the bilingual programme and the ESP group (control group) from the regular (German) programme. Both groups comprise male and female students who are all L1 speakers of (Austrian) German. At the time of data collection 1 (T1), their age ranged from 19 to 27 years (M = 23) in the focus group, and 18–25 (M = 23) in the control group. The majority of them started to learn English as a foreign language (EFL) in primary school around the same age (8 years), thus they all share a similar age of onset of L2 learning (AOL). The most crucial difference that can be observed between the two groups is the amount of exposure to the English language in the classroom: Whereas both groups have one ESP course per semester with roughly the same contents, the focus group (i.e. bilingual group) also has up to 50% of the content courses taught in English. Especially in the first two semesters, great care is taken by the organisation to ensure that in addition to the ESP class, 10 out of a total of 20 weekly semester hours are held in English. This adds up to a weekly exposure of approximately

12 hours. In the last year of the programme, however, a general decline in the number of EMI courses could be observed.

2.5 Conclusion

This chapter started off with an overview of some of the most commonly known acronyms that have come to be used in the field of English-medium teaching. Following Unterberger's categorisation of these terms, I have argued that in many English-taught courses at European universities EMI is the correct term to use as rarely are both essential components of such a programme, language and content, considered equally important. Instead, the focus is often on subject knowledge with the language learning component relegated to the sides. It is, therefore, often assumed that language learning happens 'on the go' as the subject is presented and discussed in the L2. Clearly, foreign language learning in itself is hardly ever the main reason why these programmes are adopted.

I have also discussed a number of significant political, economic and social challenges in the field of HE that have prompted many universities to introduce EMI programmes as a means to be marketable and stay competitive in the 21st century. As has been shown, this trend is currently sweeping across Europe at incredible speed and the latest figures suggest that its peak has not yet been reached. Austria has jumped on the bandwagon early on as the example of the UAS Vienna shows, where a bilingual (English/German) undergraduate degree programme was already introduced almost two decades ago.

The next chapter moves on to discuss the question of how languages are learned in the English-medium classroom.

3 Language Learning in the English-Medium Classroom

Having established in Chapter 2 that the decision by many European universities to offer English-medium instruction (EMI) courses can be traced back to the common belief of many programme designers that the students 'get two for the price of one', let us now find out if that is in fact the case. How are languages learned in the English-medium classroom if there is no explicit language teaching? How is pronunciation learned? What are the linguistic benefits of EMI? What are the phonological benefits of EMI? These are the questions that serve as the backbone of this chapter, which is subdivided into three main sections: EMI and language learning theories, language learning and second language (L2) phonology, and empirical investigations into language learning outcomes in the EMI classroom.

First, language learning theories that are frequently associated with EMI are described and critically assessed. More specifically, Krashen's Input Hypothesis, two theories based on the Input Theory, namely the Output and the Interaction Hypothesis, and Vygotsky's Sociocultural Theory (SCT) are discussed and related to the English-medium classroom. After having outlined the main tenets of each and their implications for English-medium teaching, the specifics of pronunciation learning are addressed. In this section, an overview of the theoretical underpinnings of foreign accent (FA) and the way L2 pronunciation skills are learned will be delineated. Then, the purported language benefits reported in a number of studies investigating students' pronunciation skills in the EMI classroom will be referred to. The chapter closes with insight into the findings of the present project with reference to the development of the participants' pronunciation skills.

3.1 EMI and Language Learning Theories

One of the core issues pertaining to EMI teaching and learning refers to the way language is learned in an English-medium classroom although teaching/learning does not focus on language. In order to address this fundamental question in the context of pronunciation learning, this chapter is devoted to a number of language learning theories that are commonly associated with English-medium teaching.

In the English-medium classroom, students use the target language more frequently and thus internalise it more quickly and more deeply. This is where second language acquisition (SLA) research comes in. In general, SLA refers to the study of how people learn languages in addition to their native language/s (Gass & Selinker, 2008). It should be noted here that the term 'second language' is used to denote any language that is acquired after early childhood and thus it may also be the third or any subsequent language learned.

Within the scientific domain of SLA, a myriad of theories investigating the language learning process from various angles has evolved. Attempts at categorisation (e.g. Larsen-Freeman & Long, 1991; Spolsky, 1989) have demonstrated how difficult it is to synthesise and group them. It appears that a great number of theories and hypotheses focus on one particular aspect without considering developments in other disciplines. Pincas (1996: 10) concludes that 'the most recent analysis of research into language learning [...] shows very clearly how much is lacking. Most chapters end on a note of indecision, pointing out that research is still inconclusive'. Nevertheless, the interpretations of those theories have been crucial in shaping the common understanding of what should be taught and how. They have also provided significant directions for conceiving language and language learning that occurs in English-medium classrooms. For language teachers, this means that it is essential to gain an understanding of the role the L2 plays in shaping the students' thinking and their construction of academic knowledge, how the foreign language (FL) reflects identity and how it works to establish relationships with the group(s) into which they are socialised.

In the following, some of the most significant SLA concepts that are frequently mentioned in rationales for Content and Language Integrated Learning (CLIL) will be sketched. These theories are either based on the notion that exposure to the target language is sufficient for acquisition to take place (e.g. Krashen's Input Hypothesis), or they rely on the assumption that output, practice and the social context are equally important to promote learning. The focus here will be on three major trends: (1) the Input Hypothesis; (2) two conceptualisations based on it, namely the Output and the Interaction Hypothesis; and (3) SCT. For each framework a brief overview of the tenets will be given, the main points of criticism they have triggered will be outlined and their implications for pronunciation learning in the English-medium classroom will be discussed.

3.1.1 The Input Hypothesis

Without doubt, one of the most pervasive theoretical concepts regarding SLA is Stephen Krashen's Input Hypothesis (e.g. Krashen,

1977, 1981, 1982, 1985), which he later renamed the Comprehension Hypothesis. This model is often considered the theoretical foundation of the natural approach and is largely based on the notion that if the language learner is exposed to comprehensible input within a setting that focuses on meaning rather than form, acquisition will occur naturally. Since English-medium education provides exactly the proposed learning environment, it comes as little surprise that Krashen's model has been drawn upon extensively in rationales for CLIL.

In general, Krashen's model comprises five central hypotheses and a number of other variables that need considering in SLA. The fundamental assumption upon which he bases his theories is that human beings have an innate ability that shapes and conditions the language learning process. As an example, he refers to children who learn their mother tongue simply by listening attentively to spoken language and interacting with adults.

According to Krashen's Acquisition-Learning Hypothesis, it is essential to distinguish between two independent processes by which a language is learned, namely acquisition and learning. These two concepts differ considerably in terms of their nature, quality and function. He sees language acquisition as a subconscious process (like the way children learn their first language [L1]) resulting from informal, natural communication with the focus on constructing meaning rather than on the language form. For him, L2 learning, on the other hand, is a conscious process with the learner focusing on the language form, thereby generating knowledge about the rules that govern the target language. In contrast to acquisition, learning can only act as a monitor, checking the accuracy of the acquired system.

Critics have argued that it is difficult or even impossible to test Krashen's hypothesis empirically. In addition, it seems problematic to draw a line between acquisition and learning (Mitchell & Myles, 1998: 2) as boundaries are blurred and acquired knowledge may also become learned knowledge.

Following Krashen's view, the notion is enforced that language teaching needs to support acquisition and create an environment in which language is presented in authentic communicative situations. Hence, formal teaching of, for example, grammatical items or phonemes hinders acquisition and needs to be reduced. For pronunciation teaching, for example, this means that pronunciation is an acquired skill and there is no point in formal instruction.

In addition, Krashen's Monitor Hypothesis attempts to explain the process underlying acquisition and learning. Accordingly, the acquisition system triggers an utterance and then the learning system monitors this utterance in order to detect and if necessary also correct mistakes. Krashen sees this monitor of the knowledge about the rules of a language as an editing device that operates either before production (by consciously applying the rules) or after production (via a correcting device). However, according to the Monitor Hypothesis, explicit knowledge of the rules is not enough for the monitor to be utilised; the learner must also have sufficient time to consciously think about and practice the learned rules. Krashen himself is very critical of the use of this language editor and claims that a great number of learners tend to overuse the monitor, which consequently inhibits rather than facilitates communication. Therefore, the monitor should only be used to correct deviations from 'normal' speech.

The Monitor Hypothesis has mainly been criticised for the way it is constructed and for its lack of scientific evidence. McLaughlin (1987: 56) argues that 'Krashen has not defined his terms with enough precision, the empirical basis of the theory is weak, and the theory is not clear in its precision'. Larsen-Freeman (1983) notes that the Monitor Hypothesis does not provide an explanation for the cognitive processes that underlie acquisition and learning. No matter whether this hypothesis holds water or not, as a language teacher it will always be challenging to strike a balance between the promotion of accuracy on the one hand and the achievement of fluency on the other hand.

The third hypothesis that Krashen has put forward, the Natural Order Hypothesis, is based on the assumption that language is acquired through an innate language acquisition device (LAD). He claims that there are predictable and fixed stages in the acquisition of a language that can only be observed in a monitor-free context. As soon as a learner engages in natural communication, the standard order applies and does not depend on extra-linguistic factors such as age, L1 background or exposure to the target language. This order, he emphasises, does not depend on the order in which language rules are taught in the classroom.

Since Krashen ignores the influence of L1 on L2 as well as the role of positive and negative transferences, it comes as little surprise that this theory has also generated criticism. In contrast to the assumption that L1 acquisition and L2 acquisition follow similar paths, a number of studies on morphology have pointed out that not all learners show the predicted order of acquisition. Instead, it has been suggested that inter-learner variables (such as gender, intelligence, sociocultural background and rate of learning) play a decisive role in the order of acquisition. In addition, McLaughlin (1987) claims that the learner's L1 also has an effect in as far as it can either slow down the development or modify it. He purports that a wide range of individual variation in how a learner acquires an L2 can obscure the order of acquisition. Hence, McLaughlin (1987: 33) concludes that 'Krashen's claim that an invariant natural order is always found is simply not true'.

As has already been pointed out, Krashen considers acquisition in contrast to learning as the superior way of developing language competence. In his Input Hypothesis, he claims that acquisition is the result of comprehensible input rather than of language production. The basic idea is that if the student receives understandable input, language structures will be acquired naturally. This input can be comprehensible either because of the context in which it occurs or else through intentional simplification. He further stresses the fact that input needs to go beyond the learner's level of linguistic competence ('i'), thereby providing added value ('+1') in the form of challenging linguistic forms and functions, that is 'i+1'. Based on this concept, Krashen argues that successful language teaching needs to provide the learners with extensive amounts of comprehensible input. In addition, he recommends that teachers refrain from teaching speaking skills directly as they will emerge once the learner has built up enough knowledge. It is inferred that the learner experiences a 'silent phase' until a sufficient amount of comprehensible input has been provided.

Linguists have repeatedly rejected this hypothesis mainly because it reduces the process of language learning to a merely receptive role. Bleyhl (2009: 146), for instance, argues that 'language is learnt in social interaction and not when the learner is confronted with bits and pieces of input'. Furthermore, the concept of 'i+1' has been criticised as too vague a construct that cannot be verified. McLaughlin (1987: 39), for example, asserts that Krashen's definition of comprehensible input as being both meaningful and understood by the learner is in fact a tautology. Chomsky (quoted in N. Ellis, 1994) argues along the same lines when he states that input as such is important but considered in isolation, it fails to explain L1 acquisition as it also includes ungrammaticalities and disfluencies that turn it into an inadequate source of information. Based on such input, children would not be able to decide what is grammatical and what is not. He further maintains that input alone cannot be enough for the learner to discover the rules of the L1. Ellis (1990: 106) concludes: 'The input hypothesis is a bucket full of holes'.

Clearly, the Input Hypothesis focuses on the role of the L2 in the classroom. By providing a large amount of comprehensible input, the teacher can create effective opportunities to foster the language learning process. As far as pronunciation is concerned, this also implies that the quality of the teacher's own pronunciation skills is crucial to the successful acquisition of L2 phonology.

In addition, Krashen believes that the learning situation has to be characterised by positive emotions, as laid out in his Affective Filter Hypothesis. Negative emotions, such as anxiety, self-doubt, stress and boredom interfere with the acquisition of L2 by building a mental block and impeding efficient processing of the language input. The learner needs to be open to input. Thus, the more comprehensible input the learner receives in low-stress situations with the affective filter being low, the more successful the teaching will be. Input only reaches the LAD if the affective filter provides favourable conditions. This, according to

Krashen, explains why adults and more experienced learners frequently face severe difficulties in achieving a native speaker level of proficiency. As a consequence, teaching not only has to ensure that there is extensive comprehensible input but it also has to create a positive learning environment that is meant to keep the affective barrier low. For Krashen, this means that teachers need to concentrate on meaning and not on form to reduce anxiety by refraining from overt corrections of language errors.

This theory has also been criticised by a number of researchers claiming that firstly, not all adults are struggling with mastering an FL due to a high affective filter (e.g. Gregg, 1984) and secondly, that a low affective filter is no single guarantee of a higher level of success in mastering the language (e.g. Zafar, 2009). Thus, many aspects of the affective filter remain in the dark.

To sum up, the quantity and quality of the input of the target language is of central importance in Krashen's theories. No matter how disputed his claims are, they have undoubtedly inspired research and laid the foundations for further studies into SLA. They have also directly made their way into the classroom and thus have greatly influenced teaching practice, teacher training and classroom strategies.

These ideas are undoubtedly crucial in the conceptualisation of language learning in an English-medium setting. Clearly, Krashen's theories according to which success in language acquisition depends on the focus on meaning rather than exclusively on form, on language input being just above the proficiency level of the learner and on the learning environment providing ample opportunities for meaningful interaction, are all in line with the CLIL approach, which involves conditions similar to those in L1 acquisition (Crandall, 1992). Indeed, as studies on the relation between CLIL students' motivation and language competence prove, CLIL pupils tend to show better results than regular English as a foreign language (EFL) learners.

3.1.2 The Output and the Interaction Hypothesis

As mentioned above, Krashen's Input Hypothesis model has had a major impact on developments in SLA research since the 1970s. Although it is now widely recognised that input is pivotal to language acquisition, it is also generally accepted that output and interaction are crucial determiners in the process of learning an L2. Complementary to Krashen's Input Hypotheses, two further theories have evolved that can and should be related to the EMI classroom. Firstly, Swain's Output Hypothesis purports that mere exposure to the L2 is not sufficient as learners need to use the FL actively to trigger the acquisition process. Secondly, Long's Interaction Hypothesis (IH) goes one step further by pointing out that verbal interaction, feedback, negotiation and comprehensible input are also essential prerequisites for successful L2 mastery.

The Output Hypothesis

A hypothesis that greatly challenges Krashen's Input Theory by questioning the role of input as the single most important factor in SLA, is the Comprehensible Output Theory. This theory is commonly attributed to Merrill Swain (1985, 1993) who explored the learning process of French immersion students in Canada.

Swain's (1985) hypothesis has to be seen in the context of the increasing popularity of French immersion programmes in Canada in the 1980s, the evaluation of which yielded some surprising results. Whereas the French immersion students scored similarly to the Francophone learners of the same age in listening and reading, their speaking and writing competence clearly lacked behind. Swain attributed this to two major reasons, firstly insufficient input and secondly insufficient output. She claimed that restricted input (e.g. in terms of language features such as the conditional) entailed limited acquisition opportunities. The second problem she identified was that of limited output produced by the French immersion students. Additionally, she noted that only about 19% of the grammatical errors that occurred in the students' productions were corrected by the teacher (Swain, 1996: 97). Thus, the learners were not pushed to more accurate language use as the teachers solely concentrated on meaning rather than form. Essentially, feedback and the negotiation of meaning, which incorporate the idea of being pushed toward the delivery of a precise, coherent and appropriate message, are of central concern. As Swain (1985: 248–249) sees this as parallel to that of the 'i+1' of comprehensible input, she calls it the 'comprehensible output hypothesis'. Interestingly, students' perception of being 'pushed' is, according to Swain, highest when the feedback comes from the teacher and lowest when it comes from a peer.

Swain elaborates on three distinct functions of output: Firstly, the noticing function, which states that learners notice gaps between what they intend to say and what they actually say and thus they realise what they do not know. Secondly, when learners speak, a hypothetical assumption tends to precondition the production (e.g. grammatical rules). By producing an utterance, this hypothesis is tested and ideally meets with feedback from an interlocutor. This feedback then allows them to change their hypothesis. Swain calls this the hypothesis testing function. Thirdly, learners reflect about the language and thus the output gives them an opportunity to check and internalise their knowledge of the L2 on a metalinguistic level.

Overall, a great number of scholars agree that opportunities for comprehensible input and output are also crucial for successful language learning (e.g. Shehadeh, 1991; Swain, 1985, 1995; Swain & Lapkin, 1995). The implications generated by numerous studies on the negotiation of meaning overall tend to match paradigms such as the communicative language approach, which also puts learners and learner interactions to the fore (cf. Widdowson, 1990).

It comes as little surprise that Stephen Krashen (1998) severely criticised Swain's approach in order to defend his own theory with his main argument being that output in general is scarce. This claim was further confirmed by Ellis *et al.* (1994), who investigated vocabulary acquisition and found that only a small minority of their learners engaged in the negotiation of meaning whereas the majority simply listened. Further, Krashen insists that high levels of proficiency can be obtained without any language output and refers to studies conducted in the field of vocabulary growth (e.g. Day *et al.*, 1991; Pitts *et al.*, 1989). Further, he claims that pushing students to speak is unpleasant and creates a learning atmosphere that is largely dominated by a high level of anxiety.

Bearing in mind that a traditional university course is often characterised by a teacher-fronted and monologue-based (Goffman, 1981) classroom discourse, the linguistic output produced by students by nature tends to be severely restrained. This might thus give rise to the assumption that chances to promote language learning in tertiary EMI courses are in fact slim. However, it seems that the importance of interaction in university lectures is gaining momentum. Indeed, a number of studies have recently observed a gradual shift away from being 'an institutionalised extended holding of the floor' (Morell, 2007: 223) to a more egalitarian and participatory approach where the role of the lecturer is also moving from the main provider of knowledge to that of a facilitator in the learning process (Dafouz & Sánchez, 2013).

The Interaction Hypothesis

The line of research following Krashen's Input Theory predominantly focused on Krashen and Terrell's (1983, 1996) claim that comprehensible input is sufficient to foster language learning and as a result, a number of new perspectives were brought to light, with Long's pioneering work on the IH being among the first and most influential one. The IH is based on the notion that conversation is not only a medium of practice but also the means by which learning takes place.

Closely related to Krashen's Input Hypothesis, the IH stresses the importance of comprehensible input for successful language learning. However, Long adds that the effectiveness of comprehensible input can be considerably enhanced when the learner needs to negotiate meaning. This happens when there is a breakdown in communication and when the speakers try to overcome this barrier. The participants will employ various communicative strategies to help the interaction continue. These strategies may encompass the slowing down of the speech rate, speaking in a more articulate way, asking for clarification or paraphrasing.

Long discovered that interaction may prompt language learning through what he coined 'interactional modification'. This process has been defined by Pica (1994: 418), among others, as 'the modification and restructuring of interaction that occurs when learners and their interlocutors anticipate, perceive, or experience difficulties in message comprehensibility'. Likewise, Long (1996) defines interaction as

> [...] the process in which, in an effort to communicate, learners and competent speakers provide and interpret signals of their own and their interlocutor's perceived comprehension, thus provoking adjustments to linguistic form, conversational structure, message content, or all three, until an acceptable level of understanding is achieved. (Long, 1996: 418)

Since Long's study, a growing body of research has sought to elaborate on the role that interaction appears to play in SLA. Generally speaking, interaction is claimed to change input qualitatively by making it more comprehensible and therefore more beneficial for the development of the L2 (Long, 2003: 449). For Gass and Varonis (1994: 318), for example, interaction is of paramount importance in language acquisition by providing learners with 'a forum for testing out hypotheses about the target language'. In a similar vein, Oliver (1998) argues that interaction is beneficial since it gives learners the opportunity to receive comprehensible input that is adapted to suit the individual circumstances. In addition, interaction allows them to modify their own contributions in an attempt to make themselves understood (Gass & Varonis, 1994: 373).

For the L2 language classroom, this implies that apart from the availability of comprehensible input, emphasis should be on language forms, which clearly contradicts Krashen's demands. If communication breaks down, feedback should be given, for example in the form of recasts or explicit error correction, and this in turn makes learners recognise gaps in their linguistic competence and take in the correct language forms (Long, 2003: 429). Thus, through focused negotiations of meaning, the learner resources are steered towards potential discrepancy between language knowledge and language reality.

In his evaluation of the IH, Krashen rejects it as being too vague and not empirically proven. He claims that there is convincing data proving that reading can foster language learning and that acquisition can happen without interaction. Nevertheless, he concedes that interaction can be seen as a valuable source of comprehensible input (Krashen, 1982).

As has been shown, Long's IH posits that language acquisition is facilitated by the use of the L2 in interaction. It follows that the language classroom needs to provide opportunities for interaction to support the cognitive process of successful language learning. Regarding its implementation in the EFL classroom, the IH suggests that teachers need to engage the learners in activities involving problem-solving, decision making and giving opinions as these create an ideal atmosphere for negotiating meaning. By taking advantage of these opportunities, learners make the input comprehensible through negotiation and at the same time they produce comprehensible output, which they then again make comprehensible to other learners through interaction and negotiation. Interaction is therefore seen here as a social process that focuses on the construction of meaning by both interlocutors.

Overall, the importance of the three factors – input, output and interaction – has been generally accepted in L2 learning. The findings of interactional studies clearly highlight the role of interaction and the negotiation of meaning in developing language competence, thereby asserting the importance of interaction in the production of comprehensible output, which is at the same time one of the core principles of the communicative language approach.

3.1.3 Sociocultural Theory

Having its roots in the ideas of the Russian psychologist Lev Vygotsky (1896–1934), SCT is probably the most influential of several psychological theories attempting to explain mental development in a sociocultural context. Drawing on ideas from constructivism, this theory offers a novel perspective of the language learning process by taking the broader view on the phenomenon of learning and development. Vygotsky claims that to understand a learner's development it is too narrow a view to solely focus on the individual. What is more, the external social world in which that individual lives has to be taken into consideration. By taking part in activities that require cognitive and communicative functions, 'children are drawn into the use of these functions in ways that nurture and "scaffold" them' (Vygotsky, 1978: 6–7). In other words, mental progress happens as the learner interacts with the environment, thereby actively constructing reality.

This approach to learning and teaching clearly underlines the importance of the social context and the role of discourse in enabling the construction of knowledge. In Gibbons' (2002: 25) words, 'the kinds of talk that occur in the classroom are critical in the development of how students learn to learn through language and ultimately how they learn to think'. Thus, it is crucial for students to engage in social classroom events that trigger the thinking process and develop students' conceptual knowledge.

Vygotsky claims that learning starts at birth and continues throughout one's life. One of the most important ways in which progress is made is through the zone of proximal development (ZPD), which Vygotsky (1978: 86) explains as 'the distance between the actual development level as determined by independent problem solving and the level of potential development as determined through problem solving under adult guidance or in collaboration with more capable peers'. He purported that two developmental levels need to be distinguished to grasp the relationship between development and learning: the actual and the potential levels of development. The actual level denotes those accomplishments a child can perform without help; whereas potential levels of development refer to what children are capable of doing with assistance. It follows that productive and useful interactions are in fact those that steer instruction towards the ZPD. If that is not the case, instruction will lag behind the development of the child. 'The only good learning is that which is in advance of development' (Vygotsky, 1978: 89). Development therefore occurs as children learn general concepts and principles that can be subsequently applied to new tasks and problems.

Scholars have wondered whether the ZPD is in fact the same as Krashen's 'i+1'. In their review article, Dunn and Lantolf (1998) answer this question by claiming that these two concepts cannot be compared since they are built on different ideas as to how development can be induced. According to them, the ZDP is a metaphorical place where learners co-construct knowledge together with an interlocutor. In Krashen's 'i+1', however, the input comes from outside the learner and the focus is on the comprehensibility of the input that is just beyond the learner's current developmental state.

Vygotsky's theory of constructivism is centred on three main tenets: scaffolding (Bruner, 1978), ZPD (Vygotsky, 1978) and approximation (Holdaway, 1979). Firstly, scaffolding means that a teacher detects a child's ZPD and engages the learner or group of learners in a task while providing temporary support that is gradually removed as the learners make progress in language development. Broadly speaking, scaffolding requires an instructor to demonstrate how to solve a problem, while being in control of the learning environment so that the learners can proceed step by step, expanding their base of knowledge without being overwhelmingly frustrated. Secondly, ZPD involves reciprocal teaching that provides a learning environment of open dialogue between student and teacher by going beyond a simple question and answer session. Taking their turns to lead discussions, students soon find out that they are in fact capable of assuming a leadership and instructional position. The third key element of SCT is approximation, a process in which learners imitate the language behaviours of their models. By testing their hypothesis about the new language, they increase their proficiency. Approximation largely depends on language opportunities within the context of wholes. In other words, the learners rely on listening, speaking, reading and writing as a whole, rather than as a separate entity. Consequently, it is assumed that skilful teachers engage their students in integrated language tasks in which they are expected to listen, speak, read and write in a safe environment.

Lantolf and Thorne (2006: 4) conclude that 'SCT is a theory of mediated mental development', which assumes that mediatory tools become internalised by means of social interaction and that language is an immensely powerful sociocultural tool. The authors argue that the principles of the SCT can also apply to SLA. They explain that 'SCT is grounded in a perspective that does not separate the individual from the social and in fact argues that the individual emerges from social interaction and as such is always fundamentally a social being' (Lantolf & Thorne, 2006: 217–218). It is in the social world that the language learner observes others using language and imitates them.

From Vygotsky's point of view, SLA is mediated by the learner's L1. For him, there is a clear distinction between learning an FL at school and developing one's L1. Learning a new language means using the native language as a mediator between the world of objects and the new language.

Besides describing the opposing features of the L1 and L2 acquisition processes, Vygotsky (1978) also holds the view that the conscious and intentional learning of an L2 rests on a certain level of development in the L1. Hence, learning an FL means that the child understands the native language as a single realisation of a linguistic system and as a result develops a certain potential to generalise the parameters of the native language and to gain conscious awareness of how speech in general operates.

Interestingly, SCT has also been linked to the IH in as far as the role of the interlocutor is concerned. Lightbown and Spada (2006) point out that the difference between these two views lies above all in the role that cognitive processes play. Whereas the IH highlights the cognitive process in the mind of the learner, Vygotskyan theory focuses more on the conversations themselves with learning being a by-product of the social interaction (Lightbown & Spada, 2006: 47). Thus, the crucial difference between the sociocultural perspective and that of other scholars who also consider interaction as important in SLA is that sociocultural theorists assert that 'the cognitive processes begin as external socially mediated activity and eventually become internalised' (Lightbown & Spada, 2006: 48).

The sociocultural approach has suggested implications for pedagogical practice in the FL classroom. For students, learning a language is not just an individual mental process to acquire communicative competence, to a certain extent it also entails socialisation in the L2 culture. Depending on a number of variables, this can result in conflicts or mismatches with the student's L1 culture, which in turn could affect the learner's assimilation and accommodation or manifest itself as resistance to instruction (McClintock, 2014). Research has proliferated in identifying the mismatches and conflicts faced by learners in order to help teachers provide more culturally responsive instruction to diverse students.

As Dalton-Puffer (2007) points out, in the English-medium classroom it is crucial to abandon the position that input alone triggers the acquisition process. In fact, this process is bound to be shaped by the context in which it occurs. Conceivably, a sociocultural perspective allows us to analyse the characteristics of this particular classroom within the context of the system 'school' (Dalton-Puffer, 2007: 11). Therefore, to learn at an educational institution means to learn within a particular system that inherently conditions learning opportunities (Dalton-Puffer, 2007: 293). Just like regular language classes, CLIL courses take place in the institution/school and so the conditions there are likely to be similar in both instances. She therefore concludes that simply by changing the language of instruction, the educational context as such is not altered. After all, the facilities, the stakeholders (teachers and learners) and also the discourse patterns are largely the same (Dalton-Puffer, 2007: 279).

Indeed, a number of studies conducted from a sociocultural perspective have revealed that English-medium classrooms – much like traditional classrooms – show certain limitations for learning that are typically related to the institutional context. Although English-medium teaching is generally considered to be ideal for language acquisition as it allows for extensive natural and authentic comprehensible input (Dalton-Puffer & Smit, 2007: 8), studies have shown that opportunities for language acquisition are necessarily limited by reduced input and output. These problems have been related to the discourse structures in CLIL classrooms, which are after all not very different from those in traditional EFL classes. Dalton-Puffer (2007) compares Canadian French immersion teachers with Austrian CLIL teachers and points out that the former appear to rely on lecturing techniques whereas the latter tend to resort to the initiation-response-feedback (IRF) structure of discourse (Dalton-Puffer, 2007: 54). This goes to show that in Canada as well as in Austria, CLIL programmes mirror the predominant discourse patterns of the local educational culture. Adhering to these traditionally evolved structures may lead to limitations in terms of input and output. It is important to note that not only the discourse patterns but also the discourse functions are in fact more traditional in CLIL classrooms than might be assumed. Without doubt, the CLIL approach provides pupils with the opportunity to experience the L2 as a means with which content information can be conveyed. Nevertheless, CLIL classes often fail to provide opportunities to realise the social functions that language also fulfils (Dalton-Puffer, 2007: 286). For example, pupils usually do not use the L2 among peers to criticise, to joke or to negotiate their social position in the classroom. In this respect, Tarone and Swain (1995: 166–172) detect a form of diglossia, where the pupils use the target language to discuss academic issues but then switch to their L1 to talk about private matters. Clearly, the notion that English-medium teaching provides authentic, natural and also meaningful exposure to the L2 in the classroom needs to be qualified as communication can only be natural and authentic in as far as the limitations of the contextual setting go.

3.1.4 Conclusion

The discussion of the pertinent theories that are frequently associated with English-medium teaching has shown that language learning is a highly complex process in which cognitive considerations are inseparable from sociocultural practices.

Whereas Krashen identifies comprehensible input in the form of high quantity and quality of language input together with a clear focus on meaning rather than form as decisive factors in successful language learning, it has been suggested that this input alone is not sufficient. Therefore, output produced by learners and the negotiation of meaning in the form of interaction are also crucial determiners that need to be taken into consideration. In addition to that, the sociocultural perspective has put forth that learning is not only an individual mental process but also involves a number of sociocultural variables, which are closely linked to the fact that language learning takes place in a particular classroom and a particular institution.

While these theories have enriched the common understanding of how languages are learned, they seem to fall short of the specifics required to take account of the contextual factors of the EMI classroom. It appears that the more cognitive-oriented approaches (emphasising input, output and interaction) combined with the sociocultural stance (focusing on the context as a source and resource) provide a more comprehensive and multifaceted view than a single theory can capture. For an English-medium teacher and researcher, a fundamental awareness of the implications of those theories may give rise to a wider, deeper and more accurate understanding of the language learning process. Hence, viewing these approaches as complementary pieces of a broader picture may reveal a more active, more dynamic and less linear option to learning both language and content in EMI classrooms.

Without doubt, these ideas lend themselves well to most secondary school EMI settings with input, output, interaction and context-related aspects being driving forces. In a traditional university context, however, these forces are often restricted by organisational, practical and technical constraints. Very often, overcrowded lecture halls filled with hundreds of students leave little room for output let alone interaction among the learners. At the University of Applied Sciences (UAS) Vienna, however, this is not the case. In fact, one of the proclaimed advantages of an Austrian UAS as opposed to a state university is that these institutions guarantee small groups with approachable lecturers in active learning environments. This also means that the given setting more closely resembles that of a secondary school than a university, thereby allowing us to draw on a large pool of empirical studies stemming from that level of education.

3.2 Language Learning and L2 Phonology

The previous section has tried to answer the question of how language is learned in the English-medium classroom. Before turning to research that has been conducted in the field of language development in the EMI classroom, it is crucial to consider the question of how L2 phonology is learned since the focus of this book clearly rests on this particular FL skill.

Without doubt, a clear sign that someone is an L2 learner is a certain tendency to produce speech with an FA. Even a one-word utterance like 'hello' can be enough to identify him or her as a learner. More than any other language skill, pronunciation has an undeniable impact on how a speaker is perceived in terms of language competence, sociocultural background, credibility and confidence (Gilakjani et al., 2011), and yet pronunciation is said to be one of the most challenging skills in English (Derwing & Munro, 2005). As casual observers and scholars alike will confirm, some English language learners may have lived in an English-speaking country for a long time but still have weak pronunciation skills. Other speakers seem to pick up pronunciation with very little effort, and some may even do so without ever having set foot in an English-speaking environment. This variation seems to have little to do with the level of education, or even the knowledge of grammar or vocabulary.

In language learning research, FA plays an important role not only because it is often used as an indicator of the fluency and intelligibility of learners, but also because of its close relation to other extra-linguistic factors, such as the age of learning (e.g. Flege et al., 2006; Gallardo del Puerto & Garcia Lecumberri, 2006), experience with the L2 (e.g. Flege et al., 1997a; McAllister, 2001), sociocultural variables (e.g. Al-Issa, 2003; Major, 2001) and speaking rate (e.g. Hirata, 2005; Munro, 1998). In addition, a number of other learner-dependent factors are said to be crucial to FA, such as gender, motivation, attitude, length of residence, type of formal instruction, amount of L1/L2 daily use/exposure, language learning aptitude, etc. (Piske et al., 2001).

This section aims at uncovering the most significant theoretical underpinnings related to the phenomenon of FA. First, I will define what FA means and then I will conceptualise it by discussing three significant SLA theories: the Critical Period Hypothesis (CPH), the Interlanguage Hypothesis and the Contrastive Analysis Hypothesis (CAH). These three theories have been instrumental in explaining how FA develops. Within the realm of the CPH, three models focusing on L2 phonological acquisition will be sketched. Although different in their view of the perceptual representation of L1 and L2 sound patterns, Flege's Speech Learning Model (SLM), Best's Perceptual Assimilation Model (PAM) and Kuhl's

Native Language Magnet (NLM) Model share the notion that the ability to distinguish new L2 sounds diminishes with age.

3.2.1 Defining foreign accent

In the SLA literature, the term 'foreign accent' has been defined in different, yet to a large extent overlapping, ways. For instance, Flege *et al.* (1995) observe that the accented speech of an L2 learner sets itself apart from L1 norms in systematic ways that are not pathological and entail consequences in terms of perception for the listener. A more production-related definition comes from McAllister (2000: 50) who asserts that FA 'refers consistently to the inability of non-native language users to produce the target language with the phonetic accuracy required by native listeners for acceptance as native speech'. According to Derwing and Munro (2005: 385), FA is a 'listener's perception of how different a speaker's accent is from that of the L1 community'. Scovel (1969: 38) speaks of 'phonological cues [...] which identify the speaker as a non-native user of the language'. Along the same lines, Jenner (1976: 167) sees FA as the 'complex of interlingual or idiosyncratic phonological, prosodic and paralinguistic systems which characterise a speaker of a foreign language as non-native'. This study is based on the concept that an instance of FA involves a deviation from the generally accepted norms of pronunciation of a particular L2 – in this case English – that is reminiscent of the speaker's L1, i.e. Austrian German.

Research has shown that segmental (i.e. individual sounds) as well as suprasegmental factors such as pitch, stress and intonation are crucial for effective and efficient communication. Empirical investigations exploring the concept of FA have focused on a number of aspects of L2 phonology on both the segmental and the suprasegmental level: consonants (e.g. Flege & Hillenbrand, 1987), vowels (e.g. Mack, 1982; Munro, 1993), syllables (e.g. Altenberg, 2005; Broselow, 1984, 1988) and intonation and prosody (Jilka, 2000; Jilka *et al.*, 2007; Munro, 2006). This strand of research has often focused on mature L2 learners, with the overall observation that those learners who come from the same L1 background seem to have a tendency to make similar deviations from native norms and that their FAs therefore preserve certain parameters of their L1. These manifestations of an FA can impede communication and greatly influence the listener's perception (e.g. Cutler & Butterfield, 1992; Munro & Derwing, 2008; Smith, 2005).

3.2.2 Explaining the development of foreign accent

Although the field of SLA has largely progressed over the last few decades, the area of L2 phonology has often been marginalised (Derwing & Munro, 2005: 375). In the late 20th century, Major (1998: 131) noted that 'of the nearly 200 articles published in Studies in SLA, only about a dozen focused on phonetics and phonology'. However, in the last decade pronunciation has regained some importance with university centres and the British Council actively promoting the attention to pronunciation in teaching and research (cf. Bamkin, 2010).

In this chapter, three of the most influential theories of L2 phonological acquisition accounting for FA will be discussed, namely the CPH, the Interlanguage Hypothesis and the Comparative Analysis Hypothesis, since they are instrumental in explaining the development of an FA. As will be seen, these theories partly compete with or even contradict each other. However, as Flege (1995: 234) suggests, 'the diversity of these hypotheses attests to the complexity of the phenomenon'. Beyond doubt, the most relevant for the present study is the CPH as it seeks to explore the relationship between age and L2 proficiency. This question is of crucial importance within the framework of the present project as all the subjects are university students for whom the maturationally constrained period of time during which complete acquisition is possible (as proposed by the CPH) has already closed. Against this backdrop, the CPH will be treated extensively in the following section.

The Critical Period Hypothesis

There has been a long-standing debate in SLA regarding the extent to which the ability to acquire a language can and should be linked to age.

Schouten (2009) observes that in most areas of learning, adults outperform children. Yet, when it comes to language learning, children seem to achieve considerably better results. In fact, the vast majority of young learners who are exposed to the L2 at an early age can achieve native-like competence (Schouten, 2009: 1). Among adult learners, however, proficient mastery of the target language is far less common (e.g. Han, 2004; Herschensohn, 2007; Nakuma, 1998; Scovel, 2000; Selinker & Lakshmanan, 1992). This phenomenon has triggered the question as to whether or not some kind of critical period for language learning exists.

The CPH – a core theory in SLA research – tries to explain if and why age affects language learning. According to the CPH there is a certain window in the human developmental process when the ability to learn a new language reaches its peak. Thus, if the learner is exposed to new input during this window, theorists believe that it is certain that he/she can become proficient, but once this window closes, the chances for mastery fade.

The neurologist Walter Penfield is often named as being the first to recognise the existence of a critical period in language learning. He claims that 'the human brain becomes progressively stiff and rigid after the age of nine' (Penfield & Roberts, 1959: 236). This idea was then taken up again and elaborated on by Eric Lenneberg (1967) in *Biological Foundations of Language*. He associated the declining ability to acquire an

FL after puberty with the loss of neural plasticity and the ensuing completion of hemispheric lateralisation of the brain. According to Lenneberg, learners who embark on an L2 before the end of the critical period are able to reach native-like attainment, provided they are exposed to 'sufficient input from native speakers' (quoted in Bongaerts *et al.*, 1997: 448).

A much-debated question regarding the CPH is whether the time frame is in fact a critical or a sensitive one. Mack (2003) distinguishes between the two terms by claiming that the critical period applies to the period when complete acquisition of a particular property of language is possible, while the sensitive period refers to the time frame during which only partial acquisition can be achieved. This way of defining the terms is not satisfactory since it implies that the critical period lasts throughout one's whole life span. In fact, exceptions show that even in a mature stage of learning high achievement is possible (Moyer, 2013: 26). In the literature, however, most researchers use the term 'critical period' synonymously for all such periods, as will be done in this book.

Originally, the CPH was introduced in the context of L1 acquisition. Its subsequent application in the field of SLA has triggered a controversial debate with a myriad of diverse and partly contradictory views. Basically, two main perspectives can be observed. Some researchers argue that from a neurological perspective, once the mother tongue has been acquired, the cognitive mechanisms that foster language acquisition remain intact and SLA is just as possible (e.g. Singleton & Ryan, 2004). Others argue that by the close of the critical period, neurocognitive mechanisms of language acquisition become defective so that native-like attainment is bound to fail (e.g. Thompson, 1991).

Lenneberg's view, which has been fervently rejected by some researchers like Singleton (2001: 77) who claims that the CPH is 'based partly on folk wisdom' and Marinova-Todd *et al.* (2000: 27) who conclude that '[t]he misconception that adults cannot master foreign languages is as widespread as it is erroneous', has been brought back into the limelight by Hyltenstam and Abrahamsson (2003: 578) who purport that '[…] given that maturation has the strong influence on second language outcomes that our review has indicated, it should come as no surprise that native-like proficiency is unattainable for adults'.

Among those who find a strong relationship between the age of exposure and the ultimate proficiency achieved are for instance Krashen (1982), Johnson and Newport (1989), Newport (1990) and Patkowski (1994). In their literature reviews, Long (1990) and Patkowski (1994) both maintain that the achievement of a native-like accent in an L2 is not possible unless the learner is exposed to the language at an early age. Scovel (1988) goes one step further by postulating that a critical period exists only in the realm of pronunciation. He asserts that – in contrast to other language skills – 'phonological production is the only aspect of language performance that has a neuromuscular basis' (Scovel, 1988: 101).

Despite the general consensus regarding the likely existence of a critical period for accent, some of these scholars differ in their views concerning the offset of the critical period. In general, critical periods have an onset, a peak of heightened sensitivity and an offset followed by a period of flattening. During the onset, a gradual rise regarding sensitivity to the stimuli can be observed. Once the peak is reached, exposure to the stimulus is said to be most effective. However, beyond this point the development no longer correlates with age. This means that in contrast to children, adult learners who are exposed to the same quantity and quality of input are bound to behave significantly differently. However, Long (1990) and Patkowski (1994) disagree on the time when the critical period finishes. Long states that a native-like accent is not possible unless first exposure happens before the age of 6 (Long) or between the ages of 12 and 15 (Patkowski).

Additional debate has centred on the question of whether there is more than one critical period for language learning. Long (1990), Scovel (1969) and Seliger (1978) suggest that there are in fact many critical periods for the different language skills, e.g. phonology and morphosyntax, while others conclude that some sub-skills, like vocabulary acquisition, do not have a critical period at all (Singleton, 1981, 1989). Already in 1969, Scovel surmised that there was only a critical age for accent, claiming that mature language learners are likely to keep a typical accent that bears clear reminiscences of their L1. He named this the 'Joseph Conrad Phenomenon' (Scovel, 1969) after the well-known writer who managed to reach native-like fluency in English (his L2) syntax and vocabulary while at the same time retaining a fairly heavy Polish (his L1) accent.

Indeed, adults seem to vary greatly in their L2 pronunciation aptitude – both with regard to segmental as well as suprasegmental parameters of spoken language (e.g. Golestani & Zatorre, 2009; Jilka, 2009). As a matter of fact, only between 5% and 15% of late L2 learners seem to achieve native-like speech (Birdsong, 2005; Novoa et al., 1988; Seliger et al., 1975). However, a number of studies have shown that as far as FL skills other than pronunciation are concerned, older learners are more efficient for instance in terms of L2 morphology and syntax (Fathman, 1975) and listening comprehension skills (Asher & Price, 1967).

Singleton and Ryan (2004) also fuel the notion of 'younger is better in some respects' by distinguishing between those aspects of L2 proficiency that are seen as biological endowment and those aspects that are outside the ambit of the innate mechanisms. They assert that syntax and morphology remain unaffected by a critical period. Although they acknowledge the ambiguity of neurological evidence for a critical period for accent, they refer to empirical studies that seem to prove 'that general phonological abilities are maintained in adulthood and remain available to mature L2 learners' (Singleton & Ryan, 2004: 145). In addition, they advocate that 'a loss or change in the abilities to produce and perceive new sound contrasts' (Singleton & Ryan, 2004: 149) does not exist. To them, the innate ability to master the syntax and phonology of an FL remains intact for mature L2 learners. Nevertheless, the authors concede that non-innate aspects of L2 proficiency (such as vocabulary) may very well experience age-related deterioration. The evidence they provide to support this view comes from adult learners who seem to have retained access to their original sensory abilities and are therefore capable of perceiving and producing new sounds (Singleton & Ryan, 2004: 148). In their concluding remarks, the authors admit that despite a well-founded knowledge of principles and parameters in the retention of phonemic capabilities, mature L2 learners are still bound to fail, as 'a sweeping biological explanation, [...] fails to answer the more subtle and ultimately more interesting question of what particular aspects of linguistic behaviour are affected by age' (Singleton & Ryan, 2004: 151).

Abrahamsson and Hyltenstam (2009) also investigated the various levels of language proficiency (morphosyntax, vocabulary, pronunciation, etc.) of a group of late learners who had the potential to reject the CPH. In agreement with other scholars mentioned above, they found that only a very low number of adult learners were perceived as mother tongue speakers. Interestingly, in their study the adult learner with the highest score exhibited results within the native speaker range of L2 proficiency with deviance only in certain aspects of speech production and perception.

Focusing on the notion of a critical period for accent, early studies dating back to the 1970s produced conflicting results. Ekstrand (1976), for instance, detected better pronunciation in older subjects, whereas Fathman (1975), Martohardjono and Flynn (1995) and Seliger et al. (1975) argued that in fact the opposite was true. Scovel points out that the ability to master a native accent is in fact the first to be lost around the onset of puberty. However, Seliger et al. (1975) report on a few exceptional cases of adult learners who achieved non-foreign-accented pronunciation in their L2, as well as cases of adult learners who did not. What seems striking in this respect is that there is no agreement among scholars on whether the exceptional behaviour of very few experienced learners confirms or rejects the CPH.

In a series of publications, Flege (1988a, 1988b, 1992b, 1995) shed new light on the issue by drawing attention to the distinction between perception and production. He argues that foreign-accented speech is largely perception based and not related to the end of neural plasticity. At the age of 5 or 6, the phonetic prototype categories are refined and stabilised owing to an increasing awareness in the child concerning segmental features of the L1. As a consequence, new sounds of an FL are identified and integrated into the categories of the native language. By the age of 7, the L1 categories are firmly established. In his review of the literature, Flege (1987: 174) notes that the results of most studies are 'inconsistent with the expectations generated by the critical period hypothesis'. He claims that the hypothesis is, on the one hand, difficult to test empirically and, on the other hand, it is problematic to isolate speech learning from other factors that are closely linked to age.

A number of researchers have argued that there are other factors at work that override any binding effects of age. Schumann (1975), for example, associated the success of younger learners with socio-psychological factors, according to which younger learners are in general exposed to more varied input from native speakers and are consequently more motivated to reach native speaker level. Klein (1995) rejects this view by claiming that adults neither receive less adequate input nor are they less motivated. In striking contrast to Schumann, Klein (1995: 261) insists that there is no evidence of drastic biological changes in the brain and arrives at the conclusion that no absolute barriers to the perception and production of a new sound system exist. Instead, he believes that massive and continuous exposure to the target language together with 'the different motivations that push a learner forward' are crucial prerequisites for attaining a native-like accent and thus more important than biological age.

Moyer (1999) argues along the same lines and challenges traditional views of the CPH. For her, using age effects is too simplistic and insufficient. Instead, she links age and maturation with socio-psychological factors such as learner motivation, cultural empathy, a desire to sound like a native speaker, and quantity and quality of input as essential for successful language learning. She tested her hypothesis on a group of late learners of German. And indeed, none of the subjects scored within the native speaker range on the pronunciation tasks. But those who used German in their workplace scored higher than those who did not. In addition, those who attended German pronunciation classes also achieved better results. Age of exposure was clearly an important factor, but apparently not the only one.

As already mentioned, there is scientific evidence that a low number of exceptional learners are not bound by maturational constraints. Bongaerts (1999), for example, reports on the pronunciation of highly proficient post-puberty Dutch learners of English and French. They were asked to read out a series of sentences with supposedly difficult words to pronounce. It turned out that the majority of them scored in the upper range of the native control group. Similarly, in their investigation of the pronunciation of 30 highly advanced learners of English, Bongaerts *et al.* (2000) found that two participants (out of 30) who were 21 and 14 years old passed as native speakers.

Lee *et al.* (2006) carried out a study on the production of unstressed English vowels, comparing early and late Korean and Japanese bilinguals. They found that both groups (early and late learners) were affected in the production of L2 by their L1. However, this was felt stronger in late learners.

Comparing the studies that report on the language proficiency of late L2 and early L2 learners, it appears that it is difficult if not impossible to find learners who achieve overall native-like proficiency (Hyltenstam & Abrahamsson, 2003; Moyer, 1999). The reasons for the success of the low number of exceptional leaners are attributed to increased motivation (e.g. Moyer, 1999), a high language learning aptitude (DeKeyser, 2000; Ioup et al., 1994) and intensive formal L2 instruction (Bongaerts, 1999; Moyer, 1999).

In their review article on the issue of neural plasticity, Zhang and Wang (2007) also looked at the question of whether learners lose the ability to learn with age. They purport that the loss of brain plasticity at a critical age is not complete and as a consequence, post-critical age L2 learners can still reach native-likeness in their pronunciation. Interestingly, they identify two key factors that are considerably more important than brain plasticity, namely quantity and quality of L2 input.

In recent years, there has been a shift in research in L2 phonology from production to perception. Empirical studies have shown that difficulties in L2 production are in fact rooted in perception (Derwing & Munro, 2005: 388). Further support comes from brain studies, such as Golestani and Pallier's (2007) 'Anatomical Correlates of Foreign Speech Sound Production'. They surmise that 'it is not necessary to be able to articulate sounds in order to be able to perceive them, but that it is necessary to be able to accurately perceive speech sounds in order to be able to articulate them correctly' (Golestani & Pallier, 2007: 933).

To sum up, the CPH for SLA has neither been conclusively proven nor has it been completely dispelled. The contradictory results yielded by a great number of studies investigating all the different facets show that it is difficult if not impossible to identify all its parameters in their intrinsic complexity. No wonder David Singleton (2005: 280) compares the CPH to a 'mythical hydra' with an infinite number of heads which keep producing new heads. In their review of the literature, Singleton and Ryan (2004) conclude that neither the claim that younger language learners are in every respect and in every learning phase superior to adult learners, nor the view that mature learners are in all respects and in every learning phase ahead of younger learners holds water. Nevertheless, evidence from research suggests that a critical period for the acquisition of L2 phonology seems likely. The fact that some late learners perform exceptionally well appears to refute the idea that ultimate attainment is primarily a consequence of biological maturation. Conceivably, a number of other factors such as motivation, exposure to L2, language learning aptitude, intensive formal L2 instruction and quantity and quality of input all play a decisive role when it comes to pronunciation mastery.

In relation to the CPH, a few theoretical models have been developed to explain adults' general difficulty in L2 phonological acquisition by focusing on the perceptual interference between the L1 and the L2. The most popular and most frequently mentioned models in this regard are Flege's (1995) SLM, Best's (1994, 1995) PAM and Kuhl's NLM (Iverson & Kuhl, 1996; Kuhl, 1991; Kuhl et al., 1992). Although they display differences in their views of the perceptual representation of the L1 and L2 sound patterns, they all share the notion that the ability to distinguish new L2 sounds diminishes with age and that adults' discrimination of non-native speech contrasts is systematically related to the L1 sound system. However, they differ in how they see the L1 perceptual framework. Flege's SLM primarily focuses on the notions of phonetic similarity and the construction of new perceptual categories with a clear focus on experienced L2 speakers. Best's PAM describes the variation of discrimination between L2 phonemes, depending on their phonetic ability to fit L1 categories. Kuhl's NLM is also based on segmental linguistic units. Generally speaking, these three models posit that success in pronunciation depends on the relationship between phonetic elements found in the L1 and the L2 systems. Predictions about performance in L2 segmental production are thus based on the perceived phonetic proximity between L1 and L2 sounds. Some of the main tenets of the three models will be outlined in the following.

The SLM was formulated and devised by Flege in 1995. In this model, he combines several hypotheses about L2 speech acquisition. Generally speaking, the SLM seeks to predict that if an L2 sound is clearly different from an L1 sound, it will be less difficult to acquire than an L2 sound that is fairly similar to an existing L1 sound.

The SLM is based on two major assumptions. Firstly, Flege (1995) posits that the accuracy of speech production of the L2 learner is limited by the accuracy related to their perception. That is to say, accurate perception is just as good as or better than accurate production of the sound. In an experiment, Flege et al. (1999) examined the production and perception of English vowels by highly experienced native Italian speakers of English. They found that the perception and production of English vowels significantly correlated. Flege cautions though that this does not necessarily mean that all instances of FA are perceptually motivated. For example, a Spanish speaker's pronunciation of the word 'school' as /eskul/ is not perceptually motivated. Rather, it is rooted in the phonotactics of the Spanish language.

Secondly, the SLM is also concerned with the ultimate attainment of L2 pronunciation. Assuming that age is the defining criterion in the distinction between L1 and L2 acquisition, the SLM particularly aims at examining the role this factor plays. According to Flege (1995), if L2 learning begins early on in life, L2 learners are more likely to establish new phonetic categories. This assumption is based on the notion that as phonetic L1 units develop, they attract L2 sounds, thereby hindering the development of new phonetic categories. Furthermore, with increasing age, learners lose the ability to detect such phonetic differences.

Generally speaking, the language learner can classify and process a new L2 sound in two different ways. Firstly, if the sound is very similar or even identical to an L1 sound, it will most likely be incorporated into the established L1 category (Flege, 1995: 239). Secondly, if an L2 sound is clearly different from any sound in the L1, a new category will be established that will not be tainted with an FA. Therefore, the SLM assumes that although mature L2 learners may not be able to perceive new L2 sounds accurately at first, they 'will ultimately be more successful in [perceiving them] if they differ substantially from L1 sounds than if they differ just a little' (Flege, 1992a: 187). However, it could also be the case that the new category generated by the learner is different from the corresponding L1 category simply because it has been influenced by a nearby L1 category or because the learner employs different features to discriminate categories. As an example, Flege refers to Munro (1993) who investigated Arab learners of English realising the short/long contrast in the English vowel system and found that they tend to exaggerate duration differences between the two classes of vowels. Consequently, the category representations that fail to correspond to category representations of a native speaker are inevitably realised as instances of FA.

Empirical support for the SLM is provided by Flege (1987) who purported that L1 speakers of English produced the L2 French phone /y/ accurately but not the more 'similar' phones /u/ and /t/. Additional evidence comes from experienced learners of an L2 who demonstrated more native-like perceptual patterns of L2 vowels than less experienced learners (cf. Bohn & Flege, 1990, 1992, 1997).

Nevertheless, a number of potential problems have been associated with the SLM. The earlier version was criticised for its lack of explicit criteria for the distinction between 'similar' and 'new' phones, particularly vowels (e.g. Blankenship, 1991). Another problem is that the SLM does not account for a number of results of empirical studies in the area of speech learning. For example, an investigation into native Italian speakers' productions of English vowels, (Munro et al., 1996) did not confirm the hypothesis that English vowels that are acoustically 'close' to Italian vowels are less well produced.

On the other hand, a study by McAllister (2007) lends support to the SLM, in particular as far as mastering the /s/-/z/ distinction by Swedish learners of English is concerned. In this investigation, the Swedish students were rated by native speaker listeners regarding their pronunciation of /s/ and /z/. Altogether 68 attempts were recorded to pronounce /z/ correctly, but only 15 of them were rated as successful. The author attributes this finding to the lack of contrast between /s/ and /z/ in Swedish. Hence, the apparent closeness of /s/ and /z/ prompted the Swedish students to put these two phonemes in the same phonetic category, thereby hindering the creation of a new sound category for /z/ (McAllister, 2007: 164).

To sum up, the SLM developed by Flege and colleagues attempts to describe the process of SLA, thereby taking into consideration the role of age-related factors in the occurrence of foreign-accented speech. Accordingly, accurate L2 production cannot take place unless there is accurate perception. Also, both L1 and L2 are not fully separate systems and L1 phonological acquisition capacities stay intact throughout the whole life span, which means that there is no critical period that significantly hinders the successful acquisition of an L2 sound system.

Another prominent theoretical cross-linguistic speech perception concept is the PAM, which was originally developed to account for the finding that native speakers of English are able to discriminate Zulu click consonants surprisingly well (Best *et al.*, 1988). Best argued that the reason for this was that the listeners had perceived the clicks as non-speech sounds.

Broadly speaking, PAM posits that adult L2 learners assimilate L2 phones into their L1 phonemic inventory. In other words, L2 phones are perceived in terms of their similarity to L1 phones (Best & Strange, 1992: 306). The differences between the L1 and L2 sounds are based on the properties of the articulatory organs (e.g. the lips, the tongue and the glottis).

Best's model has to be seen within the direct realist view of cross-language speech perception. She maintains that the central idea behind direct realism is that 'the perceiver directly apprehends the perceptual object and does not merely apprehend a representative or "deputy" from which the object must be inferred' (Best, 1995: 173).

In contrast to the SLM, PAM goes beyond a mere one-to-one segment comparison between the L1 and L2 sound systems and posits that two members of a non-native contrast can be assimilated to native phones in three different ways. Firstly, if two members of an L2 contrast are perceived as equally good instances of a single L1 category, their discrimination will be difficult. Secondly, if one of the two members is perceived as a better instance of an L1 category than the other (CG), their discrimination will be easy. Thirdly, if the L2 categories are mapped onto two different L1 categories (two category assimilation), they will be discriminated with ease. Thus, L2 contrasts that are assimilated to L1 phonemes can be divided into three main categories: two category (TC), category goodness (CG) and single category (SC) contrast depending on the degree of proximity between the L2 contrasts on the one hand and between the L2 and the L1 sounds on the other hand. The PAM predicts that the TC type will be the least difficult, the SC the most difficult and the CG in the middle range, depending on the degree of 'goodness' between the two phones perceived. Thus, according to the PAM, discrimination will be excellent if the L2 contrast is similar to the L1 contrast and least successful if two L2 segments are the same with respect to an L1 category. Like the SLM, the PAM allows for later acquisition, noting that 'even limited exposure [...] in adulthood can improve performance to some extent' (Best et al., 2001: 776).

As its name already indicates, the PAM highlights the perception of L2 speech and is not specifically concerned with production, i.e. FA. However, Jilka (2000: 33) speculates that the PAM implies the notion of FA in as far as L2 constellations that are assimilated to an L1 category show traces of FA, particularly when they are classified as non-ideal. Regarding the new categories in the L1 phonological sphere, it is assumed that corresponding phonemes are correctly inferred from perception and that for this reason no foreign-accented speech is produced.

To give support to their claims, Best and Strange (1992) examined Japanese students' perception of the American English sounds /w/ and /j/. They found that these sounds were indeed assimilated to the corresponding Japanese /w/ and /j/, a typical case of TC assimilation. Similarly, the English /r/ and /l/ sounds were assimilated to a single Japanese /l/, an example of the SC-type of assimilation.

Polka and Werker (1994) embarked on a study to test the perception of German vowels by native English adult speakers and English-born infants. Indeed, their results showed that the German front and back rounded vowels were assimilated to the English back rounded vowels but the ratings also revealed that the front vowels were assimilated less well to the English vowels. The authors pointed out that the listeners perceived clear differences in CG for the German vowels within each contrast. The high level of accurate performance on non-native vowels was taken as confirmation of the CG assimilation pattern of the PAM model.

In 2001, Harnsberger carried out a study that involved the testing of native speakers of Malayalam, Marathi, Punjabi, Tamil, Oriya, Bengali and American English on their ability to identify nasal consonants (Harnsberger, 2001). Again, the results showed that the discrimination scores corresponded to the claims lodged by the PAM. Similarly, Nagao et al. (2003) examined Japanese listeners from three different age groups and levels of experience with the English language on the identification and discrimination of non-native syllable structures and voicing in non-native syllables. They discovered that the Japanese listeners accurately identified non-native syllable structures and that the performance of the Japanese listeners was correctly predicted by the PAM.

As has been shown, both Best's PAM and Flege's SLM try to anticipate the difficulty with which a listener is able to distinguish between non-native phonemes, which seems to be directly related to the extent to which these sounds assimilate to different L1 phonemes. The predictions generated by Flege's SLM for inexperienced learners are much the same as those generated by the PAM, in that they are also based on perceived phonetic similarities. However, the SLM differs from the PAM in two important ways: Firstly, the SLM focuses on individual phonetic categories whereas the PAM focuses on pairwise phonological contrasts and secondly, the SLM primarily looks at L2 production with perception merely guiding it, whereas the PAM clearly focuses on perception.

In the literature, the NLM theory (Kuhl, 1991; Kuhl & Iverson, 1995) is often seen as an elaborate model of speech perception and language acquisition that details the structure and representation of phonetic and phonological categories. To explain this phenomenon, Kuhl introduces a perceptual magnet, also referred to as the NLM, which is based on the premise that prototypes act as powerful anchors for phonemic categories.

Kuhl points out that humans tend to exploit certain auditory features and so perception is changed to serve language. The perceptual magnet effect already manifests itself at the age of six months. Kuhl et al. (1992) discovered that six-month-old infants clearly recognise native prototypes. She provides the example of Swedish infants recognising /y/ as a prototype, whereas American infants identify the /i/ prototype and therefore treat the non-native sound as a non-prototype. The NLM holds that the speech representations developed in the first year of an infant's life are influenced by the surrounding language and play a crucial role in the acquisition process.

This can be illustrated by the fact that Japanese speakers show considerably less discriminatory sensitivity for vowels than Swedish speakers owing to the fact that Swedish has more vowel categories and clearer boundaries. Accordingly, in Phase 1, children perceptually divide the acoustic space that is available to them in a more general way (A). Then, in Phase B, when the learners are about six months old, they show language-specific magnet effects that are closely related to their language experience. Finally, in Phase C, specific phonetic boundaries seem to disappear and magnet effects alter the perceived distance between stimuli (cf. Kuhl & Iverson, 1995: 139).

The NLM can also be extended to L2 phonological acquisition as it takes account of typical instances of foreign-accented speech such as the frequently reported problem that Japanese L1 speakers experience regarding the distinction between /r/ and /l/. For them, these two speech sounds are drawn perceptually towards one L1 phonological category only, which renders them difficult to distinguish. Hence, the speakers are not capable of generating perceptual representations for both sounds and subsequently they fail to produce them accurately. This recognisable link between perception on the one hand and production on the other hand is further reinforced by the fact that the perceptual representations for any given language are essentially seen as aims to acquire accurate articulatory gestures which are essential prerequisites for accurate production. It follows that if the representations of some L2 sounds do not correspond to those sounds' actual phonetic features, they will essentially give rise to the production of foreign-accented speech.

In their study, Iverson *et al.* (2003) examined the perception of English /l/ and /r/ by a group of German English as a second language (ESL) learners (who also distinguish between the two phonemes in their L1), a group of Japanese ESL learners (whose difficulties with the two sounds are well known) and a control group of native speakers of American English. Their results showed that whereas the English and German speakers managed to differentiate between the two English liquids, the Japanese subjects were comparatively insensitive to differences at the /r/-/l/ boundaries. The L1 speakers of English were in fact found to display the sharpest between-category distinctions and the poorest within-category discrimination. Overall, the German ESL learners seemed to follow the English pattern but with considerably less between-category discrimination. Although Japanese ESL learners had significantly poorer between-category discrimination, they showed higher accuracy in terms of within-category distinctions than both the German and the native English speakers. Apparently, Japanese adult learners are most sensitive to an acoustic cue that appears to be irrelevant regarding the English /r/-/l/ categorisation. Conversely, German adults showed a fairly high sensitivity to more critical acoustic cues.

Obviously, one of the most crucial problems for L2 learners has to do with the fact that speech sounds in the L2 are confronted with perceptual magnets and perceptual boundaries that are inherently associated with their L1. Those L2 speech sounds that are similar to existing L1 categories are bound to be influenced by the magnet and so they may either not be perceived independently at all or their perception is significantly shaped by the distorted perceptual space. The NLM therefore provides support (Kuhl & Iverson, 1995: 143) for the SLM hypothesis that 'the greater the perceived phonetic dissimilarity between an L2 and the closest L1 sound, the more likely it is that phonetic differences between the sounds will be discerned' (Flege, 1995: 239)

To sum up, the SLM, the PAM and the NLM hypothesise that adult L2 speech production problems are due to the perception and assimilation of L2 segments to L1 categories and that achievement in SLA pronunciation diminishes with age.

The Contrastive Analysis Hypothesis and Markedness

Apart from the CPH, a second theoretical conceptualisation that is frequently associated with attainment in L2 phonology is the CAH as developed by Lado (1957). The CAH claims that the challenges an L2 learner faces essentially result from the direct transfer from the learner's L1 to the target language. These difficulties may arise when '[w]e tend to transfer to [the foreign] language our phonemes and their variants, our stress and rhythm patterns, our transitions, our intonation patterns and their interaction with other phonemes' (Lado, 1957: 11). According to Lado (1957), the adult speaker of an L2 cannot easily hear language sounds other than those of his/her L1. Consequently, L2 phonemes are often perceived incorrectly. He argues that those features of the FL that are similar to the learner's L1 will be easy to learn and those features that are different will be more challenging.

CAH theorists claim that mistakes in the language acquisition process result from the negative transfer between the L1 and the L2 (Brown, 2000: 208). Here, two main reasons are given. First, this can happen when the L1 phonological system lacks sounds that exist in the target language. For a Spanish learner of English this would mean that as the sound /dʒ/ in words such as jail does not exist in Spanish, it is often replaced with the sounds /tʃ/ (as in chica) or /j/ (as in yuyo) (Kenworthy, 1987: 153). For German learners of English the pronunciation of the English /ð/ in words such as *this* or *that* is often difficult because this sound does not exist in German and is therefore often confused with /d/. Second, the sounds exist in L1 and in L2 but they are used differently (Brown, 1992: 10). Hence, a Spanish learner of English might encounter problems distinguishing the phonemes /d/ and /ð/. In this case, in English the spelling helps to differentiate between these sounds (in words, like *those* vs. *dose*). In Spanish, however, it is the position within a word that provides the cue for the accurate production of 'd'. As a consequence, 'the letter "d" can be pronounced as /d/ at the beginning of a word like *díme* or as a fricative /ð/ in the middle as in *cada*' (Lado, 1957: 14).

A considerable amount of research in this field focuses on the segmental level due to the fact that 'prosodic errors in stress placement or rhythm, may contribute less to FA than do segmental errors' (Flege, 1992b: 589). Nevertheless, proponents of the CAH have also pointed to the relevance of contrastive analysis at the suprasegmental level (e.g. Tarone, 1984: 63; Young-Scholten, 1995: 115). In 'The Role of the Syllable in Interlanguage Phonology', Tarone (1984), for instance, argues for the importance of investigating syllable structures by referring to a study conducted by Briére in 1966. This study examined the English phonemes /ʒ/ and /ŋ/. In the English language, both phonemes exist but neither of them is found in word-initial position. The American subjects in the study experienced great difficulty with the accurate pronunciation of the sound /ŋ/ in word-initial position. The possible explanation is that as opposed to /ʒ/, which occurs syllable initially in English (as in *pleasure*), /ŋ/ does not. Therefore, the American subjects had problems trying to pronounce the Vietnamese *ngao*. Hence, this study clearly identified the position of a sound within a syllable as a crucial aspect to be considered when discussing language transfer (Tarone, 1984: 64). In addition, Tarone sought to provide an answer to the question of whether syllable structures are directly transferred from the learners' L1 or whether there are in fact universal syllable structures that lie at the core of the transfer.

In her analysis of data collected from Korean, Portuguese and Chinese learners, she concludes that

> [...] there is observational and experimental evidence in second-language acquisition research to suggest that the universal intrinsic structure of the syllable has some influence on the shape of IL phonology. Further, there is evidence that transfer of NL syllable structure rules into TL sequences does occur, and is also influential in shaping the IL phonology. (Tarone, 1984: 71)

Regarding the contrastive analysis of stress patterns, an empirical investigation conducted by Mairs (1989) deserves to be mentioned. Seeking to shed light on the notion of word stress, she analysed interviews with Spanish L1 learners of English. In accordance with Tarone, Mairs (1989) also detects a clear effect of L1 tendencies to influence L2 syllable structures. However, her findings on stress patterns appear to diverge:

> The results of this analysis further suggest that while transfer of constraints on native language syllable structure may be important in developing interlanguage grammars and influencing a number of different levels of grammatical structure, the tendency to transfer stress rules from the learners' native language may be less pervasive. (Mairs, 1989: 282)

In contrast to the CPH, the CAH does not focus on the ultimate attainment in L2 learners. Although there are some examples of adult L2 learners who are compared with children (e.g. Beebe, 1984: 57; Gussmann, 1984: 33), CAH theorists did not manage to provide a clear definition of an adult L2 learner, nor did they speak in favour of children's exceptional ability and advantages regarding language learning. However, what needs to be discussed is the process of interlanguage production since it is closely linked to the notion of FA. Whereas Selinker considers interlanguage a sum of the 'learner's attempts to produce a target language', later advocates of the CAH tend to see IL 'more as a creation of an active and resourceful constructor, an L2 learner' (Gussmann, 1984: 33). From this constructivist view, the explanation related to learners' negative transfer may be either that 'they constructed the correct representations but failed to implement them in the native-like manner or they constructed a representation close to the correct one but not close enough' (Ard, 1990: 254). This view is largely based on data collected by Beebe (1984). Her study, which relies on sound files of native Asian learners of English, rejects some of the claims made by the CAH. Beebe points out that the L2 learners' phonological repertoire is largely conditioned by the level of acquisition:

With training, they [L2 learners] may add to their phonetic repertoire, and a large number of approximations may occur as they advance to the intermediate level. Finally, however, as they progress to an advanced level of proficiency, they will realise TL norms more frequently and eliminate some of the approximations they formerly relied on. (Beebe, 1984: 57–58)

In addition, Beebe claims that the concept of sociolinguistic variation is of central concern when discussing IL. For instance, her data shows that for Thai learners of English the production of the sounds /l/ and /r/ strongly depends on the social context rather than on their ability to pronounce these sounds accurately (Beebe, 1984: 59). Beebe (1984: 60) concludes that 'a contrastive analysis can never be detailed enough to be able to account for all of the existing variations in pronunciation'.

Although the CAH was a major breakthrough at the time, it cannot be used to explain all pronunciation errors made by L2 learners (Eckman, 1987). However, in defence of the CAH, Eckman (1987: 68) states that 'the CAH should be revised to incorporate a notion of degree of difficulty which corresponds to the notion of typological markedness'.

Typological markedness has its origins in the Prague School of Linguistics and in the theories of Nikolai Trubetzkoy (1969) and Roman Jakobson (1969). Eckman (1977: 320) explains the notion of markedness as follows: 'phenomenon A in some language is more marked than B if the presence of A in a language implies the presence of B; but the presence of B does not imply the presence of A'. Accordingly, the basic idea underlying the concept of markedness is that two polar opposites of certain phonemic properties (e.g. voiced and voiceless obstruents) are in fact not considered to be binary contrasts. Instead, one of the two opposing members is regarded as privileged in as far as it has a wider distribution. The other – less frequent one – is labelled marked, indicating that it is more difficult and less natural. In the example given above, voiceless obstruents would be considered unmarked and voiced obstruents would be seen as marked.

Trying to predict potential problems that learners of any L2 may have, a number of advocates of the Markedness Differential Hypothesis (MDH) basically compare L1 and L2 systematically and add the notion of markedness. According to the MDH, those areas of the L2 that are different from the L1 are marked and thus prone to cause difficulties. The more marked a certain feature of the L2 is, the more difficult it is to acquire. As a consequence, it is easier to learn unmarked elements than marked ones (Eckman, 1977: 321). To give an example, Eckman's MDH postulates that native speakers of German learning English will experience problems learning the difference between final voiced and unvoiced consonants because in German, obstruents are always voiceless in word-final position (*Reis* vs. *rice-rise*).

The Interlanguage Hypothesis and Fossilisation

A third hypothesis that deserves due attention in the discussion of L2 phonological acquisition concerns the concept of interlanguage, which is based on the notion that an L2 learner employs a language system that does not correspond to either the L1 or the L2. It is in fact a third language that has an intermediate status between the L1 and the L2. This interlanguage shows the learner's attempt to approximate the target language.

The term 'interlanguage' was coined by Selinker in 1969 and further elaborated by Selinker in 1972. A number of alternative terms have also been used by other researchers to refer to the same phenomenon: 'in-between' language or grammar, 'transitional competence' (Corder, 1971) or 'approximative system' (Nemser, 1971).

Based on his observation that 95% of L2 learners never reach native speaker competence, Selinker (1972) attributed this to the phenomenon of fossilisation. He saw fossilisation as a process whereby the interlanguage ceases to develop. 'The argument is that no adult can hope to ever speak a second language in such a way that s/he is indistinguishable from native speakers of that language' (Selinker, 1969: 5). Similarly, Nakuma (1998: 247) defines fossilisation as 'a state of permanent failure on the part of an L2 learner to acquire a given feature of the target language'.

In the literature, the labels that have been given to this phenomenon are numerous and thus a myriad of terms referring to the same or a similar concept have been suggested, e.g. backsliding, stabilised errors, learning plateau, typical error, persistent non-target-like performance, de-acceleration of the learning process, ingrained errors, systematic use of erroneous forms, cessation of learning, structural persistence, ultimate attainment, long-lasting free variation, persistent difficulty and inability to fully master target language features (cf. Wei, 2008: 1).

A great number of researchers have attempted to investigate this phenomenon (e.g. Adjemian, 1976; Nakuma, 1998; Schumann, 1990; Selinker, 1972). The questions they sought to answer were mainly related to reasons (Adjemian, 1976; Schumann, 1976, 1978, 1990, 1997; Seliger, 1978) precipitating conditions (Schumann, 1990), the kind of linguistic material that tends to be fossilised (Selinker & Lakshamanan, 1992; Todeva, 1992) and the relation between type of learner and fossilisation (Adjemian, 1976; Scovel, 2000; Selinker *et al.*, 1975; Vigil & Oller, 1976).

Investigating the causes of fossilisation, scholars have concentrated on four main aspects that seem to play a decisive role, namely biological, motivational, psychological and affective factors. One possible biological explanation is assigned to the CPH, as discussed in detail in Chapter 3: Section 3.2.2 of this book.

A second factor of obvious relevance in determining the causes of fossilisation is motivation (e.g. Gardner, 1988; Gardner & Smythe, 1975) to meet the learner's communicative needs (Corder, 1978; Nickel, 1998; Ushioda, 1993). In this respect, concerns have been expressed regarding adult learners' lack of empathy with L2 native speakers and their culture. According to researchers such as Guiora et al. (1972a, 1972b), adult learners often lack the motivation to change their accent and to strive for native-like pronunciation. In contrast to children, adults tend to be less open to L2 cultures and they therefore have more 'rigid language ego boundaries' (Guiora et al., 1972a: 421). Thus, mature learners tend to establish and reinforce their cultural and ethnic identity, and this they do by keeping their stereotypical accent. Interestingly, in this particular study the researchers sought to mitigate the empathy level of their informants by administering increasing amounts of alcohol. They found that the learners' L2 pronunciation improved to a certain degree and then declined again with the consumption of increasing amounts of alcohol. However, another reason could be that alcohol relaxed the learners' muscles, which in turn may have had a positive effect on their articulation of the L2 sounds.

Acton (1984: 71) expressed the view that as soon as a learner reaches puberty, his/her 'ability to learn a second language, including the possibility of acquiring a native-like accent, begins to deteriorate'. He argued that learners' pronunciation becomes fossilised as soon as they become functionally bilingual.

At this point there seems to be little consensus of what triggers phonological fossilisation. Apparently, none of the above-discussed theories provides deep insights into a highly debated phenomenon. There is substantial evidence that argues in favour of the existence of different constraints that shape the language learning process. However, it is far from clear whether FA is determined by insufficient phonetic input, by gradual deterioration of speech learning mechanisms or simply by the inability to keep the L1 and L2 phonological systems apart.

3.2.3 Conclusion

The theoretical considerations and empirical investigations I have outlined in this section discussed the concept of FA. As has been shown, various researchers have looked into the question of how and why adult FL learners struggle with this seemingly unavoidable challenge. The review of those theories that are frequently mentioned in the context of foreign-accented speech has revealed that each hypothesis approaches the phenomenon from a different angle, thereby treating accent as a perplexing theoretical puzzle whose pieces still need to be identified and assembled. Whereas the CPH identifies biological constraints as the main reason for the failure of adult learners to acquire native-like pronunciation, the CAH focuses on the direct transfer of L1 phonology into the learners' L2 phonological inventory in order to predict potential problem areas. The third theoretical concept discussed here, the Interlanguage Hypothesis, describes the learner system as a separate entity that does not corresponds to the learners' L1 or their L2. What these theories seem to suggest is that age and L1 matter, the extent of which, however, remains uncertain.

Although the aim of this book is not to empirically validate the models and hypotheses discussed above, the results of this study still need to be seen in light of these theoretical assumptions. As the students in this project are all adult learners of English whose L1 is Austrian German, it will be interesting to see how far these two factors play a role in determining the development of the degree of FA.

3.3 Language Learning Outcomes in the English-Medium Classroom

Having discussed a number of SLA language learning theories commonly associated with the EMI classroom as well as the theoretical underpinnings of the development of FA, I will now turn to empirical investigations into the potential language benefits of English-taught courses in higher education.

As mentioned before, a distinctive feature of a traditional EMI classroom at university is the absence of attention to language. English is essentially seen as a vehicle through which content is transferred (e.g. Coyle et al., 2010: 15). In this respect, it is often assumed that language learning happens incidentally. This means that in the case of EMI, the mere exposure to comprehensible English will trigger the language learning process. Järvinen (2008: 83), for instance, purports that 'the affordances view of input – what the context can "afford" in terms of learning language' also fosters the general understanding that in English-medium programmes (EMPs) students are given a myriad of possibilities to acquire the respective language. At the same time, it may be claimed that the students need to actively take advantage of these opportunities to ensure that learning does take place. In the case of a great number of institutions of higher education, this is severely restricted owing to large student numbers and a general lack of interaction between teacher and student. Exceptions in this respect are many private universities or UAS.

3.3.1 Linguistic gains

As discussed in Chapter 2, the current trend towards teaching content courses in English as a means to facilitate the European notion of integration and multilingualism has been gaining momentum in the last decade. However, as this is still a fairly new approach to language learning and teaching, studies into the linguistic gains of EMI in tertiary education seem scarce. Researchers are only now beginning to explore this emerging field, which means that research to date appears to be predominantly descriptive and exploratory in nature (cf. Ament & Pérez-Vidal, 2015). Hence, it makes sense to draw upon the CLIL experience in primary and secondary school settings for further insight into what can be expected at the tertiary level.

Generally speaking, CLIL is believed to be an effective way of improving students' FL skills (Dalton-Puffer & Nikula, 2006; Ruiz de Zarobe, 2008; Zydatiß, 2007a). One of the most common arguments in favour of CLIL is the assumption that increased exposure to and use of L2 in the classroom lead to increased language proficiency. In addition, CLIL is often associated with advantages not only in terms of the learners' linguistic abilities but also regarding their intercultural competence as well as motivation and confidence to study both the language and the content (cf. http://ec.europa.eu/languages/policy/language-policy/bilingual_education_en.html). Nevertheless, empirical research seems to suggest that under CLIL conditions certain competences are enhanced more than others. According to Dalton-Puffer (2008), receptive skills, vocabulary, morphology, creativity, risk-taking, fluency, quantity and affective outcomes benefit most, whereas syntax, writing, informal language, pronunciation and pragmatics seem to remain unaffected. Interestingly, pronunciation appears to be the least affected of the speaking dimensions (Dalton-Puffer, 2008).

Taking into account that CLIL students usually continue with their regular EFL classes alongside their CLIL content courses, it comes as little surprise that they tend to outperform their non-CLIL learners (Dalton-Puffer, 2011). This expectation is clearly corroborated in a number of studies (e.g. Lasagabaster, 2008; Mewald, 2007; Ruiz de Zarobe, 2008; Zydatiß, 2007a, 2007b). However, these studies vary considerably in their design and methodology and therefore general conclusions can hardly be drawn. The question of how much and in what respect CLIL students are in fact better remains in the dark, as does the question of why (Dalton-Puffer, 2011).

Although the findings reported from secondary school scenarios are insightful and valuable, simply transferring them to the tertiary level of education would essentially mean ignoring the peculiarities of learning and teaching at universities regarding language and education policy, institutional interests as well as learners and instructors involved (cf. Unterberger, 2014). Despite the fact that in tertiary education a vibrant research scene has established itself, it seems that studies into the linguistic gains of EMI are scarce. Airey (2004), for example, pointed out that the number of research projects assessing language competence through EMI programmes at university level is rather limited. Actually, he could not find any projects on the effects of EMI on students' linguistic competences. In the Austrian context, it is interesting to note that students who choose an EMI course expect their English language competence to increase and report this to be one of the prime factors for choosing the respective programme (Tatzl, 2011). To date, however, there seems to be little empirical evidence to support this claim.

Among the very few empirical studies into the linguistic gains of tertiary EMI is a study conducted by Loranzc-Paszylk (2009) in the academic year 2006/2007 at the Academy of Technology and Humanities in Bielsko-Biala, Poland. The results of her investigation into reading and writing skills lead her to conclude that systematic text-responsible writing increases the undergraduate students' linguistic gains as far as reading skills are concerned. Therefore, she concludes that in an EMI classroom a particular linguistic skill (i.e. writing) may in fact be transferable to another skill (i.e. reading).

Rogier (2012), in her longitudinal study into the linguistic progress of EMI of students enrolled in higher education in the United Arab Emirates, explored score gains on the International English Language Testing System (IELTS) exam after four years of undergraduate study. Her findings clearly indicate that the students achieved significantly higher scores in all four of the English language skill areas tested by the IELTS exam. The most noticeable gains were reported in the area of speaking, followed by reading, writing and then listening.

Recently, a longitudinal study conducted at a Catalan university has caught the attention of researchers as it has – for the first time – tried to measure long-term linguistic gains in four skills, namely listening, writing, grammar and speaking. For their project, Ament and Pérez-Vidal (2015) chose a pre-test post-test design over a period of one year to capture the language development. They compared two groups: a focus group with 100% exposure to English through EMI and a control group with 18%–41% of their courses taught in English. They discovered a trend towards improvement in both groups. Interestingly, they report significant gains in grammar in the control group but not in the focus group. Regarding the lack of improvement in terms of listening skills, the authors note that the lecturers were non-native speakers of English. Accordingly, they attribute the lack of gains in the students' listening skills to the lack of native accent input.

3.3.2 Phonological gains

As discussed above, the area where the clear superiority of the CLIL students is detectable is spontaneous oral production. In this respect, a number of quantitative surveys (e.g. by Lasagabaster, 2008; Ruiz de Zarobe, 2008; Zydatiß, 2007a) purport that CLIL students are generally ahead in this respect. This result is largely based on self-reports obtained in student interviews where learners frequently displayed increased fluency and speaking confidence. Other studies (e.g. Hüttner & Rieder-Bünemann, 2010; Maillat, 2010; Moore, 2009) have also found that CLIL students show greater flexibility and listener-orientedness together with more self-assuredness in getting their message across even if they may momentarily lack the necessary linguistic resources (cf. Nikula, 2007).

As far as pronunciation is concerned, however, the impact of CLIL instruction seems to be more moderate (e.g. Gallardo del Puerto *et al.*, 2009). Indeed, reviewing the latest and most relevant studies related to the effects of English-medium teaching on language competence, we find that spoken production in general and pronunciation in particular have only received minor attention, especially as far as the tertiary level of education is concerned. Nevertheless, a number of researchers – mostly from Spain – have looked at pronunciation and FA in secondary school settings.

In her longitudinal case study, Ruiz de Zarobe (2008) compared the oral language competence of secondary CLIL students with EFL students in terms of pronunciation, vocabulary, grammar, fluency and content. She concludes that in every category the CLIL group outperforms the non-CLIL group. Interestingly, she observes that there appears to be no significant increase in proficiency over a longer period of time.

In their research, Gallardo del Puerto *et al.* (2009) contrasted the degree of FA of learners in the CLIL classroom with that in the traditional FL classroom. They argue along the same lines and maintain that no statistically significant difference in the degree of FA can be detected and claim that this, again, can be attributed to a lack of native speaker input. Much to their surprise, the evaluation of the communicative effects of the FA in a narration task shows that the learners in the CLIL group were judged to be more intelligible.

A study conducted by Rallo Fabra and Juan-Garau (2011) in 2010 explored the effects of CLIL instruction on Spanish-Catalan learners' perceived comprehensibility and accentedness in a reading-aloud task. The authors claim that CLIL has a modestly positive effect on the learners' overall intelligibility but does not seem to contribute to ameliorating the degree of FA in the short and mid-term (after one year), speculating that the main reason for this lies in the fact that most of the language input comes from non-native teachers of English. Also, it has to be noted that in their sample the students only had one or two subjects taught in the FL.

A fourth project from Spain that needs to be mentioned was carried out by Gallardo del Puerto and Lacabex (2013) who sought to measure the influence of additional (i.e. +30%) CLIL exposure on secondary school learners' oral production in a story-telling task. Their findings go along with earlier research showing that learners' productions were perceived to be more fluent and more accurate in terms of vocabulary and grammar. Yet, no differences were found for pronunciation.

In the German-speaking context, the only study that attempted to shed light on the impact of CLIL on learners' pronunciation was conducted by Varchmin (2008), who investigated the effects of CLIL at the segmental level, focusing on final devoicing and the pronunciation of dental fricatives. She compared a group of CLIL and a group of non-CLIL students in Germany and concludes that for her study no connection between the teaching method and the students' pronunciation skills can be discerned.

To the best of my knowledge, empirical studies into the effects of tertiary EMI on students' pronunciation skills are practically non-existent. In this respect, the two studies that could be identified appear to be only partly relevant for the present project in that they are either set in an English-speaking country (i.e. New Zealand) or rely on self-reported linguistic gains that are not validated by listeners.

Firstly, a small-scale longitudinal study on the effects of English as an additional language (EAL) on pronunciation at university level comes from New Zealand. Examining the changes in pronunciation that occur in four Asian immigrants in New Zealand within three years of studying, Romova *et al.* (2008) claim that a number of changes in the learners' pronunciation can be observed both in terms of FA as well as fluency. It has to be noted, however, that the findings of this study can only be loosely linked to the project at issue since English is an official language in New Zealand and therefore provides considerably more exposure to the English language than Austria. Furthermore, their subjects received explicit formal pronunciation training.

Secondly, Maiz-Arevalo and Dominguez-Romero (2013) report on the self-perceived linguistic gains of business students at Madrid University in speaking, reading, writing and listening. As far as pronunciation is concerned, about half of the sample believed that the EMI classes had led to a significant improvement in their pronunciation. About one-fourth, however, stated that their pronunciation had not changed much. The authors see the reason in the fact that the emphasis in these courses is on the content and not so much on the language.

In summary, it can be said that findings from secondary school contexts suggest that pronunciation is one of the skills that seems to remain largely unaffected by EMI. The main reasons why EMI does not impact the students' pronunciation skills are threefold: quantity of input (only a few courses are taught in English), quality of input (referring to the teachers' own pronunciation skills) and a lack of long-term observation. Clearly, this scarcity of empirical data on the effects of tertiary EMI on learners' pronunciation skills calls for further investigations into an area that has been conspicuously neglected in the literature so far. This oversight is particularly striking when taking into consideration that one of the overall aims of English-medium teaching as such is communicative competence of which pronunciation is undoubtedly a key component. This is exactly where the present study can make a significant contribution.

3.4 Insights from the UAS Vienna

The discussion of language learning outcomes in English-taught courses has shown that little empirical evidence is available suggesting that phonological gains in an EMI classroom are in fact likely. By examining the development of the students' pronunciation skills in a specific EMI programme where up to 50% of the content courses (quantity) are held in English by native speakers of the language (quality) over a duration of roughly three years (longitudinal design), this project provides the ideal avenue to effectively address a vital question that undoubtedly deserves to be explored.

Building on the theoretical and empirical work in the field of language learning in the EMI classroom as discussed in the previous sections, this section now turns to my own research project. First, some of the challenges I was confronted with in my endeavour to measure the phonological development of the learners are described. Then, I will present the results derived from the sound file rating. After the presentation of some descriptive statistics, I will discuss the findings in more detail and relate them to the literature.

3.4.1 Measuring the development of the degree of foreign accent of the learners: The challenges

Trying to measure the pronunciation development of EMI students, I was confronted with a number of challenges, especially in terms of choosing appropriate tasks, developing a useful rating tool and selecting qualified listeners for the project. For this reason, it was immensely helpful for me to find another researcher at the University of Vienna who was also working on the question of why some language learners are better or more talented than others when it comes to pronunciation learning. Susanne Reiterer, then a guest professor at the Department of English and American Studies, was working on a large-scale project together with the universities of Stuttgart and Tübingen, Germany, investigating the neural correlates of pronunciation talent, i.e. the differences in the brain activity between talented and untalented speakers (cf. Dogil & Reiterer, 2009). To cover all possible manifestations of talent and to find correlations between a number of supposedly significant factors and the overall talent score, psychological and behavioural tests and questionnaires were administered as well as tasks assessing phonetic and general linguistic aptitude. After intensive talks and discussions with Susanne Reiterer, I decided to draw on her study and use some of the data collection tools that had already proven to be successful in her project (i.e. the questionnaires, the choice of text types, the online rating tool) as the basis for the development of my own data collection instruments and assessment tools and tailored them to the specific needs of my own study. By doing so, it is also hoped that the results of the present study complement and add a longitudinal view and a novel perspective to the information gathered by the German researchers.

Most studies investigating the perceived degree of FA have included two main types of tasks, namely controlled production tasks (e.g. the reading of a text or the repetition of a recorded model) and extemporaneous production tasks (e.g. picture stories, personal narratives, interaction). Whereas the former approach has the advantage that it allows the researcher to elicit predetermined, clearly specified speech material from the speakers, the language is bound to lack naturalness as it is not formulated by the speaker (cf. Munro, 2008: 202). Less controlled tasks, such as the narration of a picture story, may compensate for the weaknesses of controlled tasks by producing more natural speech; however, the output may not contain those predetermined features of the language that the researcher is interested in and thus it will also be difficult to compare two speakers or groups. Owing to the drawbacks of both approaches to how speech can be elicited, it seems sensible to rely on more than one task type in order to be able to draw reliable conclusions about a particular accent. In line with Dogil and Reiterer's project, I decided to include the reading of a short text ('The North Wind and the Sun') as well as the narration of a Gary Larson (cf. Jilka, 2009) cartoon in the present study.

Among others (e.g. Horgues & Scheuer, 2014; Meng *et al.*, 2009) 'The North Wind and the Sun' was also used by Gass and Varonis (1994) in their study into the comprehensibility of non-native speech. The reason why this text enjoys such great popularity in the field of pronunciation research goes back to the early 20th century when the International Phonetic Association started to invite linguists to contribute phonetic versions of the text in different languages and dialects. This corpus has proven to be an exceptionally valuable resource for the comparison of the pronunciation of different language varieties and accents. Not only is a considerable number of descriptions of its rendition in a wide range of languages available, but transcriptions have also been provided for many English accents, ranging from Californian American English (Ladefoged, 1999) to Tyneside British English (Watt & Allen, 2003) and received pronunciation (RP) British English (Roach, 2004). In addition, on the CD-ROM in Schneider *et al.* (2004), more than 30 different varieties of English from around the world including English-based creoles are recorded. This extensive use of the text together with the detailed descriptions provided by a number of researchers investigating the phenomenon of FA makes it highly appropriate for the present project.

To account for a more natural type of speech, the students were also asked to narrate the Gary Larson cartoon, which was also used in Dogil and Reiterer's study. This quasi-spontaneous task was included as it primarily promised to best reflect the learners' overall pronunciation abilities and secondly, output can – to a certain extent – be controlled and more effectively compared (Jilka, 2009). Notably, words like cow, farmer, door, bell, house and grass are likely to occur. The decision to choose this particular story was also prompted by the fact that it does not require any advanced technical or business terminology. Rather, it relies on the students drawing on their knowledge of very basic vocabulary, which means that they can tell the story quickly and without much preparation.

A further – more pragmatic – advantage of these two tasks has to do with the length of the text, which was an important criterion for the recording and the rating process as well. Each task took no longer than one minute to record, which was considered advantageous for both the speakers as well as the listeners.

Having selected the appropriate task types for my research, another challenge was related to finding a suitable rating tool. Despite the growing body of empirical research into FA, there is still no standard scale for measuring the degree of FA. Piske *et al.* (2001) point at this lack and raise the question of whether the various utilised rating scales ensure equally valid and reliable measures of the degree of L2 FA. Indeed, the objective characteristics of FA remain elusive (see Section 3.2.1). In this regard, Southwood and Flege (1999: 344) purport that there are no physical units in which an accent can possibly be measured, and that there is therefore a certain danger in an FA experiment of the raters applying a contraction bias, which means that they might overestimate small differences and underestimate large ones.

Although there is great diversity in the type of assessment, most studies on the perceived degree of FA have been based on the listeners' intuition to place speakers on a scale ranging from native speech to strongest FA (Thompson, 1991). Whereas some studies explicitly ask listeners to rate the degree of FA on a particular scale (e.g. Flege *et al.*, 2002), others label only the endpoints of the scale as 'native' and 'non-native' (e.g. Moyer, 1999), 'very good pronunciation' and 'very poor pronunciation' (Yeni-Komshian *et al.*, 2000) or more vaguely in relative terms such as 'close to native English' and 'less close to native English' (Magen, 1998), respectively.

Owing to this lack of a standard measuring tool and scale (cf. Major, 1987), I decided to refrain from designing yet another rating tool with another rating scale that would significantly complicate the comparison across empirical findings. Instead, I opted for the replication of a model that had already proven to be effective. Thus, the evaluation tool created by the researchers in Reiterer's project (cf. Jilka, 2009) served as the basis for the development of a suitable online rating instrument. With the help of a professional software programmer, a few minor changes were made to the model in order to meet the requirements of the present project.

In particular, a clearer focus on the rating of foreign-accented speech – rather than intelligibility or fluency – was expressed in the basic instructions provided for the listeners.

First, the raters needed a username and a password to access the tool. They were then asked to fill in a short form asking them to provide a few personal details such as gender, L1 and experience in teaching pronunciation courses. After a brief demonstration of how to use the tool correctly, the self-timed rating process of the sound files started. It should be noted here that all the raters were asked to use earphones for listening as the importance of controlled quiet conditions in the research-related sense cannot be underestimated. These sound files appeared in random order with all the raters listening to the reading of 'The North Wind and the Sun' first, followed by the narration of the cartoon (Figure 3.1).

As Figure 3.1 illustrates, the raters listen to the stimuli (using headphones), see the pictures to be narrated or the text to be read and use the rating bar where they can directly indicate the degree of foreign accent. This rating bar features a visual analogue scale (VAS), which consists of a vertical line with the two poles labelled. The scale that has been used in the present study, as shown in Figure 3.1, is unipolar and denotes the lack of the degree of FA of 0 at one end and its maximum intensity (10) at the other end of the line. Any click along the scale is assigned to a corresponding numerical value. On the scale, no further marks are provided, which allows for little orientation for the listeners, but is at the same

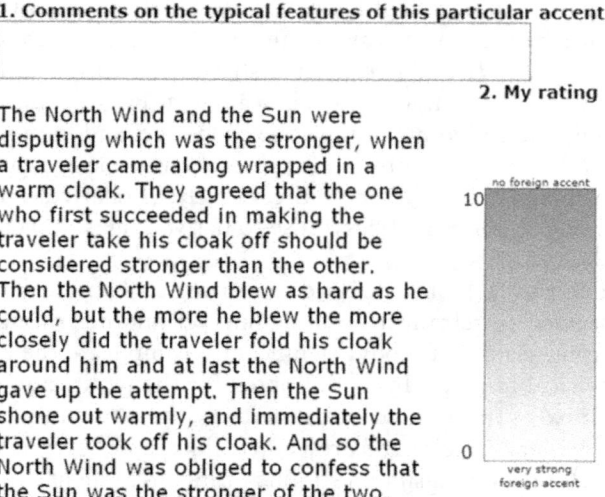

Figure 3.1 Screenshot of the rating bar

time assumed to provide a more uniform distribution of scores along the scale's entire length (cf. Scott & Huskisson, 1976).

VASs are said to be easily understood, quickly processed and also account for fine discriminations. Indeed, by using this particular tool information can be obtained very quickly from any number of raters who do not require any special training. This way, a holistic and intuitive assessment of a speaker's perceived degree of FA can be provided. As the screenshot of the instructions for the listeners in Figure 3.2 shows, at the beginning of the rating process a chart providing an approximate orientation was given with five subcategories ranging from 'speaker sounds like a native speaker of English with NO foreign accent' to 'very strong foreign accent'. In addition, the listeners could also leave comments if they wished.

Instructions for using the rating bar

Please use the rating bar in a holistic and intuitive way. Just click on the approximate area in the rating bar, where you would roughly put the person's foreign accent. The picture below should give you an approximate orientation:

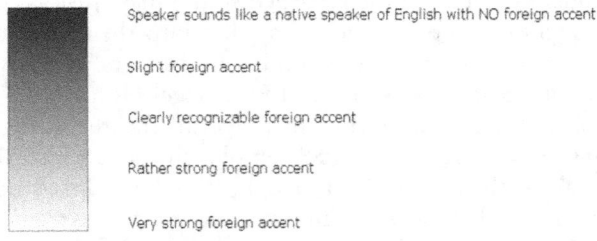

Speaker sounds like a native speaker of English with NO foreign accent

Slight foreign accent

Clearly recognizable foreign accent

Rather strong foreign accent

Very strong foreign accent

In addition, you will find a box for comments.
There you can note down anything about the performance that you consider to be strong features of the particular foreign accent displayed (segmental or super-segmental features, prosody, etc.).
Any comment is optional but highly appreciated!

**Please note that once you have clicked on the rating bar, the next file starts and you cannot go back. If you would like to add a comment, you need to do this BEFORE you rate:
Step 1: comment
Step 2: rate**

Figure 3.2 Screenshot of instructions for using the rating bar

A further aspect that needs to be mentioned here concerns the fact that the scores also reflect fine discriminations, as in this case the scale underlying the rating bar 0–10 in fact consists of 100 rather than 10 units. This means that, for example, a listener who clicked on the middle of the rating bar in fact clicked the value 50 rather than 5, which allowed for more precise and distinct differences to be established among the speakers. Apart from the already mentioned small extent of orientation a VAS can give the rater, another possible drawback could lie in the indistinct definition of what exactly is meant by 'maximum' and 'minimum' on the scale, which allows for different interpretations by different listeners. Nevertheless, the absolute values for the overall degree of FA are not the top priority in the present study as its purpose lies in the investigation of the development of FA, i.e. the comparison of the values obtained at T1 and T2 rather than ultimate attainment.

Another potential weakness of global FA ratings (FAR) is based on the assumption that FA can be captured on a unidimensional, linear scale or simply assigned to one of a given number of discrete categories. This view is of course a simplification of a phenomenon that comprises a wide range of features on both the segmental (sound) as well as the suprasegmental level (stress, pitch, tone, intonation, speech rate and rhythm) (cf. Munro & Derwing, 1995; Southwood & Flege, 1999). In addition, disfluency and hesitation markers also play a role in the assessment of foreign versus native speech (Yu, 2005). As in the present project, the aim is to monitor the development of FA and not to identify specific features of it, the use of FAR is certainly justified. It goes without saying that for the identification of those features of the Austrian accent in English that are least susceptible to change, a different approach needs to be taken.

A third challenge in the course of my research constituted the selection of listeners or judges evaluating the recorded sound files. Just as the number of speakers included in experimental studies into the degree of FA appears to vary greatly, so too does the number of listeners who have been involved in the rating process. Snow and Hoefnagel-Höhle (1977), for example, used only one single listener to judge all the recordings, whereas Anderson-Hsieh and Koehler (1988) employed more than 200 raters, although not all of them rated every single stimulus. Most studies, of course, can be located somewhere in between the two extremes. On logical grounds, Piske *et al.* (2001) put forward the claim that generally a large number of listeners is needed for the reliable detection of differences between speakers.

Beyond numbers, of course, the linguistic background of the judges for the rating task is also an important consideration that needs to be taken into account. This being said, in the vast majority of cases, 'experts' of the target language have been used to make judgments of L2 language performances or to validate rating scales. However, it is not always clear how 'expert' is defined and operationalised. As a consequence, 'expert' has come to denote the self-reported familiarity with foreign-accented speech (e.g. Munro *et al.*, 2006a) or the degree of exposure to L2 speech (Kennedy & Trofimovich, 2008) or phoneticians (e.g. Cucchiarini *et al.*, 2002) or ESL teachers with extensive teaching experience (Calloway, 1980) or just native speakers of the target language (Wrembel, 2010). Still others have used some combination of these different criteria (Huang, 2013). These inconsistencies of course render cross-study comparisons very difficult.

Generally, studies investigating the relationship between rater background and scoring performance have yielded conflicting results. For instance, some researchers (e.g. Johnson & Lim, 2009) failed to find a consistent correlation between listeners' language background and measures of their performance in rating oral responses. However, other studies concluded that raters' background variables partially accounted for some scoring differences. Interestingly, Carey *et al.* (2011) examined familiarity in accented English and found that a significant number of non-native-speaker listeners scored candidates from their own home country higher than candidates from a different country. In his study, Thompson (1991) compared the FAR provided by an experienced group (i.e. learners who spoke at least one FL, attended language classes and had frequent contact with native speakers) and a novice group (i.e. learners who spoke no FL fluently, did not attend language classes and rarely had contact with native speakers). He found that the novice group generally evaluated the recordings as decidedly more accented than the experienced raters.

Similarly, Flege and Fletcher (1992) drew a comparison of the FAR of students with a university degree in neuroscience (who were classified as 'experienced') and students who were less familiar with FAs. Surprisingly, in this particular study the ratings were in fact comparable, suggesting that, in contrast to Thompson's findings, judges who are inexperienced need not automatically be less reliable. Along the same lines, Bongaerts *et al.* (1995, 1997) and Anderson-Hsieh and Koehler (1988) also reported good levels of agreement between ratings made by experienced and inexperienced listeners.

As far as training in phonetics is concerned, the literature seems to suggest that this does not affect FARs. Groups of phonetically trained and phonetically untrained raters overall seem to display great agreement in their overall ratings (e.g. Hopp & Schmid, 2013), even though inter-rater reliability is generally found to be higher among trained raters (e.g. Thompson, 1991; Xi & Mollaun, 2011). After careful consideration, I decided to employ phonetically trained rather than untrained judges as the latter might rely on factors other than phonological/phonetic cues when assessing the FA of learners' productions (cf. Gallardo del Puerto *et al.*, 2007), such as grammatical accuracy (Varonis & Gass, 1981) or fluency (Anderson-Hsieh & Koehler, 1988) or content (Ludwig, 1982). A pilot experiment carried out in the preparation phase of this project with a number of untrained listeners clearly confirmed this assumption.

All in all, nine potential judges were identified to be suitable listeners for the present project. They had all taught English pronunciation courses and assessed students' pronunciation skills at the University of Vienna for about 10 years. Three male and six female lecturers from various linguistic backgrounds (L1 speakers of American English, British English and Austrian German) were included to ensure a wide range of perspectives. Furthermore, in their courses, they had always assessed the (predominantly Austrian) students' pronunciation skills in pairs which means that they were largely familiar with the Austrian accent and due to their extensive experience and common understanding of grading foreign-accented speech, a high degree of reliability, validity and homogeneity was to be expected. All potential listeners were contacted and agreed to participate. None of them reported any hearing impairment. After T1 rating, however, it turned out that two of the raters had experienced major technical problems and as a consequence their ratings could not be used. The remaining seven listeners each rated all the sound files, i.e. approximately 140 sound files at T1 and 120 sound files at T2.

Language data collection for T1 and T2 was performed on two consecutive days in Semester 1 and Semester 6, respectively, split up into two groups (focus group/control group) with each group taking approximately one hour. The students were initially informed by email in which it was stressed that the project was being carried out within their own institute. For them, this meant that their contribution would be of immediate relevance to their own studies and also for the next generation of students in the bilingual programme.

In this particular study, a potential risk inherent in any longitudinal experiment was related to student attrition. In order to obtain data from as many students as possible, I had to ensure that the students participated voluntarily. As a known member of staff, it was not difficult for me to persuade English language lecturers to set aside half an hour of one of their in-class sessions for my data collection. On the agreed day, the students were collected from their classrooms and accompanied to the soundproof radio studio where the recording was to take place. This way, it was guaranteed that a maximum number of students participated as the project was part of the English class, the students knew me and the whole procedure only took 60 minutes.

The English for specific purposes (ESP) teachers had agreed to set one hour of their in-class teaching time aside. In practice, this meant that I picked up the whole group about one hour before the end of their regular English language class and accompanied them to the radio studio assigned to another degree programme, which was located in the same building but on a different floor. Each student began by filling in a brief language background questionnaire, which is included in Appendix A. At this stage, my presence turned out to be very helpful in that it enabled any queries or uncertainties to be addressed immediately and it also ensured a good response rate. In addition, I made sure that all the questions were completed and filled in correctly. This way, information from a great number of respondents could be gathered quickly and correctly.

One by one, the students were then asked to go to the enclosed sound-attenuated room where they met one of my colleagues (who teaches radio broadcasts and who knows how to handle the sound mixing console) to ensure the highest possible quality of the recordings. The students were given a headset, the sheet with the text they had to read and the cartoon they were to describe. They were given about a minute to prepare and then they read the text and narrated the story wearing a head-mounted microphone. The entire task took two to three minutes for each participant. The two tasks were recorded separately and saved as jpg files on a USB stick.

Recordings of four L1 speakers of English (exchange students from the United States) were included in the corpus to serve as distractors for the raters on the one hand and as baseline data to assess the learners' performance on the other hand (cf. Dogil & Reiterer, 2009).The recordings were then transferred to the online rating tool, and passwords were distributed to the raters together with an email containing general information about the project. The rating process as such ran over several weeks in Semester 1 and then again in Semester 6. Upon entering the language rating site, the listeners found basic information about the project and were asked to provide details concerning their age, gender, years of teaching pronunciation, L1, etc. Then they were shown a sample to ensure that the instructions were clear. In random order (which varied from listener to listener), they rated the stimuli with all the files for the reading task appearing first and then all the files for the story coming next. Throughout the rating process, the extreme values 'no native speaker' (1) to 'native speaker' (10) were displayed on the rating bar. The listeners were permitted as much time as they needed to rate. The sound files could be played again, but once given the rating could not be altered. The next sound file started immediately after each rating response was given. Space was also provided to make comments but the raters very rarely took advantage of that option. If necessary, they could listen to the same sound file several times before clicking the rating bar. As the whole rating process took between two and four hours, they could also log out and continue later. On the whole, it took roughly two months to collect the ratings from all seven listeners.

3.4.2 Analysing the development of the degree of foreign accent: The results

In order to answer the question if and to what extent the learners in this project developed their pronunciation skills, the main source of information was the data set comprising the sound file ratings. As already mentioned, the informants in the two participating groups, the focus group from the bilingual programme ($n = 25$) and the control group from the German programme ($n = 30$), were recorded at the beginning of their studies (T1) and then again shortly before graduation (T2). The informants were asked to read the text 'The North Wind and the Sun' and to narrate a picture story by Gary Larson. Each sound file was subsequently rated by seven carefully selected pronunciation experts from the University of Vienna. These listeners used a VAS ranging from 'very strong foreign accent' (0) to 'no foreign accent' (10). A statistical analysis of the inter-rater reliability (two-way mixed) was carried out by the consulted statistician and revealed that the raters were using the measurement technique correctly and consistently, reflected by intra-class correlation coefficients ranging from 0.816 to 0.876 across the four experimental conditions A to D (i.e. two pre-tests and two post-tests).

Comparative analysis of the two groups

One of the core objectives of this research project was to compare and contrast the mean scores received from the expert judges for the focus groups with those for the control group. A statistical analysis of the data derived from the sound file ratings shows the results for both groups and tasks for T1 and T2, respectively (Table 3.1).

Table 3.1 Descriptive statistics of the scores obtained for the two groups at T1 and T2 by skill

	Mean (SD)		t-test	
	Focus group	Control group	t	p
Reading T1	5.7 (±1.5)	4.0 (±1.1)	4.69	0.000
Reading T2	6.8 (±1.7)	4.6 (±1.7)	4.75	0.000
Speaking T1	6.2 (±1.5)	4.4 (±1.0)	5.19	0.000
Speaking T2	7.2 (±2.0)	5.0 (±1.7)	4.50	0.000
Average T1	5.9 (±1.4)	4.2 (±1.0)	4.75	0.000
Average T2	7.0 (±1.8)	4.8 (±1.6)	4.86	0.000

Source: Richter (2017).

Table 3.1 illustrates the results of a *t*-test for independent samples, which reveal a significance level of <1% as far as the difference between the two groups is concerned. This can be seen at both T1 and T2 for all three aspects analysed (reading, speaking and average). The rather unexpectedly high degree of difference clearly supports the methodology adopted in this research project which sought to explore the *development* of the learners rather than their *ultimate attainment*. Accordingly, it can be seen that already at the time of the first recording (T1) the focus group (average mean 5.94) significantly outperformed the control group (average mean 4.2) and the same trend can then be observed again at T2 with the scores for the control group (average mean 4.8) distinctly lagging behind the focus group (average mean 7.0). This initial superiority of the students in the EMP comes as little surprise as other empirical studies into the linguistic benefits of secondary school CLIL students have shown that this particular teaching method seems to appeal to a very specific group of learners. In this respect, Sylvén in her study on the effects of CLIL on Swedish learners remarks that

[t]here is (normally) a requirement of a certain level of proficiency before entering a CLIL class. Therefore, students who enjoy, and are interested in, English are more likely to find the CLIL method appealing than those who are less interested in English. (Sylvén, 2004: 180)

Similarly, Rumlich (2016) finds that CLIL programmes ostensibly appeal to learners with higher levels of language learning motivation and linguistic talent. Without doubt, this assumption is also in line with the findings of the present project. Clearly, a mere cross-sectional comparison of the differences in ultimate attainment in the two groups would not have produced any new insights in this respect.

These results overwhelmingly exceed all expectations and hopes raised by other empirical studies into the phonological gains of EMI at secondary school level as discussed in Section 3.3. As outlined there, a number of investigations conducted in the Spanish context (Gallardo del Puerto *et al.*, 2009; Rallo Fabra & Juan Garau, 2010; Ruiz de Zarobe, 2008) found that CLIL at secondary school level does not seems to contribute to the amelioration of the degree of FA in the short or mid-term (after one year). The Spanish researchers mainly attribute the reason for this to a lack of exposure to native speakers on the one hand and a very low number of subjects taught in English on the other hand. My study now provides pioneering and evidence-based data according to which tertiary EMI can indeed have a positive effect on the learners' pronunciation skills provided that favourable conditions are given. Ostensibly, the design of the bilingual programme at the UAS Vienna with increased quantity and quality of native speaker input as central parameters has produced clear and convincing results.

Another noteworthy observation revolves around the fact that the scores for elicitation task 1 (the reading of the short text 'The North Wind and the Sun') were clearly lower than for elicitation task 2 (the narration of the Gary Larson cartoon) for both groups at T1 and T2, respectively. This finding is generally supported by other empirical studies of L2 foreign-accent which employed both elicitation methods. For instance, Oyama (1976) found that overall the read speech of Italian-English subjects was more heavily accented than their spoken speech tokens. In this respect, Munro and Derwing (1995) hypothesised that these effects might be largely related to the nature of the task type, since the speakers cannot leave out words and expressions which they find challenging when they read a text. Another crucial aspect which merits further examination – especially when it comes to adult learners – is related to orthography. Bassetti and Atkinson (2015), who examined the role of orthography in adult L2 learners' speech production, confirm that orthographic forms indeed have an impact on the pronunciation of known words, albeit to a lower degree in immediate word repetition than in read-aloud tasks. In addition, culturally and pedagogically conditioned classroom practices may have played a role. In Austria – and in many other European countries – asking students to read out a given text in class is not common practice. For the past decade or more, reading aloud seems to have been generally discouraged in communicative language teaching methodology (e.g. Gibson, 2008). In brief, the main reasons why the scores assigned to the read text were considerably lower than those for the narration of the cartoon might be threefold: difficult words and/or sounds cannot be omitted, orthography may have interfered and reading-out aloud is a skill rarely practiced in Austrian classrooms.

The development of foreign accent

Having explored the main differences in achievement between the two groups, the next aspect to focus on is the development of the FA. Table 3.2 presents the statistical analysis of the scores obtained for both groups at T1 and T2.

Table 3.2 Descriptive statistics of the development of FA

Group	Task	Mean (SD)			t-test	
		T1	T2	Average difference	t	p
Focus group	Reading	5.7 (±1.5)	6.8 (±1.7)	+1.1	−6.37	0.000
	Speaking	6.2 (±1.4)	7.2 (±2.0)	+1.1	−5.12	0.000
	Average	5.9 (±1.4)	7.0 (±1.8)	+1.1	−6.65	0.000
Control group	Reading	4.0 (±1.1)	4.6 (1.7)	+0.6	2.56	0.016
	Speaking	4.4 (±1.0)	5.0 (1.7)	+0.6	2.56	0.016
	Average	4.2 (±0.9)	4.8 (±1.6)	+0.6	2.89	0.007

A t-test for independent samples performed on the data revealed that both groups experienced a significant improvement in the development of their pronunciation skills. The figures derived from the comparison of the results obtained for the focus group are highly significant with $p<0.01$. The scores for the control group are also significant albeit to a lower extent with $p<0.05$. Still, both groups distinctly managed to ameliorate their foreign-accented speech. While the focus group improved their speech production by an average of 1.1 points, the control group in the German programme scored significantly lower at 0.6 points.

When considering the development of the two skills (reading and speaking) separately, it can be seen very clearly that for both tasks the scores have undergone a favourable development. In order to find out whether these observations are in fact significant, it was necessary to conduct a t-test (Table 3.3).

Table 3.3 aims to illustrate the differences in the development of the learners' FA at T1 and T2 for the two elicitation tasks (reading and speaking). As can be seen very clearly, these differences are in fact not significant ($p>0.05$). Nevertheless, the fact that the two values calculated for reading

Table 3.3 Differences between groups according to tasks

	Mean (SD)		t-test	
	Focus group	Control group	t	p
Reading	1.1 (±0.9)	0.6 (±1.2)	1.95	0.056
Speaking	1.1 (±1.0)	0.6 (±1.3)	1.55	0.127
Average	1.1 (±0.8)	0.6 (±1.1)	1.99	0.052

Source: Richter (2017).

(0.056) and average (0.052) are extremely close to significance level 0.05, it might be assumed that a larger sample size could have resulted in a higher significance level. It has to be noted, however, that the mean difference for 'speaking' (0.127) stands out as it is clearly far from significant. This shows that the mean scores for the development of the students' foreign-accented speech as measured in the read-aloud task are statistically significant, while the scores obtained from the raters for development of the FA in the narration of the cartoon is considerably less pronounced.

The most striking results obtained in this study can be found in the fact that both groups managed to ameliorate their FA, albeit to different degrees. Although I had sound reasons to expect moderate improvement on the part of the focus group owing to favourable conditions provided by the UAS (such as increased L1 input in the EMI classroom), it does come as a surprise that the values calculated for the control group at the time of the second recording also indicated a significant progression towards less accented speech.

Evidently, these findings substantiate the view that the pronunciation skills of adult language learners are not necessarily inhibited by maturational constraints of the aging brain as proposed by the CPH. It can be safely assumed that the language learning process of the subjects in the present project has not been compromised by age and that under favourable circumstances further progress can be expected. In line with other studies into the existence of the CPH (see Section 3.2.2), the results presented here support the view that the CPH does not provide a full explanation for the development of the foreign-accented speech of adult learners. Contrary to the tenets of the CPH, a steady and gradual rise in the level of speaking proficiency was revealed across both groups.

In addition to the determination of the group scores at T1 and T2, it was also intriguing to investigate the range of distribution within the two groups. To visualise the range of distributional characteristics, I decided to conduct a box plot analysis displaying the statistical variance for both groups. Figure 3.3 presents the difference in the distribution of the average difference (i.e. development) within the focus group and the control group, respectively.

What Figure 3.3 clearly shows is that the box plots for the two groups are generally similar in size but uneven in distribution and height. As for the focus group, the median is roughly 1.0 and the second quartile is the

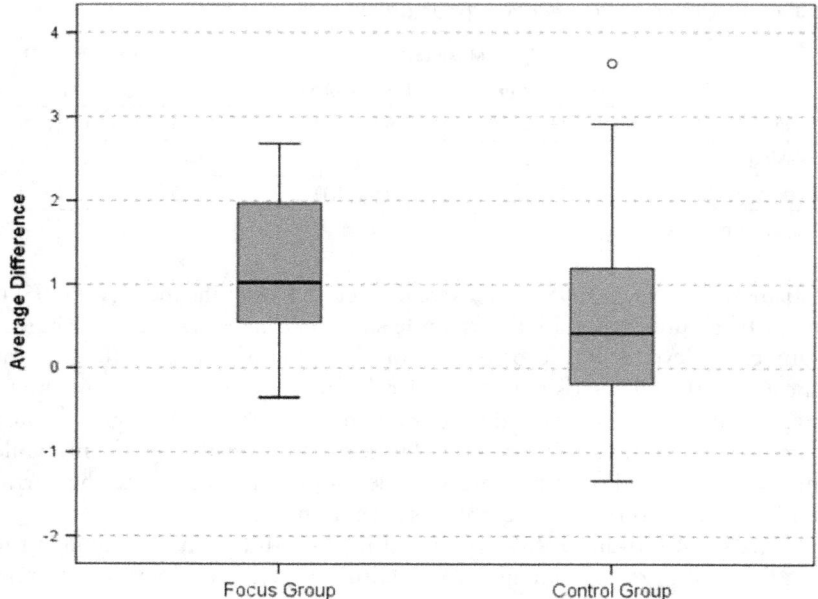

Figure 3.3 Distribution of average difference

largest in size. In contrast, the median for the control group is approximately 0.5 and here the largest quartile seems to be the upper one spanning nearly 2 points. The most outstanding difference between the two box plots is the distribution range from –0.4 to +2.8 in the focus group and –1 to +2.9 in the control group. This means that in the focus group, the learners are generally much more homogeneous in their development than those in the control group.

Overall, these results confirm the findings presented above according to which the focus group experienced a more substantial improvement than the control group. However, within the control group the difference is considerably more varied in its distribution. In the focus group, about 75% of the learners experienced an overall improvement of up to 2 points whereas 75% of the participants in the control group only reached an improvement of up to 1 point. The outlier in the control group turns out to be an exceptional student whose performance deserves special attention and will be discussed separately in Chapter 4: Section 4.2.1.

Self-assessment versus FA ratings

Apart from an examination of the figures presented above that show the learners' development of FA as rated by pronunciation experts, I also considered it noteworthy to compare those scores with the students' own views of the progress they had made regarding their pronunciation skills.

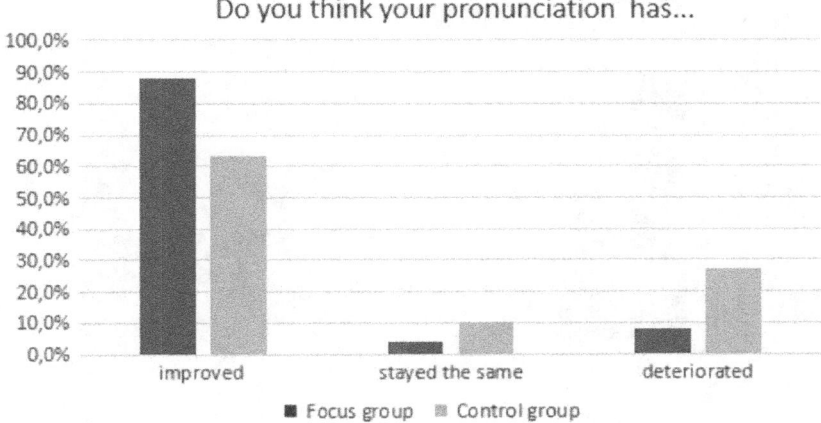

Figure 3.4 FA – self-report

As many teachers would agree, there is often a great deal of disparity between how students see their own progress and how teachers rate them. As I was interested in finding out whether there was any difference between self-perception and the FARs of the listeners, I included a number of probing questions in the questionnaires about their own feelings in terms of their English language gains in the course of their studies. Specifically, they were asked to rate their competence in different skills and language areas both at T1 and T2. Hence, Figure 3.4 shows the learners' self-perceived progress at T2.

In both groups, about half of the learners had the impression that their pronunciation had improved. However, 46% in the focus group and 32% in the control group said that they saw no changes. The main difference to be detected between the two groups can be found in their view concerning the deterioration of their pronunciation skills. In this respect, the figures diverge considerably with 4% in the focus group and 16% in the control group believing that their pronunciation skills had experienced a considerable decline during their studies. In stark contrast to that, the scores from the FAR experiment exhibited the results shown in Figure 3.5.

As Figure 3.5 convincingly shows, the vast majority (88%) of the learners in the focus group managed to ameliorate their foreign-accented speech, 4% stayed the same and for 8% the score at T2 was below that at T1. In the control group, 63% improved their accent, 10% stayed the same and 27% were in fact downgraded at T2.

These findings suggest that for both groups a clear mismatch between self-reported L2 phonological competence and the actual FAR can be discerned. Whereas 50% of the students in the focus group believed that their pronunciation had improved, the actual figure from the FAR was

Figure 3.5 FA – rating

considerably higher with 88%. Likewise, only 52% of the learners in the control group expressed the view that they felt they had improved. However, the FA score for them was 63% and therefore also clearly higher. An interesting detail that deserves due notice is related to those students who perceived their pronunciation to be at a lower level at the end of their studies than three years previously. In fact, there was only one single student from the focus group (i.e. 4%) who indicated that his pronunciation had deteriorated. A closer look at the information he provided in Q2 reveals that among other aspects, he spent one semester in Argentina where he spoke mostly Spanish.

By nature, self-perception is subjective and may therefore fail to correspond to external indicators of proficiency. Although some studies have shown that self-assessment can be a valuable tool for student placement (LeBlanc & Painchaud, 1985), it is clear that language students sometimes underestimate or overestimate their language ability. In this respect, a number of studies have reported that some learners systematically underestimate their abilities (e.g. DesBrisay, 1984). Fiske and Taylor (1991: 216) proposed that 'by leading the self to expect poor outcomes or poor performance, one lays the groundwork for defending against loss of self-esteem in the event of failure'. In the present context, this might mean that the students may have rated their own performance lower in order to protect themselves from disappointment.

The marked divergence displayed here between the learners' self-perceived L2 phonological development and the actual competence as rated by pronunciation experts also seems to hint at the role pronunciation learning and teaching assumes in the given context. At the UAS, this particular sub-skill of spoken language competence is relegated to the sides not only in the EMI courses but also in the ESP classes, where language learning is primarily seen in business-related contexts such as meetings, telephoning or negotiations where the focus is more on intelligibility and comprehensibility rather than form and accuracy. This inattentiveness on the part of the programme designers and teachers alike together with a general lack of capability to assess their own accent seems to result in many students generally underestimating their own pronunciation skills.

3.4.3 Conclusion

The findings emanating from the data gathered in this study have convincingly shown that the FA of the learners in both the focus group and the control group improved considerably. However, the difference in the degree of development of the two groups is highly significant as the EMI students decidedly outperformed their peers in the control group at the beginning of their studies as well as at the end. Over a period of almost three academic years, the focus group improved their FA by an average of 1.1 points, whereas the control group in the German programme scored significantly lower at 0.6 points. The initial superiority of the learners in the focus group gives rise to the assumption that those students from the UAS Vienna who are accepted into the bilingual programme already possess better pronunciation skills than the students in the German programme. This head start is then further reinforced in the course of their studies (most likely through increased exposure to English in the form of EMI classes, exchange semesters and internships abroad) and leads to a clear edge towards the time of graduation. A comparison of the scores obtained for the two tasks reading and speaking revealed that the former developed less whereas the latter was rated considerably higher. In addition, a wider distribution range of performances could be observed in the control group whereas the EMI group was found to be more homogeneous in their linguistic abilities. Also, a clear mismatch concerning the students' own perception of their development and the FAR was revealed. This could perhaps be attributed to the fact that although the students in the focus group were exposed to a considerable amount of L1 in their EMI courses, the general lack of attention to language in those classes may have given rise to the students' believing that the input they received was mostly valuable in terms of increased subject knowledge but not in terms of enhanced English language skills.

4 Factors Influencing L2 Pronunciation Mastery

One of the main tasks that lies at the heart of second language acquisition (SLA) research is to unravel the puzzle of why some learners seem to be more successful than others. The most frequently given explanation for this much debated phenomenon is age and the impact of a critical period for language learning in general and for pronunciation in particular (see Chapter 3: Section 3.2.2). Whereas there seems to be little doubt about the potential correlation between the age of the learner and the ultimate level of his/her pronunciation mastery, there is more scholarly dispute regarding the question of whether age is the single most important reason for incomplete acquisition. In fact, the amount of variation in pronunciation attainment that can be observed among mature second language (L2) learners suggests that age can hardly be the only factor that plays a role. Instead, other non-linguistic individual factors have been named as crucial to ultimate attainment. Thus, a considerable body of linguistic research has focused on an investigation of these factors and their relative importance in inhibiting or fostering a learner's phonological competence in the L2. Sociolinguistic research in SLA, for example, has shown that a number of social, cultural and psychological variables play a decisive role. Indeed, among scholars there is steadily growing interest in how these aspects impact the learner's degree of foreign accent (FA). As Moyer (2013: 49) points out, language learning is now seen as 'chaotic, messy, and far less predictable than previously assumed'. In response to changing environments, a constant interplay between psychological, cognitive and social mechanisms renders FA a dynamic construct that is largely characterised by its complexity and fluidity (Moyer, 2013: 49).

In this chapter, I will highlight the most significant individual difference (ID) factors that are claimed to account for phonological variance in foreign language (FL) learning. In particular, the focus will be on affective variables such as (1) attitude and identity, (2) motivation and (3) anxiety; educational aspects like (4) formal pronunciation instruction; as well as other individual factors like (5) gender, (6) musicality and (7) exposure to the target language (TL); all of which dominate the scientific discussion in this field and are put to the test in the present study. It should be noted, however, that a number of other variables (e.g. neurolinguistic predisposition, working memory, first language [L1] aptitude, IQ, learning styles) have also been considered by researchers (e.g. Dörnyei, 2005; Dogil & Reiterer, 2009), but will not be included here.

Before embarking on a detailed literature review of the relevant learner variables, a crucial aspect concerning the nature of the respective parameters deserves due notice. A closer look at these individual factors gives rise to the assumption that there is a high degree of ambiguity and complexity involved in discussing them in isolation. Rather, there appears to be a constant interplay between a number of learner propensities contributing to the development of an individual's L2 pronunciation. Some indicators clearly interrelate and function as preconditions or the effects of other factors, but to what degree and how this happens remain unknown. As a consequence, research has recently shifted away from a linear view of these factors to a more overarching theoretical perspective of the issues at stake. According to Ellis (2004), for example, future research needs to focus on how these skills and traits condition the learners' perceptions about language and language learning, and how these, in turn, influence other aspects such as learning strategies.

Essentially, the theory will need to grapple with what is perhaps the overriding issue in SLA today – the role of consciousness. It will need to specify for example, whether the influence of ID factors such as motivation and language aptitude is mediated by learner cognitions and learning strategies, which by definition are conscious actions performed by the learner, or whether they have a more direct effect on opportunities to learn and acquisitional processes that arise without awareness on the part of the learner (Ellis, 2004: 547). What seems to be evident here is that Ellis strikes a new note by postulating an interrelated approach that puts the issue of consciousness at the centre of SLA.

In a similar vein, Dörnyei (2006: 62) also argues in favour of a new, more 'concerted approach' that does justice to the fact that ID variables interact and that 'combinations of traits have more predictive power than traits in isolation'. For this reason, the following subsections will highlight the most important research findings for each variable; however, where appropriate, links with other factors will be provided.

Furthermore, it should be noted that the empirical studies discussed here vary greatly in terms of their design and methodology (subjects studied, elicitation and rating techniques used, stimuli chosen, etc.). These methodological differences, as Piske *et al.* (2001) in their review point out, can – to a certain extent – be held responsible for the often conflicting results that have been yielded. Therefore, the comparability and validity of these studies outside the given context need to be treated with due caution as generalisations are bound to be hazardous and speculative.

4.1 Individual Variables

4.1.1 Attitude and identity

One of the most frequently mentioned predictors of the acquisition of L2 pronunciation is the learner's attitude towards the TL and culture. Indeed, research has found that pronunciation mastery needs to be examined within the context of the learner's values, attitudes and socio-schemata (e.g. Pennington, 1994). Hence, a particular attitude towards the L2 can either support or hinder the development of L2 pronunciation. Stern (1983: 386), for example, purports that 'the affective component contributes at least as much and often more to language learning than the cognitive skills', and this is evidenced in studies postulating that affective variables indeed exert a remarkable influence on language success (e.g. Eveyik, 1999; Saracaloğlu, 2000).

As a matter of fact, the – conscious or unconscious – decision whether or not to adopt or imitate a particular accent can often be traced back to the speaker's relation to the TL and community. In this respect, Kenworthy (1987) notes that

> [s]ome individuals seem to be impervious and even after a long time will absorb only some turns of phrase and the pronunciation of a few individual words. Others seem very receptive and begin to change their accent almost as soon as they step off the plane! (Kenworthy, 1987: 7)

Clearly, there are large differences between those who seem to be able to switch to a particular accent in no time and those who retain a certain kind of reluctance towards the FA.

In his work on acculturation and language learning, Schumann (1986) points out that learners will acquire the L2 to the extent that they acculturate. Accordingly, the learner's openness to the target culture paired with the desire to be socially integrated in the L2 culture can predict the amount of L2 that he/she acquires. In other words, the learner's views of and attitude towards the culture of the TL will impact the sounds of that language. Along similar lines, Brown (1992) notes that students with a positive attitude towards speakers of the TL are likely to master pronunciation skills more successfully as they are more willing to accept a second identity that may emerge within them. Much in the same vein, Ellis (1994) notes that affective factors influence the level of L2 attainment by individual learners who are in turn themselves affected by this success. This means that those learners who hold positive attitudes and who are successful, will experience a reinforcement of these attitudes, whereas learners with negative views may be strengthened by their lack of success.

Already in the 1970s, Guiora *et al.* (1972a) suggested that pronunciation mastery should be linked with psychological factors. They claimed that learners who wish to change their pronunciation need to develop what they called an 'English language ego' by addressing fundamental issues about their personality. In their study, 87 students from the University of Michigan were given moderate amounts of alcohol and after 10 minutes their ability to imitate the pronunciation of an unfamiliar FL was tested. They found an increased ability to authentically pronounce the L2. It appears that alcohol produces a temporary change in ego boundaries. This language ego permeability, i.e. the reluctance to give up control, is then held responsible for the fact that adults experience difficulties learning FLs. The authors conclude that giving up this control is a fundamental prerequisite for learning a new language. They see the process of learning an L2 as an act of extending the self so as to take on a new identity. Furthermore, they identify pronunciation as the most outstanding expression of the language ego, the most challenging skill to acquire in a new language and also the most difficult to abandon in the native language.

Given that identity and the concept of self are driving forces for the successful acquisition of L2 phonology, concretising this accent–identity link has proven to be a challenging endeavour. Norton Peirce (1995), for instance, sees identity as a 'multiple and shifting' concept, pointing out that the conscious control and manipulation of accent is a phenomenon that needs to be considered in research. In this respect, Moyer (2004) found that some advanced learners enjoyed taking on a particular accent when traveling abroad in order to be taken for a native speaker (NS) of the L2. On the other hand, some learners may hold on to their FA to ascertain the link to their linguistic origin (Moyer, 2004). Clearly, identity plays a major role in shaping a learner's attitude towards the TL.

By and large, empirical research seems to suggest a firm connection between learner attitude and pronunciation learning. In their study, Suter and Purcell (1980) devised a list of 20 variables, which were believed to have an influence on pronunciation. They investigated the English-speaking skills of 61 non-native speakers (NNSs), which were rated by a panel of 14 native English-speaking judges. Among the variables that turned out to be the most strongly related to pronunciation accuracy was the learner's attitude and the strength of his/her concern about his/her pronunciation.

In his research on the pronunciation accuracy of tertiary-level students studying Spanish as an FL, Elliot (1995) set out to measure students' attitudes towards the importance of pronunciation teaching in the classroom on the one hand and their own assessment of their pronunciation skills on the other hand. The participants' responses were then correlated with their abilities as measured by a test of their pronunciation. Elliot asserted that the learners' attitudes towards acquiring a native-like pronunciation was the most important variable. This suggests that those students who cared more about their own accent had in fact better pronunciation than those who cared less.

In 2007, Moyer focused on the relationship between learner attitudes and foreign-accented speech. She measured the significance of learner attitudes against two other aspects, namely age of onset of learning (AOL) and length of residence (LOR) in the country where the TL was spoken. The participants in her study were 42 non-native and 8 native US university students who were asked to complete a questionnaire on their language learning background as well as their attitude towards the English language and American culture. They were also given a series of tasks including a read-aloud text and free speech with prompts to measure the degree of their FA. Moyer (2007) found that the L2 users clearly differed from their NS controls in terms of accent rating, but she also considered LOR and AOL to be significant factors. However, language-directed attitudes seemed to be more closely linked to achievement than culture-directed attitudes, although both were considered to be significant. She postulates that a combination of experience together with a positive orientation appears to be particularly important for L2 pronunciation mastery.

The research outlined above seems to support the notion that there is indeed a positive correlation between learners' attitudes towards the FL and the respective cultural environment on the one hand and their ultimate attainment in L2 pronunciation on the other hand.

4.1.2 Motivation

A second crucial ID variable that calls for closer examination is motivation. According to Moyer (2004: 39), the learner's motivation is 'a construct that uniquely represents many orientations simultaneously: conscious effort, intentionality, and planning towards a specific goal'. Accordingly, it is based on 'interest or curiosity to know more, along with perceived likelihood of success and reward' (Moyer, 2004: 39) and has been named the strongest and most influential factor determining the success or failure of learning an L2 (Dörnyei, 2001). Thus, if learners are motivated to improve their L2, they will put more time and effort into it and therefore they are likely to achieve better results. On the other hand, if they do not see the value of it, they will be less motivated and less successful.

The importance of motivation in learning an L2 has been investigated by a great number of researchers (e.g. Deci & Ryan, 1985; Dörnyei, 1994, 2001; Gardner, 1993, 2003; Gardner & Lambert, 1972a, 1972b; Gardner & Tremblay, 1994; Smit, 2002; Smit & Dalton-Puffer, 2000). In their work, they address the various aspects of language learning; however, there seems to be a paucity of research into students' motivation to improve their speaking skills. Specifically, research on pronunciation issues is still very rare.

In an attempt to conceptualise the dynamics of motivation in SLA research, various viewpoints have been brought to bear. Despite clear differences in terms of approach, scholars mostly agree that motivation is indeed a key player in SLA as it has a direct impact on how often students use L2 learning strategies, how much they interact with L1 speakers of the language, how much input they receive in the L1, how successful they are on achievement tests, how high their general language proficiency level becomes and how long they preserve and maintain L2 skills once their language studies are over (Oxford & Shearin, 1994: 12).

In the late 20th century, the scientific debate mainly concerned the question of whether motivation triggers achievement or vice versa. Whereas Gardner (1985) argues that motivation triggers achievement, Ellis (1996) indicates that this is far from clear. In this context, the Resultative Hypothesis, as coined by Hermann (1980), postulates that learners who are successful in learning an FL are therefore likely to be more motivated to learn the language. A motivated pupil mostly achieves good results in the L2, which confirms and sometimes even intensifies the existing motivation. This also explains the beliefs of less motivated language learners. Pupils who are less motivated to learn an L2 will probably achieve lower results, and consequently their enthusiasm to acquire the L2 will decrease even more. In brief, Ellis notes that there is a constant interaction between motivation and achievement.

Dörnyei (2005: 65) suggests a broader view by claiming that to a certain extent all factors involved in SLA presuppose motivation, as 'it provides the primary impetus to initiate L2 learning and later the driving force to sustain the long and often tedious learning process'. Other scholars, too, have recently seen motivation at the core of all affective variables, describing it as a kind of 'super construct' that incorporates many other factors (Moyer, 2013: 68).

As far as different types of motivation are concerned, it appears that various taxonomies are used in the literature. One very common categorisation juxtaposes instrumental and integrative motivation. While instrumental motivation denotes a situation where the purpose of language learning is to obtain a benefit (e.g. getting a job), integrative motivation refers to language learning prompted by the desire to affiliate with the particular language and its culture. Another scale that tends to be used to measure motivation contrasts intrinsic and extrinsic motivation depending on whether the stimulus for the behaviour comes from outside or inside the individual (e.g. Deci & Ryan, 1985).

Theoretical approaches to L2 motivation have also undergone various paradigm shifts over the years, starting with Gardner's social-psychological approach in the 1950s, to the more cognitive approach in the 1990s and the latest neurobiological research, suggesting that the topic of L2 motivation has not lost its appeal.

In this regard, the key framework that has driven much of the research was introduced by Gardner (1985). With his model, he aims to show that motivation directly influences L2 achievement and is itself affected by certain social and psychological factors. One of these variables that has been discussed extensively in the literature is the learner's orientation, i.e. the learner's long-range goals for learning the TL (Gardner, 1985, 1988). According to Gardner and Tremblay (1994), the main difference between orientation and motivation is that a student might display a particular orientation, without actually being motivated to achieve that particular goal. For instance, a learner might see that proficient English language skills are crucial in finding a desirable job, but at the same time he/she feels a lack of motivation in terms of studying the relevant business terminology.

By and large, Gardner's social-educational model builds on integrative and instrumental orientation (Gardner & Lambert, 1972a). While the authors see integrative orientation as genuine and personal interest in the L2 culture, for them instrumental orientation focuses on the pragmatic value of learning a new language, i.e. a higher salary or a job promotion (Gardner & MacIntyre, 1991). Gardner purports that integrative orientation is the most crucial determinant of motivation as the learner's ultimate goal is not just to reach a certain level of language competence but to be integrated into the L2 community. Thus, in his studies on Canadian students learning French, Gardner linked the students' success in learning the FL with their desire to become part of the French culture. He concludes that students with integrative orientation tend to show greater motivational effort in learning the TL than those with instrumental orientation, and consequently, master higher levels of L2 competence.

On the other hand, recent research has shown that motivation is more complex and dynamic and needs to go beyond a mere distinction between integrative and instrumental motivation (e.g. Dörnyei, 1994). As Major (2001: 66) points out, 'motivation and success are mutually reinforcing: motivation can lead to success, but success can also lead to motivation'. In striking contrast to Gardner, Dörnyei (1990) argues that integrative orientation only plays a secondary role for FL learners since in an English as a foreign language (EFL) context, students hardly engage with the people and the culture of the L2. In his study of the motivational components of Hungarian English learners, Dörnyei (1990) concludes that instrumental goals – rather than integrative goals – contribute significantly to motivation for FL learners. He then goes even further and proposes an L2 Motivational Self System model (Dörnyei, 2005), which incorporates the notions of identity and identification in the form of the Ideal and Ought-To L2 Selves – the linguistic facets of the type of person a learner would like to be, and feels obliged to be.

Findings from a number of recent studies conducted in Asia reveal that students' aspirations are also more instrumental than integrative owing to the fact that English has become a global or international language. For example, Lamb's (2004) empirical research of Indonesian EFL students indicates that English may have lost its association with particular Anglophone cultures. Lamb points out that it may no longer be relevant to consider whether learners have a favourable attitude towards the culture where English is spoken as an L1. His study shows that these learners attach great importance to the status and prestige of the English language. In addition, he argues that sometimes it is difficult to separate the concepts of integrative motivation and instrumental motivation since aspirations, such as meeting people from the West, understanding music, studying abroad, travelling to a foreign country or pursuing a desirable career, are all associated with English as an integral part of the globalisation processes. As Lamb (2004: 16) puts it, 'the English language is so important to this "world citizen" identity because it is both a means and an end'. Therefore, the learners' role models may no longer be English speakers, but rather other global citizens.

Humphreys and Spratt (2008) report similar findings in their study involving 526 Hong Kong tertiary students. Their research reveals distinct patterns of motivation towards various languages where English was perceived as having greater value and in affective terms was regarded more positively.

Along the same lines, a recent study from Shanghai has found that career aspects ranked highest in high school students' reasons for learning English while integrative motivation came second (Kyriacou & Zhu, 2008). These findings indicate that, due to the role of English as a global language, Chinese pupils' motivation to learn English is dominated by instrumental reasons related to career enhancement and getting access to a good university.

Another study by Wu (2008) involving 243 Chinese English as a second language (ESL) learners at a vocational school in business administration confirms that instrumental motivation is more prevalent than integrative motivation. The majority of the students surveyed regarded English as paramount to finding a suitable job. Without doubt, the two instrumental motivators that stand out above all others concern education and employment opportunities.

Noels *et al.* (2003) introduced the application of intrinsic and extrinsic motivation in the context of language learning. Accordingly, in SLA, intrinsic motivation (rooted in the learner's internal desire to achieve a particular goal) positively correlates with achievement (e.g. Pae, 2008).

To date, there is very limited research examining the effects of motivation on language learning across national borders. An interesting example, however, is provided by Kouritzin *et al.*'s (2009) study of English language learners in Japan, France and Canada. Their findings reveal that the French view language study as a way to increase their value in the job market, and the Canadians consider FL learning valuable because jobs in the civil service and government favour English–French bilinguals. However, the undergraduate learners of English in Japan attach a high social value to the learning of English.

Turning to the interrelation between motivation and pronunciation achievement, research yields a fairly consistent and clear picture. It has been suggested that a personal or professional goal for learning the English language can positively affect the need and desire for native-like pronunciation (e.g. Bongaerts *et al.*, 1997; Bernaus *et al.*, 2004; Gatbonton *et al.*, 2005; Moyer, 1999). In the concluding remarks of their review of research on adult acquisition of English, Marinova-Todd *et al.* (2000) assert that adults can become highly proficient – even native-like – speakers of L2s, if motivated to do so.

Cenoz and Lecumberri (1999), in their analysis of the attitudes of Basque and Spanish learners of English, used motivation as one of the four predominant factors to explain the perceived difficulty and importance of segmental and suprasegmental features of the English language (the other three factors are contact with NSs, proficiency and ear training). It turned out that the learners themselves considered motivation as a prominent aspect in order to improve their English pronunciation.

In two studies examining the pronunciation of EFL learners in Austria, Smit and Dalton-Puffer (2000) and Smit (2002) propose a three-part model as regards motivation in pronunciation. This model incorporates firstly, learner-related factors (e.g. language use anxiety and self-perception of L2 accent); secondly, classroom-related factors (e.g. learning strategies and teaching styles); and thirdly, subject-related factors (e.g. integrativeness and intrinsic/extrinsic motives). In their study of 132 advanced pronunciation learners in Austria, the authors found the majority of them to be highly motivated to improve their English pronunciation with a goal of near-nativeness. In the final stage of her study, Smit (2002), however, did not find a strong link between motivation and achievement, revealing instead that the perceived relevance of the pronunciation course in which the students were enrolled seemed to be the most decisive factor.

It has also been proposed that integrative motivation affects two related outcomes: the development of native-like pronunciation and the development of anomie (a concern for the loss of identity) (Lambert *et al.*, 1963, cited in Spolsky, 2000). In order to learn a language and overcome this anomie, there has to be a strong wish to integrate into the L2 community. Findings from Moyer's (2007) study of 50 immigrant English language learners in the United States indicate that the learners who reported comfort with cultural assimilation significantly correlated with accent ratings. The study also shows that the learners who seemed more likely to be concerned with their accent were those who intended to stay in an English-speaking country for a longer period of time. However, that is not the case for all learners. In fact, some learners prefer not to sound native-like in order to preserve their cultural identity. For example, a study by Ladegaard and Sachdev (2006: 105) examined the motivations of 96 Danish EFL learners and found that it is feasible 'to prefer (certain aspects of) the American culture, and at the same time, not wanting to speak with, or even dislike, an American accent'.

Research shows that tensions between language identities and group affiliations may influence a language learner's motivation to adopt a particular accent (Gatbonton et al., 2005; Piller, 2002). As speech is an essential marker of social belonging, the way one speaks depends on the impression that one hopes to leave in a particular context (Levis, 2005). Learners who identify with NSs in an L2 community are therefore more likely to sound like NSs, while others who wish to emphasise their identification with their own culture often consciously or unconsciously retain an FA as a social marker (Levis, 2005). Hence, learners may regard accurate pronunciation in the FL as disloyal to their L1 ethnic group and may prompt a fear of assimilation rather than integrative motivation.

Gatbonton et al. (2005) conducted two studies to investigate the relationship between learners' L2 accent and ethnic group affiliation. The studies were carried out 30 years apart and involved learners from two different sociopolitical Canadian contexts: Francophone and Chinese. The researchers claim that language learners are subject to social forces that arise from both the L1 and the L2 communities, which prompt them to constantly reflect, renegotiate and reconstruct their identities as members of both groups. Both studies present the finding that the more that learners sound like speakers of the L2 community, the more they are labelled as disloyal to their L1 community by fellow learners. As a consequence, this connection between accent and affiliation might influence the English learner's wish to acquire a particular L2 accent. Clearly, when learners are subject to increasing pressure from their L1 community, they may lose their motivation to improve their pronunciation.

A number of studies have looked at motivation in combination with gender differences. Several of these, for example, suggest that women generally show a higher degree of motivation than men in acquiring an L2 (Baker & MacIntyre, 2000). For instance, Irish girls were found to be more motivated to learn French (Wright, 1999); British women were significantly more motivated to learn French and German (Williams et al., 2002); and Canadian girls consistently exerted more effort than boys in learning French (Kissau, 2006).

In the Turkish context, Polat and Mahalingappa (2010) also embarked on uncovering gender differences in motivation and L2 pronunciation mastery among young Kurdish learners of Turkish. Their findings revealed that overall, girls obtained much higher native-like accent ratings than boys. Integrative orientation was identified as a significant predictor of accent native-likeness for both male and female learners, but the relationship was considered to be stronger for boys. The authors relate this to the sociocultural context in which this study was conducted. It appears that in Turkey, women's access to an L2 is somewhat limited because traditionally for men the learning of an L2 is an essential prerequisite for finding a desirable job, whereas the designated workplace for women is still in the home (Norton & Toohey, 2004; Rockhill, 1993). This restriction may prompt women to believe that learning an L2 is simply irrelevant. Interestingly, Polat and Mahalingappa (2010) caution that female superiority in SLA in one setting may not apply to others. Clearly, motivation is not a fixed factor for L2 learners. Rather, it is essentially located in sociocultural contexts in which gender roles and identities play a crucial role in shaping the learner's motivation.

To conclude, it appears that research has moved away from the dichotomies of instrumental/integrative or extrinsic/intrinsic motivation in SLA to a broader approach that regards motivation as a multifaceted and dynamic construct that is closely linked to other variables. What the studies reviewed here all have in common is a fairly unanimous suggestion that learners with a high degree of motivation as regards the FL in general and pronunciation mastery in particular are likely to achieve better academic results than those whose motivation is low.

4.1.3 Anxiety

A further factor that merits examination and is in fact closely linked to motivation is the notion of foreign language anxiety (FLA). Scholars have claimed that the FL learning process is particularly prone to arousing anxiety (e.g. Campbell & Ortiz, 1991; Horwitz et al., 1986; Reid, 1999). It has been claimed that even in ideal conditions 'students can experience destructive forms of anxiety' (Reid, 1999: 297). More specifically, Campbell and Ortiz (1991: 159) estimate that almost half of all language students at some point experience debilitating levels of language anxiety (LA). Recently, Liu and Huang (2011) and Olivares-Cuhat (2010) have gone as far as to claim that LA should in fact be considered the strongest and most powerful (affective) predictor of success in FL learning.

As the first theory that pays tribute to the specific nature of LA, Horwitz et al.'s (1986) theoretical conceptualisation of FLA has been used in quite a number of studies in the field. In their view, FLA is 'a distinct complex of self-perceptions, beliefs, feelings, and behaviors related to classroom language learning arising from the uniqueness of the language learning process' (Horwitz et al., 1986: 128).

To measure the extent of anxiety a learner experiences in the classroom, they developed the so-called Foreign Language Classroom Anxiety Scale (FLCAS). This theoretical framework involves three components: communication apprehension, test anxiety and fear of negative evaluation. Taking these components into account, pronunciation can be expected to play a major role regarding FLA. Without doubt, the

FL learner's level of pronunciation mastery has a direct impact on how he/she is understood by others, which, in turn, determines the level of communication apprehension. Weaknesses in pronunciation affect the impression made on classmates and the teacher's assessment, which, when consistently negative, can enhance both test anxiety and the fear of negative evaluation. In this context, Shams (2006: 55) points out that the students' pronunciation skills contribute 'to fear of negative evaluation when the speaker fears what others may think of the way he/she sounds'.

The different types of anxiety that impact on L2 learning and achievement have been widely discussed among scholars. In this respect, two main categories of anxiety, namely state and trait anxiety, are often named. State anxiety denotes the type of anxiety that is triggered in response to a specific situation and trait anxiety is more generally applicable across a number of situations and contexts (cf. Horwitz, 2010: 154). Gardner and MacIntyre (1991) argue that as far as the language learning process is concerned, the notion of state anxiety rather than trait anxiety seems to apply. In addition, two further types of anxiety, namely facilitating (i.e. fostering language acquisition) and debilitating (i.e. hindering language acquisition), have been mentioned. Facilitating anxiety appears to keep students alert, and thus can lead to increased language proficiency; debilitating anxiety, on the other hand, is often negatively correlated with L2 success resulting in poor performance in achievement tests (Oxford, 1998).

These differences in the types of anxiety may also be responsible for the fact that especially early studies investigating LA and achievement have yielded conflicting results. Whereas some studies carried out in the 1970s found a negative relationship between anxiety and L2 achievement, others found no or even a positive relationship between anxiety and L2 proficiency (e.g. Kleinmann, 1977). Scovel (1978) offered a rational solution to this enigma by pointing out that the various studies used different anxiety measures and concluded that language researchers need to be more explicit about the type of anxiety they are trying to measure. However, since the introduction of the FLCAS and other specific measures of L2 anxiety, studies have discovered a fairly consistent negative correlation between learner anxiety and L2 achievement, typically regarding final course grades.

It has been suggested that the connection between FL pronunciation and FLA might be both physiologically as well as affectively motivated. The former dimension sees LA as a set of 'emotional reactions and motivations of the learner; they signal the arousal of the limbic system and its direct intervention in the task of learning' (Scovel, 1978: 131). Consequently, a high level of anxiety may lead to neuromuscular problems by physically impeding the FL learner's speech. The affective connection between pronunciation and FLA, on the other hand, has been addressed in very few studies only. Derwing and Rossiter (2002), for example, found that 60 out of 100 respondents reported a significant shift in their pronunciation skills when experiencing anxiety and nervousness. In an experiment conducted by Horwitz and Young (1991: xiii), one learner was quoted saying: 'I hate it when the teacher calls on me to speak. I freeze up and can't think of what to say or how to say it. And my pronunciation is terrible'.

A plethora of studies have emerged investigating the connection between the extent of anxiety felt by a learner and its impact on various FL skills such as reading and writing (e.g. Saito *et al.*, 1999), listening (e.g. Elkhafaifi, 2005) and grammar (e.g. VanPatten & Glass, 1999); however, it is spoken production that has received the most attention in this context (e.g. Phillips, 1992; Price, 1991).

In line with the observations discussed above according to which LA seems to have a negative influence on FL mastery in general, studies investigating oral production/pronunciation and learner apprehension have found negative correlations (e.g. Liu, 2006; Stephenson Wilson, 2006; Woodrow, 2006). For instance, learners are sometimes reported to experience anxiety when giving presentations in class, interacting with an NS or being corrected while speaking (Mak, 2011). Anxious FL learners also mention challenges that are directly linked to pronunciation. For example, they complain about difficulties discriminating the sounds and feel embarrassed because of their pronunciation errors (Price, 1991). Ohata (2005) points out that unrealistic beliefs can cause greater anxiety and frustration, particularly when beliefs and reality do not match. He asserts that if learners believe that pronunciation is the single most important aspect of language learning, it comes as little surprise that they will be frustrated to find the reality of their poor speech pronunciation even after learning and practicing for a long time.

The reciprocal relationship between anxiety and pronunciation has been discussed by a number of scholars (e.g. Horwitz *et al.*, 1986; Price, 1991) who claim that pronunciation can be considered a significant cause of LA. An issue that remains unsolved is the question of causality, i.e. does anxiety interfere with FL ability and impair FL performance, or does poor FL performance lead to anxiety as a consequence? (Gardner & MacIntyre, 1991). Price (1991), who also touches upon this topic, established a direct link between pronunciation problems as perceived by the learner and classroom-related anxiety. In this study, the author compared anxious learners' articulation to that of NSs. He found that the learners felt greatly embarrassed by their inability to pronounce FL words correctly. In interviews, Price asked students what aspects of FL classes troubled them the most. Again, the answer was 'the greatest source of anxiety was having to speak the target language in front of peers' (Price, 1991: 105). Similarly, Young (1991) also stressed the fact that LA is derived from the fear of mispronouncing words. Insufficient knowledge of how to pronounce certain sounds or words can generate concern about not being intelligible or being ridiculed by peers. The author points out that the difference between self-perceived language competence and reality can be the reason for high levels of anxiety in particular if a student regards pronunciation as the most important skill to be learned in an FL. Yet, in reality the majority of the students, 'unless they are highly motivated, will not sound like a native speaker' (Young, 1991: 428).

Interesting data from a study carried out by Shams (2005) compared the effectiveness of two different approaches to pronunciation teaching (i.e. in a listening laboratory and in a computer laboratory) in reducing FLA. Among other things, the study proved that a seven-week pronunciation course resulted not only in the improvement in this particular skill but also in a significant decrease in FLA, irrespective of the pronunciation teaching approach. It has to be taken into consideration, however, that the lower level of FLA upon completion of the pronunciation course may have resulted not only from the actual improvement in pronunciation but also from the subjects' belief in their improved pronunciation skills and their increased self-confidence after intensive practice.

These self-perceived pronunciation problems as indicated by anxious learners have been investigated by a few researchers. For instance, Feigenbaum's (2007) results revealed that there is no notable difference regarding pronunciation accuracy when comparing two different types of learning environments, namely group work and teacher-fronted activities. However, she finds a significant negative correlation between LA and pronunciation accuracy in the teacher-fronted environment, which prompts her to conclude that LA only impacts negatively on pronunciation during teacher-fronted activities.

A similar study was conducted at Granada University by Stephenson Wilson (2006). The students' performance was assessed in an oral test consisting of two parts: the first was a free discussion on a given topic and the second consisted of a role-play. The results, once again, confirmed a statistically significant negative correlation.

In the Australian context, Woodrow (2006) also detected a negative, interactional relationship between spoken language competence and speaking anxiety. In this case, quantitative data were collected from more than 200 participants studying English for academic purposes (EAP) in Australia. Interestingly, the author distinguished between two different concepts, namely in-class FLA and out-of-class FLA. Her findings clearly supported this distinction by showing that both types of anxiety can in fact be related to the learners' speaking performance.

Recently, a study conducted by Szyszka (2011) in Poland investigated the connection between LA and the pronunciation competence of 48 teacher training students. In her study, the results of the pronunciation self-perception questionnaire indicated a significant negative relationship between FLA and self-perceived competence in pronunciation, thereby confirming that those students who claimed to be affected by higher levels of FLA also declared lower pronunciation competence. Szyszka concludes that apart from intonation, segmental as well as suprasegmental aspects of L2 pronunciation significantly and adversely correlated with FLA.

The interrelation between FLA and achievement has spawned a plethora of work in the Chinese environment. Cheng (2005), for instance, pondered over the question of how FLA affects spoken English language competence. Again, significant negative correlation was discovered between FLA and the final scores of the Chinese subjects' spoken English language competence. This was further confirmed by Zheng (2010) who also found that LA had a negative impact on achievement. Similarly, in their study, Lu and Liu (2011) tested a number of students who attended obligatory English language classes. Again, a significant, albeit moderate, negative relationship between FLA (as measured by FLCAS) and the learners' English language competence (as measured by exam scores) was observed. The authors arrive at the conclusion that low LA is an essential element for enhancing students' learning outcomes.

As has been shown, the fairly complex notion of FLA has given rise to a myriad of studies that by and large provide evidence that LA has a negative impact on FL achievement in general and pronunciation proficiency in particular.

4.1.4 Formal pronunciation instruction

The role of pronunciation teaching in the classroom has been subject to various changes in paradigms as far as approaches to teaching FLs are concerned. The question that has been fervently debated in this context is whether pronunciation should be taught explicitly or not. Can pronunciation instruction contribute to enhancing learners' pronunciation skills or is it a forlorn hope, a waste of time and effort on the part of both the teacher and the students?

It appears that only very few studies so far have looked into the effectiveness of pronunciation instruction (e.g. Derwing & Munro, 2005) despite its prominent role in successful communication. The question of whether an increased quantity of L2 input in the form of formal instruction impacts both child and adult SLA is dealt with in studies by, e.g. Bongaerts *et al.* (1997), Moyer (1999) and others. These studies have yielded inconsistent results suggesting that the link between formal pronunciation instruction and the students' pronunciation is not statistically significant (Elliot, 1995). At this point it should be noted, however, that although quite a contradiction in the range of results presented is apparent, the diversity of those results might again be due to differing designs and methodologies applied in the particular experiments.

Suter (1976) was among the first to report an insignificant relationship between formal pronunciation and students' pronunciation of EFL.

In contrast, Neufeld and Schneiderman (1980) and later Murakawa (1981) found that adult learners did manage to master near-native fluency which they claimed can be achieved in a relatively short time when adequate pronunciation training is provided. Although MacDonald *et al.* (1994) tried to grasp the short-term effects of different types of instruction, they failed to draw clear conclusions.

Some classroom-based studies have focused specifically on the teaching of suprasegmentals. Derwing *et al.* (1997), for example, reported a positive effect for formal instruction that focused on general speaking habits rather than individual sounds. The authors concluded that attending courses dealing with segmental and suprasegmental accuracy can give rise to improved pronunciation competence. Along similar lines, Couper (2003) also considered pronunciation courses to be beneficial. Yet, he failed to provide evidence as to the reasons for this. Clear positive short-term effects of pronunciation instruction have been seen in a number of studies involving the production of individual phonemes, prosody or overall fluency (e.g. de Bot, 1983; de Bot & Mailfert, 1982; Murakawa, 1981).

In their study, Flege and Liu (2001) found a close relation between formal pronunciation teaching and the LOR in the country where the TL is spoken. Their study further suggests a positive effect of formal instruction on adult learners' performance.

Olson and Samuels (1973, 1982) provided phonetic training in German over a period of three weeks to 20 NSs of English. Their results showed that older subjects obtained significantly higher accent ratings than younger students. This prompted the authors to conclude that older learners would benefit more from pronunciation training than younger learners.

By the same token, Elliot (1995) tested the effect of pronunciation instruction on 43 adult NSs of English learning Spanish in the United States over a period of one semester. Interestingly, the learners appeared to significantly differ in their pronunciation scores between the pre-test and post-test. In other words, their pronunciation of Spanish improved as a result of the phonetic treatment they had received.

At the turn of the 21st century, a number of studies on successful ultimate attainment of L2 phonology by late learners were published in which formal instruction – to a certain degree – did account for the subjects' mastery of L2 phonology. One of these studies was conducted by Bongaerts *et al.* (1997) and aimed to examine the degree of FA of late Dutch learners of English. Their subjects did not start to learn English before the age of 12 but received intensive training on received pronunciation (RP) at university. NS judges rated a sentence production task on a five-point scale. The results showed that the mature learners were assigned scores in the NS range. These findings clearly reject two assumptions in SLA: firstly, that late learners cannot achieve L2 pronunciation proficiency and secondly, that formal explicit pronunciation instruction is in vain. On the contrary, the authors suggest that the amount of formal instruction – in this case, 'intensive training both in the perception and in the production of the speech sounds of British English' (Bongaerts et al., 1997: 463) – may very well contribute to the late learners' successful pronunciation mastery.

A further study investigating the influence of formal instruction on late learners' L2 pronunciation skills comes from Moyer (1999). The author looked into the spoken performance of 24 NSs of English learning German in the United States. All the subjects were highly motivated late learners, who had been first exposed to the TL in a formal setting at the age of 11 and who had spent on average 2.7 years in Germany. The learners' mean accent ratings given by German NS judges were found to be more foreign-accented than those of the German controls, except for one NNS subject. A favourable effect of input was observed in that some subjects who had received explicit feedback on their pronunciation received a more favourable FA rating than those who had not. Thus, although most late learners did not perform at a native-like level on any of the tasks, the phonological input the subjects had received seemed to have played a decisive role in achieving native-like pronunciation in some cases.

In 2006, Couper (2006) showed in his classroom-based study that pronunciation teaching can indeed help students improve. He set out to determine the immediate effect of formal instruction on specific forms in L2 pronunciation. His subjects were immigrants (mostly of Asian origin) living in New Zealand. The pronunciation training over a period of two weeks explicitly focused on epenthesis (adding an extra sound) and the inappropriate dropping of a consonant. He claimed that the error rate in this group had in fact decreased dramatically, whereas the control group (without any pronunciation instruction) did not make any progress. This led the author to conclude that appropriately focused instruction can lead to changes in learners' pronunciation mastery.

A longitudinal study from New Zealand by Romova et al. (2008) investigated the changes that occurred in the pronunciation and fluency of four advanced, adult English as an additional language (EAL) learners (mostly immigrants from Asia) over three years of tertiary education. They were provided with explicit instruction in pronunciation, including a variety of models from which they could choose. Their data was obtained from two pre-study and post-study parallel tests and post-study individual interviews. The findings for pronunciation were presented as four case studies, meaning that the pronunciation of each subject was compared between the pre-study test and the post-study test. They found that all four students seemed to have enhanced both their fluency and pronunciation, although to varying degrees. Their answer to the often posed question 'Can I change the way I speak?' is a resounding yes.

And they add that the extent to which this happens depends more than anything on motivation – conscious or unconscious.

To sum up, divergent results have been reported as to the effects of formal instruction on L2 pronunciation mastery. It seems that quality of input (e.g. specific phonetic training) is of greater importance than quantity (i.e. time spent studying the pronunciation of the TL). Taken all together, the studies on the amount and type of input have not provided enough convincing evidence upon which variance in L2 phonological acquisition might be solely based. In spite of the finding that late L2 learners can benefit from formal phonological instruction, the input they receive should not be looked at in isolation. Rather, other factors such as attitude, motivation, age of learning, LOR, etc., are likely to play a role too.

4.1.5 Gender differences

Intuitively, gender seems to be a very appealing variable in SLA. After all, the commonly held folk wisdom that girls are better language learners than boys still exists. However, research findings are not conclusive regarding female advantage in FL learning in general (e.g. Brantmeier *et al.*, 2007) and pronunciation learning in particular (e.g. Elliot, 1995; Purcell & Suter, 1980).

As far as SLA in general is concerned, Gardner (1985) relates gender differences to motivational issues, assuming that women are more motivated to learn languages than men. Furthermore, according to Gardner and Lambert (1959), women show more positive attitudes towards the NSs of the FL. More specifically, Ludwig (1982) points out that male learners hold more instrumental motivations, which means that they are more likely to learn an L2 for a particular reason.

Apart from the above-mentioned difference, there are also sociocultural implications that need to be taken into account: without doubt, the role of men and women in society, class or ethnicity also leave an imprint on language learning. Ellis (1996), for example, sees the generally observed enthusiastic attitude of females towards language learning from a cultural perspective. Particularly in Europe, females – more than males – consider FLs as an essential prerequisite for acquiring a desirable position in a company. In Asia, however, men generally have better English language skills owing to the fact that their jobs provide them with opportunities to communicate with NSs of English. Many Asian women, on the other hand, are housewives and therefore neither have the opportunity nor the desire to learn an FL, let alone develop any attitude towards FL learning.

Research into variance in L2 pronunciation skills between men and women has yielded interesting results that are also relevant for SLA. For example, L1 studies examining the relationship between pronunciation accuracy and gender have put forward that women in Western societies have a certain tendency to use more formal and prestigious phonological patterns when speaking their native language (e.g. Silva-Corvalan, 2001; Trudgill, 1974). For example, in her experiments, Byrd (1992) shows that men speak faster and tend to reduce their vowels to schwa more often than women. Similarly, Henton (1995) purports that women are likely to produce more open vowels than men, which means that female speech shows a tendency to be more phonetically explicit. She claims that this has socio-phonetic reasons related to the conceptualisations of male and female roles in society. Along the same lines, the experiments by Whiteside (1995, 1996) show lower rates of syllables per second for women who seem to realise consonant clusters more fully. Simpson and Ericsdotter (2003) also found that men tend to elide or reduce vowels and consonants, which results in shorter sentence durations.

In addition, a number of studies have reported differences in male and female vowel duration patterns. Various studies investigating American English (Hillenbrand et al., 1995), German (Simpson, 1998) and Swedish (Ericsdotter & Ericsson, 2001) revealed that overall, females outperformed males in most vowel durations. Producing longer vowel lengths can be seen as one of the effects of speaking more clearly, an attribute that – as has been mentioned above – is frequently assigned to female speech (Elyan, 1978). Similar findings have been suggested by Gussenhoven (1979), Broeders (1982) and Hiang and Gupta (1992) who reported that females were more likely to use prestige forms in comparison to their male counterparts and that female learners in general had better pronunciation than males.

There are, in fact, very few studies that solely focus on gender and pronunciation. Instead, gender is often combined with other variables such as attitude, motivation, AOL or LOR. In this vein, Asher and Garcia (1969) link gender with AOL on the one hand and LOR in the target culture on the other hand. They reported that girls under the age of 6 had an initial advantage over boys when acquiring L2 pronunciation. This was later confirmed by Flege et al. (1995). With increasing LOR, however, Asher and Garcia (1969) argue that gender differences appear to diminish.

Similarly, Tahta et al. (1981a, 1981b), who looked primarily at the transfer of accent from L1 to L2, identified gender as the most significant predictor of degree of FA in an L2, with women receiving higher scores than men. This finding was also confirmed 10 years later by Thompson (1991), who investigated the English pronunciation of Russian learners.

In contrast to that, a great number of the studies in this field (e.g. Elliot, 1995; Purcell & Suter, 1980; Snow & Hoefnagel-Höhle, 1977; Suter, 1976) have not identified gender as a significant predictor of the degree of L2 FA.

More recent research findings from Asia, however, suggest that female learners slightly outperform their male counterparts. In his attempt to determine Thai students' pronunciation competence, Khamkhien (2010) identified gender as the most significant factor contributing to the participants' test scores. This confirms earlier findings by who were investigating the pronunciation proficiency in the L1s and L2s of Korean-English adult immigrants in the United States. Although their general focus was on age effects, they found that females had higher scores than males.

Conversely, a study from Iran by Jahandar *et al.* (2012) involving 53 undergraduate university students studying English, arrived at a slightly different conclusion. They caution that, although female students outperformed their male colleagues in producing accurate consonants (but not vowels), this does not give rise to assume the complete superiority of female over male subjects.

In the Arabic context, Badran (2001) examined the relationship between both extraversion/introversion and gender and the pronunciation accuracy of Arabic-speaking Egyptian college students learning EFL. He claimed that extroversion/introversion correlated positively with English pronunciation accuracy, i.e. extroverted students scored higher than introverted ones and that male students outperformed their female counterparts.

In an altogether very different experiment carried out in Germany on L2 pronunciation talent, Dogil and Reiterer (2009) noticed a significant gender difference in one of their tasks, namely the imitation of Hindi sounds, where the scores for the male imitators were higher. For them, this result was unexpected. They speculate that the reason for this may lie in the task type that required a speech imitation skill, which was devoid of syntactic and semantic operations. Apparently, when it comes to motor skill learning, recent evidence (Dorfberger *et al.*, 2009) shows that male learners have a significant advantage over their female counterparts. Interestingly, giftedness research in general suggests that gender differences are greater in gifted than in average ability individuals (Preckel *et al.*, 2008). They attribute this to the fact that evolutionary theories predominantly consider males as more located in the extremes of the normal distribution curve, whereas females tend to be more represented towards the mean (with respect to any kind of ability). Accordingly, male predominance is more frequently found at the upper end of the ability scale in gifted populations and at the lower end of the scale, a wide range of developmental problems such as disorders of the voice and tone-deafness seem to be more prevalent in males than in females (Howard & Angus, 1998).

In total, the literature shows that gender does not seem to significantly influence the pronunciation accuracy of learners. Although there is a slight tendency of females to outperform males in terms of vowel articulation and vowel duration, this does not seem to result in the complete superiority of female over male students. Finally, many SLA researchers concede that investigating the connection between L2 achievement and gender from a merely biological point of view may be limited as gender categories and roles are formed within the learners' sociocultural and situational context (Ehrlich, 1997).

4.1.6 Musicality

It is commonly believed that people who are skilled at music have a sensitive ear and can discriminate between sounds more accurately and consequently imitate sounds better. This means that musically trained individuals have an advantage over non-musicians in as far as they pick up various aspects of an L2, in particular the pronunciation of L2 sounds, more easily. Hence, the question that scholars from across academic fields have tried to answer is whether there is a link between musical ability and language proficiency. Does musicality constitute an advantage for phonological learning?

Research findings are – again – not entirely conclusive. Those who argue in favour of the music–language link mostly base their assumptions on three tenets. Firstly, both language and music are considered human universals that show structural parallels (e.g. Patel & Daniele, 2003). Secondly, neuropsychological studies indicate that certain regions in the brain that are often assumed to be language-specific are also involved in musical processing (e.g. Levitin & Menon, 2003; Tillmann et al., 2003). And thirdly, musical ability, like language ability, appears to be prone to affective impacts (Richard-Amato, 2003).

On the other hand, several studies failed to establish a clear link between self-ratings of musical aptitude and L2 performance (Flege et al., 1995, 1999a; Tahta et al., 1981a, 1981b; Thompson, 1991). Stokes (2001) also saw no correlation between musicality and SLA in adult learners. Thus, it remains unclear whether or not musicality improves human potential in language acquisition.

Given this lack of conclusive evidence, it is tempting to conclude that the popular conjecture that musical ability matters for L2 learning is a myth. However, more specific research into musical aptitude and its influence on L2 pronunciation mastery shows a fairly clear picture.

In her study involving French beginner and intermediate learners, Morgan (2003) sought to explore the relationship between music perception and speech perception on the one hand and music production and speech production on the other hand. The findings of her study revealed a positive correlation of all those aspects investigated.

Pastuszek-Lipińska (2004) conducted a study involving the shadowing of speech (i.e. stimuli repeated just after listening). Among other tasks, she recorded 106 musicians and non-musicians (NSs of Polish) repeating the question 'May I help you?' after they had heard it three times. These productions were subsequently rated by seven NSs of English. The data showed that the musicians received higher scores and that their productions were rated as being closer to that of NSs. Pastuszek-Lipińska interpreted the result as evidence that musicians are indeed superior to non-musicians in terms of perceiving and producing FL sounds.

In their study, Slevc and Mijake (2006) investigated the link between musical aptitude and L2 proficiency in adult learners in four domains, namely receptive phonology, productive phonology, syntax and lexical knowledge. One of the tasks involved the participants (50 NSs of Japanese) reading aloud a short English text passage. Two NSs were asked to rate overall pronunciation, intelligibility and prosody on a nine-point scale, ranging from very strong FA to no FA. They observed that musical ability predicted L2 phonological ability (both receptive and productive) but not L2 syntax or vocabulary. The authors conclude that musical skills seem to foster the acquisition of L2 sounds and see this as evidence for the link between phonology and music.

Also, it has been demonstrated that musicians tend to detect L2 sentence-final words faster and more accurately than non-musicians. Marques *et al.* (2007), for instance, investigated musical aptitude and its influence on the detection of pitch variations in an FL they did not speak. Adult French musicians and non-musicians were confronted with sentences in Portuguese. The final words of these sentences were prosodically congruous (i.e. spoken at normal pitch height) or incongruous (pitch was experimentally increased). Results showed that musicians outperformed non-musicians when the pitch deviations were small and difficult to detect.

Two further studies conducted in 2008 yielded inconclusive results. Gottfried (2008) found that musicians were more successful in perceiving and producing a particular set of tones in Mandarin; however, both musicians and non-musicians struggled with other tones. Overall, Gottfried concludes that musical talent may be more related to experience rather than cognitive abilities. On the other hand, Milovanov *et al.* (2009) confirmed that learners with more advanced English pronunciation skills also had better musical skills.

Nardo and Reiterer (2009) consider language and music as interrelated phenomena, perhaps even two sides of the same coin. In their research, they found a strong connection between rhythm and singing abilities on the one hand and pronunciation proficiency on the other. Production scores evidenced that musicians performed better than non-musicians in their experiment.

Milovanov *et al.* (2009) examined the pronunciation of Finnish young adults with higher education. They concentrated on words containing potentially problematic English phonemes. And once again, the results showed a strong correlation between musical aptitude and English pronunciation achievement. They point out that the greater the general musical aptitude the participant reported in the musicality test, the higher the scores received in the English pronunciation test.

Although the studies discussed above differed in their design and aim, most recent findings seem to cautiously support the assumption that musicality may affect SLA in a positive way.

4.1.7 Exposure to the target language

The last variable to be discussed here is also the most important for the present project as increased exposure to the TL is a core concern that is being investigated in the context of English-medium instruction (EMI) at the University of Applied Sciences (UAS) Vienna. It is often taken for granted that exposure to the L2 has a positive effect on a learner's pronunciation skills. Research, however, seems to indicate that increased exposure to English in itself does not necessarily speed up the acquisition of English (Snow, 1992). Quite rightly, Kenworthy (1987) notes that exposure can be a contributory factor but it cannot be the one and only factor in the development of L2 pronunciation.

As discussed in Chapter 3, some SLA theories suggest that learners' exposure to large amounts of comprehensible input paired with opportunities for interaction fosters the acquisition of the L2 in general and the features of L2 pronunciation in particular. However, there are also non-linguistic aspects of a language that carry meaning and yet are usually not learned through explicit instruction, but rather through experience with the TL and culture. As Shumin (1997) notes, a lack of exposure to the L2 and a lack of contact with NSs of that language, may be the reason why mature English language learners often fail to achieve a native-like production, not only as far as linguistic skills are concerned but also in terms of cultural pragmatics, such as gestures, body language and facial expressions.

Generally speaking, exposure to the TL can have a variety of meanings depending on the degree of intensity in terms of quality and quantity. This may range from living and working in the country where the language is spoken to simply listening to NSs on the radio. It should be noted, however, that living in the country of the TL does not always mean that the L2 is actually used. For example, some people may live in an English-speaking environment but still predominantly use their L1 with their families and friends. Conversely, learners who live and work in a non-English-speaking country may still use a considerable amount of English in many everyday situations. Thus, it comes as little surprise that Flege *et al.* (1997b) found that learners who live in an L2 environment but interact primarily with speakers of their L1 generally retain more salient accents than those who use the L2 more often.

In the field of SLA, the factor exposure to the TL appears to be researched as two different variables: firstly, the LOR in the respective L2 environment and secondly, the amount of L2 input the learner receives in his/her everyday life, mostly in the form of media exposure. While LOR is commonly related to immersion settings, that is L2 learning in an L2 environment, the second variable predominantly focuses on exposure to the L2 in an L1 context.

As far as immersion settings are concerned, previous research has produced conflicting evidence concerning the importance of LOR for L2 pronunciation accuracy and therefore its significance for accent seems to be rather unreliable. For instance, Flege and Fletcher (1992) and Riney and Flege (1998) observed positive effects (although not necessarily significant) whereas others have not observed an influence of LOR (e.g. Flege et al., 1995; McAllister, 2001; Meador et al., 2000; Piske et al., 2001).

Two studies that identified LOR effects need to be mentioned here. In their study, Flege and Fletcher (1992) examined English sentences produced by two groups of late Spanish–English bilinguals with differing LOR in the United States. They reported that the experienced subjects obtained considerably higher ratings than those with less experience. Yet, LOR was not found to be a significant predictor of the degree of L2 FA, which identified AOL as the most reliable predictor of the degree of L2 FA. A further study by Riney and Flege (1998) relates exposure to age. They proved that living in surroundings where the L2 is spoken has a positive effect on mature L2 learners' overall pronunciation. In this regard, Flege (1987) surmises that after a speedy initial phase of learning, LOR does not seem to influence the degree of L2 FA in adults. Therefore, the assumption that the longer the learners stay in an L2 environment the better their pronunciation skills does not hold water.

By contrast, a number of studies failed to find LOR effects on L2 phonological competence. McAllister et al. (2000), for instance, investigated the acquisition of the Swedish quantity contrast in subject groups with three different L1s. Their findings suggest that LOR may not be a reliable predictor of L2 performance. Similarly, Meador et al. (2000) arrived at the same conclusion, asserting that those subjects who were highly experienced in their use of the L2 did not manage to change their degree of FA. Therefore, Piske et al. (2001) conclude that experience with the L2 may lead to less foreign-accented speech only in the early phases of L2 learning, thereby confirming the results obtained by Flege et al. (1995), Riney and Flege (1998) and Meador et al. (2000).

The assumption that input from NSs does play a crucial role in L2 pronunciation is supported by the findings of a study conducted by Flege and Liu (2001) who investigated the influence of LOR in an L2-speaking environment. The authors claim that additional years of living in a predominantly L2-speaking environment does not, in itself, lead to progress in learning an L2 and that LOR only provides a good predictor of L2 competence when learners come into regular contact with NSs of the L2. Along the same lines, Moyer (2013: 75) purports that 'extended in-country residence confers real advantages for phonological attainment if it signifies rich target-language experience'.

Within the field of LOR research, one strand, namely the study abroad (SA) context, seems to have attracted considerable attention recently. In the context of the current social, cultural and educational changes owing to globalisation and internationalisation endeavours (see Chapter 2: Section 2.1), these programmes have come to play an important role in L2 learning policies particularly as a means to promote multilingualism (cf. Kinginger, 2009). Hence, SA programmes have become very popular in Europe and students are increasingly encouraged by language teachers, programme administrators and researchers alike to seize this opportunity. In this vein, Smit and Dalton-Puffer (2000) point out that teachers need to continue advising their students to spend some time abroad, although they caution that this might not necessarily have the desired effect.

A widely held assumption in this respect is that students who study abroad return home with substantially increased FL competences, particularly in areas such as fluency, pronunciation and vocabulary. In fact, Freed (1998: 50) describes the profile of the language skills of students who spent time abroad as follows: '[They] appear to speak with greater ease and confidence, expressed in part by a greater abundance of speech, spoken at a faster rate and characterised by fewer dysfluent-sounding pauses'. He also found that they were capable of expressing more complex and abstract ideas by drawing on a broader range of complex communicative strategies and styles. Apart from linguistic gains, stays in a foreign country are also frequently considered to foster students' motivation to learn and improve their L2 (Serrano Lopez, 2009).

Research has mostly concurred that SA can indeed be a beneficial way of acquiring an FL (e.g. Lafford, 2006; Lafford & Collentine, 2006). While a great number of studies on the effect of SA on SLA have been carried out in the field of selected morphosyntactic areas (e.g. Howard, 2005; Isabelli, 2007; Isabelli & Nishida, 2005), less work is available discussing the specific effects of SA on L2 pronunciation.

As mentioned above, the literature is overwhelmingly consistent regarding students' development of oral fluency, as a great number of scholars, even those who initially did not concentrate on this particular aspect, claim that SA students appear to be more fluent than their at home (AH) counterparts (e.g. Collentine, 2004). Freed (1995), for example, reported that students who had spent a semester in a foreign country spoke more and faster. In addition, their speech tended to contain longer stretches of continuous speech. In their study, Segalowitz and Freed (2004) point out that SA students – in contrast to the AH group – were in fact the only ones who experienced gains in fluency. This was further confirmed by Freed *et al.* (2004).

With a focus on the pronunciation of SA vis-à-vis AH learners, Díaz-Campos (2004, 2006) looked at the production of a small number of Spanish sounds that are commonly considered problematic for L2 learners. Díaz-Campos found that although both groups made progress, there was no consistent advantage for the SA group. Concerning the oral production of native-like variants, however, this study revealed that SA students appeared to generate more target-like variants than AH students in informal (i.e. conversational) settings (Díaz-Campos, 2006: 37), whereas no significant differences between groups could be observed in more formal (i.e. reading aloud) settings.

Lord (2006) examined students' pronunciation and mimicry abilities in Spanish before and after SA. Again, she argued that learners' overall pronunciation skills did not improve significantly. However, there was some improvement in terms of their capacity to repeat sounds. She attributed these results to the phenomenon of phonological memory.

Recently, Avello *et al.* (2012) explored the perception of FA in an SA context by assessing the effect of a three-month SA programme on the pronunciation of a group of 23 Spanish learners of English. The participants in their study were recorded reading a text before and immediately after their stay abroad. These recordings were then rated by 37 proficient non-native listeners, trained in English phonetics. Although they discovered a slight yet non-significant improvement in perceived FA, a significant decrease was detected in pronunciation accuracy scores after SA.

Apart from LOR, media exposure to English in the form of cable TV, the internet, computer games, music and radio has also been researched in connection with L2 attainment, although on a much smaller scale. As Uskoski (2011: 16) points out, increased access to the internet and the growing influence of the global community have strongly influenced language learning since the 1990s. Owing to technological advances, access to the English language outside the classroom is rapidly spreading all over Europe. According to Livingstone (2002: 286), 'the media today operate as pervasive, yet often imperceptible, elements in the everyday cultures of children and young people'. She purports that the media can and do have a favourable effect on students learning English as an L2, due to the fact that a great number of media genres in Europe are now available in English. In the context of SLA research, it comes as little surprise that media exposure studies have discovered that receptive skills (i.e. listening and reading) benefit most, whereas productive skills (i.e. speaking and writing) are less affected (e.g. Pickard, 1996).

In their article on EFL in the European Union, Rubio and Lirola (2010) claim that TV broadcasting of films in the original version is a major facilitator for FL learning. According to Rubio and Lirola (2010: 32), European countries where English-speaking programmes are shown captioned or subtitled have a higher number of L2 speakers of English. As an example, they compare Greece, which uses subtitles in television broadcasting, and Spain, which does not. In spite of sharing similarities with the Spanish culture and education system, Greece is said to have twice as many L2 speakers of English who are able to hold a conversation (48%). Similarly, Germany (56%) has a much lower number of English speakers than Sweden (89%) (Rubio & Lirola, 2010: 33).

As Sweden is often named as an example of good practice regarding the use of English outside the classroom, a doctoral project carried out by Sundqvist in 2009 deserves due notice. She examined the possible effects that outside-of-school English (which she termed extramural English [EE]) has on oral proficiency and vocabulary. The study was based on data collected from Swedish learners of English aged 15–16 over a period of one year. Her results show that there is a clear correlation between high exposure to English outside of school and good oral proficiency (Sundqvist, 2009: 193).

In the Finnish context, Uskoski (2011) confirms the claim that EE activities, in his case video games, can be beneficial for the students' English language skills. Accordingly, students who played video games on a regular basis had significantly higher English grades than those who did not (Uskoski, 2011: 56).

To the best of my knowledge, there is no study focusing on the phonological gains related to out-of-class English in Europe to date. Without doubt, this field of research, still in its infancy today, will have to be seen as an increasingly important factor in SLA studies and therefore calls for closer attention.

To sum up, the review of the literature focusing on the ID variable 'exposure to the target language' has revealed divergent results. Not every study has shown a significant effect of exposure to the TL on the degree of L2 FA. Those studies that found a measurable LOR effect also indicated that the variable LOR was a less reliable predictor of the degree of foreign-accented speech than, for example, age. Moreover, for adults, additional years of experience in the L2 do not seem to lead to a significant increase in pronunciation mastery. In the early phases of L2 learning, on the other hand, increased exposure may very well lead to a decline in foreign-accented L2 speech. The SA context seems to exert a beneficial influence on oral SLA (in particular fluency), but it remains unclear what specific areas of SLA benefit from this experience and to what degree. Regarding media exposure to the L2, it can be concluded that there seems to be a general consensus among researchers that increased exposure in the form of TV, movies and social media may have a positive effect on the language learning process. Yet, its influence on pronunciation mastery has not been examined. On the whole, research tends to suggest that exposure to the TL does matter and may lead to increased L2 proficiency provided that the input is of high quality, preferably from NSs.

4.1.8 Conclusion

All in all, it can be stated that to date we are faced with an abundance of views on ID variables that impact on L2 pronunciation proficiency and their relevance to SLA. Although some of the driving forces linked to phonological development seem likely to affect L2 pronunciation achievement, it is not an easy endeavour to demonstrate their relative effects in empirical investigations. This is not only rooted in the notable absence of concise definitions and established methods to be used in experiments assessing individual variation, but it is also blurred by the notion that those individual factors appear in a number of combinations that are after all unique compounds in each individual learner. In other words, a learner seems to be the product of his/her genetically determined qualities that are exposed to highly volatile environmental influences in the course of the learning process. The outcome therefore is always unique and, in terms of empirical research, difficult to capture.

Despite the fact that in the last decade considerable importance has been attached to the examination of the complex interactions of ID variables, it has proven challenging to predict how a certain learner's characteristic features will affect the learning outcomes. This is precisely the question that the present study intends to shed light on. Nevertheless, let us speculate at this point on the profile that emerges of an L2 English language learner who has the potential to achieve complete L2 pronunciation mastery: conceivably, the learner (1) began to learn English in early childhood; (2) has a positive attitude towards the English language and culture; (3) cares about his/her FA and is highly motivated to improve his/her English pronunciation; (4) is not afraid to speak English; (5) has attended pronunciation classes; (6) is probably female; (7) plays a musical instrument or enjoys singing; and (8) has been exposed to a large amount of L1 English both inside and outside the classroom (cf. Richter, 2017).

4.2 Insights from the UAS Vienna

As discussed in Chapter 3: Section 3.4, both groups from the UAS Vienna reported impressive gains in their phonological development over the course of their studies. Having discussed potential factors that may have influenced the learners' pronunciation development in Chapter 3, this section now seeks to unveil which of these individual variables may affect the pronunciation learning of the students and if the profile of a high-potential (HP) pronunciation learner sketched above can indeed be verified.

The data to be discussed here were largely generated from Questionnaire 1 (Q1) and Questionnaire 2 (Q2), which were administered to the students at the beginning of their studies in Semester 1 (T1) and then again in their last (sixth) semester (T2). On the one hand, these questionnaires were meant to take account of the demographic variation of the student population in the two groups and, on the other hand, these variables are also a valuable resource to investigate individual learner beliefs and learner characteristics. As far as the design of the questionnaire is concerned, the 75 questions in Q1 covered the following main areas:

- personal data (gender, date of birth, education, language/s spoken at home);
- exposure to English (inside and outside the classroom);
- (self-reported) musicality;
- (self-perceived) L1 and L2 competence;
- attitude and motivation.

A number of open-ended questions (e.g. for stays abroad) but mostly closed questions on either a five-point scale (especially for rating their own language skills) or a seven-point scale (for attitudes and motivation) where the respondents are asked to indicate the extent to which they agree or disagree were included.

For T2, a much shorter questionnaire consisting of only 10 items to elicit crucial data covering the period between T1 and T2 was designed. Therefore, the following aspects were addressed:

- stay abroad (internship, exchange semester, summer holidays in English-speaking countries);
- (self-perceived) language competence and (self-perceived) progress made in English;
- satisfaction with the degree programme and suggestions for improvement.

The last item regarding their opinion of the programme was included to create a sense of responsibility among the respondents for future generations of UAS students, making it clear to them that their answers could make a difference in the running of the programme.

In the following, I will first present the results of the analysis of these variables in an attempt to determine the driving forces behind the development of the phonological competence of all 55 learners. Then, the answers provided by the informants in Q1 and Q2 will be examined with a view to identifying distinguishing features between the two groups. As the factor 'exposure to the target language' is of particular importance for the present project, it will be treated in more detail. Lastly, one learner from the upper and one learner from the lower end of the performance scale will be portrayed in order to provide an insight into the student population and to speculate on the impact these ID factors might have had on the individual student's success or failure.

4.2.1 Individual factors

Trying to identify the strongest predictor for the changes in the perceived degree of foreign-accentedness, the biographical data collected in Q1 were matched with the average difference calculated for pronunciation development. An analysis of variance (ANOVA) with the difference in the development as the dependent variable revealed the results shown in Table 4.1.

What emerges from the data is that no single variable was found to be highly significant ($p < 0.001$). The following four factors, however, were detected to be significant ($p < 0.05$):

- motivation (to improve one's pronunciation and to improve one's English skills in general);
- lack of language learning anxiety;
- self-reported musicality;
- EMI (i.e. adherence to group: focus group or control group).

To measure the effects of these independent variables and possible interactions, it was deemed conducive to calculate partial eta-squared. In this case, partial eta-squared showed that the influence of the variables was very high with values greater than 0.9. Yet, no relevant interaction effects were disclosed. Contrary to expectations, the most crucial factor in the present context, 'exposure to the target language' (as in media exposure, internship abroad and exchange semester abroad), did not yield any statistically significant results.

In a nutshell, these findings suggest that no single factor alone – not even increased exposure to the TL – can be held responsible for the observed pronunciation development. Instead, a combination of different

Table 4.1 Factors influencing pronunciation development

	Variable	p	F	Partial eta-squared
Biological	Gender	0.115	7.256	0.784
Psychological	Motivation to improve pronunciation	0.018	53.781	0.964
	Motivation to improve English language skills	0.012	80.102	0.976
	Attitude	0.442	0.902	0.311
	Language learning anxiety	0.022	43.977	0.956
	Musicality	0.026	38.319	0.991
Sociocultural	EMI	0.019	51.564	0.963
	Media exposure	0.128	6.360	0.761
	Internship abroad	0.613	0.352	0.150
	Exchange semester abroad	0.058	15.852	0.888

Source: Adapted from Richter (2017).

variables seems to have played a pivotal role in fostering learning. This rather unexpected observation can be seen in light of the Dynamic Systems Theory (DST) proposed by Larsen-Freeman (1997), suggesting that language learning as such is an inherently dynamic process that is largely determined by a set of interdependent variables that interact over time (cf. de Bot et al., 2007). Applying a DST approach to SLA is said to capture both social and cognitive aspects, thereby showing how their interaction can lead to development (de Bot et al., 2007: 19). This view is largely substantiated by the results obtained in this project, corroborating the notion that language learning in general and the development of FA in particular are distinctly shaped by an interconnected web of variables. Without doubt, every learner brings to bear a unique set of personality traits and preferences that affects the language learning process. Taken together, these *a priori* factors are said to interact dynamically with the learning context. In other words, socially and psychologically dependent variables are particularly prominent for any learner and may influence the effort the learner puts into trying to sound native-like. Although the parameters found in the questionnaires provide revealing insights into the learning background of each individual student, it is difficult to extrapolate and interpret their relative value for each group.

So far, I have concerned myself mostly with Austrian learners of English as a group, either the focus group or the control group, as the project was primarily designed to compare these two groups rather than individual learners. However, as the discussion of the factors related to L2 phonological acquisition has shown, FA is subject to individual propensities that are difficult to assign to a particular group. If we are to understand the roles these individual factors play, it is therefore paramount to zoom in on the individual learner's perspective. For this reason, it was deemed noteworthy to look at the development of two specific learners' performances, thereby shedding light on common as well as contrasting aspects that may have come to the fore in those particular cases.

The students whose performances were selected for a more detailed description are high-achiever Anna with the most remarkable progress regarding the mitigation of the foreign-accentedness of her speech (overall +3.6) and low-achiever David whose scores showed the lowest development (overall −1.3). In the following, the data gathered in Q1 and Q2 from both informants will be sketched and correlated with the results obtained in the rating to see if any key ID variables can be identified that may have contributed to the development of the respective learner.

Anna

Table 4.2 shows the scores that Anna received at T1 and T2, respectively. As can be cleary seen, the difference between the scores assigned to Anna at T1 and T2 displays a consistent improvement of M = +3.6

Table 4.2 Anna: FA rating scores

	T1	T2	Diff.
Text	4.9	8.4	+3.5
Story	4.4	8.2	+3.8
Average	4.7	8.3	+3.6

overall, more specifically +3.5 for the text and a slightly higher score for the story with +3.8. This means that her progress in the speaking task was rated slightly higher than that for the reading of the text. Interestingly, the scores for the text were both times higher than that for the narration of the picture story, which goes against the general trend discussed above.

In order to gain a more comprehensive picture of this particular student's performance, it seems crucial to look at the ID variables that may have impacted on her development. At the time of T1, Anna was a 21-year-old female student in the German programme at the UAS Vienna. She had started to learn English at the age of 6 (kindergarten). Both her parents were L1 speakers of Austrian German whose only FL was English. She did not have relatives or close friends in an English-speaking country with whom she had regular contact. Her level of English was clearly above average as she claimed to have passed the Cambridge Business English Certificate BEC Higher in 2010. Apart from English, she also learned Spanish as an FL at school.

Regarding exposure to the TL, at T1 she reported spending a few days in England, two weeks in the United States and three months working in Malta at a hotel reception as part of her secondary school education. As far as media exposure is concerned, Anna sometimes watched movies or TV programmes in English, read books or newspapers in English and occasionally visited English websites. However, she never listened to English radio stations. Musicality was not a trait she associated with herself, as she neither played a musical instrument nor enjoyed singing.

To account for the attitude that Anna had towards the English language, the items from Q1 that were assigned to this particular variable yielded a fairly consistent picture (Table 4.3). Clearly, this shows that Anna holds an overwhelmingly positive attitude towards the English language in general and sees spoken language skills and pronunciation as particularly important. In line with that, the information she provided for the variable 'anxiety' reinforces the statements made in Table 4.3 by revealing that she is not afraid to speak English inside and outside class.

In terms of motivation, the answers provided again exhibit an extremely high degree of commitment and dedication, as detailed in Table 4.4. Not only did Anna intend to spend some time during her studies abroad (as an exchange student and/or as an intern), she also managed to turn this idea into reality. By the time of Q2, Anna had

Table 4.3 Anna: Attitude

	1	2	3	4	5	6	7
I like the English language.	x						
I think the English language sounds good.	x						
I enjoy speaking English.	x						
English is an important part of a business degree programme.	x						
Good English skills are important for my future career.	x						
Good pronunciation is more important than grammatical accuracy.	x						

Note: 1 = fully agree; 7 = do not agree at all.

Table 4.4 Anna: Motivation

	1	2	3	4	5	6	7
I would like to do my internship abroad.	x						
I would like to improve my pronunciation.	x						
I would like to sound like a native speaker.	x						
I would like to have more classes in English.	x						
I would like to do an exchange semester abroad.	x						
Speaking English well is an important goal in my life.	x						
I would like to learn everything related to the English language and culture.			x				
When I am finished with my studies, I would like to live and work in a foreign country.		x					
I would like to improve my accent.		x					
I would like interlocutors to think that I am a native speaker.			x				

Note: 1 = fully agree; 7 = do not agree at all.

in fact done a four-month internship in San Francisco, after which she took a two-month holiday in Hawaii. So, all in all, she spent six months in an English-speaking country in the last year of her studies at the UAS Vienna. When asked what she considered important factors outside class that contributed to the improvement of her English skills, she claimed that friends and holidays had played a major role.

Another interesting aspect that needs to be addressed here is Anna's self-perception regarding her English language skills. When she filled in Q1 in the first semester of her studies, she provided the answer to the question: How would you rate your English language skills at the moment? shown in Table 4.5.

At T2 (2014), she was again asked to rate her language skills at the beginning of her studies. This time her answers were different (Table 4.6).

Table 4.5 Anna: Self-assessment of English language skills at T1

	1	2	3	4	5
Grammar		x			
Vocabulary		x			
Pronunciation		x			
Fluency		x			

Note: 1 = excellent; 5 = very poor.

Table 4.6 Anna: Self-assessment of English language skills at T1 as reported in Q2

	1	2	3	4	5
Grammar		x			
Vocabulary			x		
Pronunciation			x		
Fluency		x			

Note: 1 = excellent; 5 = very poor.

Apparently, looking back to the beginning of her studies, she has become more critical of her own language competence, particularly regarding vocabulary and pronunciation. However, this difference in perception at T2 needs to be seen together with the question: How would you rate your English language skills now? (at T2) (Table 4.7).

Table 4.7 Anna: Self-assessment of English language skills at T2

	1	2	3	4	5
Grammar		x			
Vocabulary		x			
Pronunciation		x			
Fluency		x			

Note: 1 = excellent; 5 = very poor.

It appears that at T2, Anna felt that she had improved in the areas of vocabulary and pronunciation, although a comparison of her own perception of her competence in the various skills at the beginning of her studies yielded diverging results. In this context, it is also interesting to note that she rated her own accent as rather Austrian at T1 and then at the end of her studies as more American.

Having speculated on the profile of a HP pronunciation learner in Section 4.1.8, let us now reconsider the claims I have made there: Conceivably, the learner (1) began to learn English in early childhood; (2) has a positive attitude towards the English language and culture; (3) cares about his/her FA and is highly motivated to improve his/her English pronunciation; (4) is not afraid to speak English; (5) has attended pronunciation classes; (6) is probably female; (7) plays a musical instrument or enjoys singing; and (8) has been exposed to a large amount of L1 English both inside and outside the classroom.

By and large, Anna fulfils the majority of the criteria outlined here. The most noticeable deviations, however, are related to two aspects; namely, the fact that she has not received explicit pronunciation instruction and that she neither plays a musical instrument nor enjoys singing. What clearly stands out in her language learning biography seems the fact that she pursued an internship in the United States in the course of her studies at the UAS Vienna. An international internship typically denotes a practicum or work experience with a company abroad to apply theoretical knowledge acquired in the classroom in a real-world setting in order to gain a more comprehensive view of how businesses operate globally (cf. Nolting et al., 2013). Depending on the degree programme, these international placements can be optional or voluntary. This type of exposure is an aspect that I believe deserves to be looked into more closely in future SLA research. When comparing the SA context (see Section 4.1.7) with the work-abroad context, it appears that the latter often makes greater demands on the students. I would argue that during an international internship, the students are required to engage more deeply in the target culture and at the same time they use the L2 for a wider range of purposes (cf. Richter, 2017). Thus, they are challenged not only to grow professionally, but also socioculturally and linguistically as the placement with a company ideally requires a fair amount of theoretical knowledge of the subject matter (i.e. business concepts), sociocultural competence in the daily interaction with colleagues and customers stemming from different cultural backgrounds as well as a high level of language competence required to deal successfully with both content and language matters. Without doubt, students gain professional experience through such an internship, while at the same time developing global skills through their international stay.

To the best of my knowledge, no empirical investigation so far has looked into the linguistic gains to be derived from an internship abroad. While the field of SA seems to enjoy increasing popularity among researchers (see Section 4.1.7), the domain of working abroad has been largely neglected. One reason for this perhaps lies in the sheer novelty of this trend and the observation that very slowly programme designers at tertiary educational institutions are beginning to realise the full potential of implementing such a decisive cornerstone in their curricula. As far as Austria is concerned, UAS with their vocational and practice-oriented focus seem to be paving the way in this respect. As already mentioned, as with regular university programmes, UAS degree programmes tend to comprise an obligatory professional practical training in their curricula. What is fairly new, however, is that some of these study programmes include internships that the students need to undertake outside the country in order to complete their degree. As Taft (2015) notes, international internships are clearly on the rise as students are increasingly becoming aware of the fact that studying abroad may not be enough to enhance their employability and career skills. For the students, such an international internship may be a distinct asset in their curriculum vitae and a decisive step in climbing their professional career ladder.

Owing to a general dearth of data available on the effects of internships abroad on the learner's language competence, we have to draw on results obtained from SA contexts. Clearly, it cannot be taken for granted that contextualised and meaningful exposure to the L1, as in a professional context, automatically translates into increased FL proficiency. In her case study of American students' language gains after an exchange semester in France, Kinginger (2008) stresses that enhanced language competence needs to be seen in connection with 'durable contacts with local inhabitants', stressing in particular that *internships* and other activities facilitate these deeper social connections' which she sees as reliable predictors of language gains (Kinginger, 2008: 110). Accordingly, working in a foreign country for a limited period of time may provide students with valuable social interactions and active engagement with L1 speakers of the language, which may eventually trigger language learning and result in notable linguistic gains. Such an internship in a foreign country is perhaps one of the most accomplished forms of content and language integrated learning as the students pursue both language learning and content learning aims by integrating fully – though temporarily – in the L2 community and culture (cf. Richter, 2017). Still, we need to keep in mind that linguistic gains to be had from this experience have not been validated empirically and always need to be seen in the context of all the other ID factors, especially motivation and attitude. Therefore, further research is necessary to substantiate the effects of an internship abroad on the language competence of the university students.

David

The second learner to be portrayed here is called David. He was chosen for closer scrutiny as the scores he received for T1 and T2 showed the most noticeable decline in pronunciation skills. More specifically, he was the student for whom the comparison of the ratings obtained at the beginning of his studies and at the end showed the steepest drop of all the students recorded. This means that of all the 55 informants, the development of his FA was rated by the listeners as the least favourable of all the participants. His pronunciation was clearly considered to be more heavily accented at T2 than at T1. To relate this negative development to

Table 4.8 Scores obtained for informant #49

	T1	T2	Diff.
Text	3.2	1.5	−1.7
Story	2.9	2.0	−0.9
Average	3.0	1.7	−1.3

potential factors that may have played a role, it is crucial to analyse the information he provided in Q1 and Q2.

David is a male student from the German control group who was 20 years old at the time of the first recording. As Table 4.8 illustrates, the student's scores for each category (text, picture story and average) display a considerable decline.

David started to learn English at the age of 10 when he entered secondary school. His parents are both L1 speakers of Austrian German. His father also speaks English but his mother does not speak any FLs. The student claims to have no relatives or friends with whom he speaks English in his free time. In addition to English, he also learned French at school.

Regarding exposure to the English language, he spent three weeks in the United States in 2008 and then again in 2009. Furthermore, he reported that he never watched films in English, never read English books or newspapers/magazines and never listened to English radio stations. Only occasionally, he watched English TV and visited English websites. The student did not consider himself a musically talented person as he neither liked singing nor played a musical instrument.

At the beginning of his academic career at the UAS, David reported that he would like to improve his vocabulary, pronunciation and fluency and generally considered pronunciation as the most important skill in an FL as opposed to grammar, vocabulary or fluency (Table 4.9).

The information provided in Table 4.9 shows that the student generally held a very positive attitude towards the English language and saw spoken language skills and pronunciation as particularly important. This

Table 4.9 David: Attitude

	1	2	3	4	5	6	7
I like the English language.		x					
I think the English language sounds good.		x					
I enjoy speaking English.		x					
English is an important part of a business degree programme.	x						
Good English skills are important for my future career.		x					
Good pronunciation is more important than grammatical accuracy.	x						

Note: 1 = fully agree; 7 = do not agree at all.

Table 4.10 David: Motivation

	1	2	3	4	5	6	7
I would like to do my internship abroad.	x						
I would like to improve my pronunciation.	x						
I would like to sound like a native speaker				x			
I would like to have more classes in English.					x		
I would like to do an exchange semester abroad.	x						
Speaking English well is an important goal in my life.	x						
I would like to learn everything related to the English language and culture.						x	
When I am finished with my studies, I would like to live and work in a foreign country.					x		
I would like to improve my accent.	x						
I would like interlocutors to think that I am a native speaker.							x

Note: 1 = fully agree; 7 = do not agree at all.

information was further reinforced when looking at the variable 'anxiety' which revealed that the student was not afraid of speaking English either in the classroom or outside and at that time had not had any negative experiences with the language.

In terms of motivation, the answers provided in Table 4.10 show a more diverse picture. Despite the fact that David exhibits a high degree of motivation to go abroad during his studies, either in the form of an internship or an exchange semester, he seems rather undecided as far as his long-term future career abroad is concerned. Similarly, he sees good English language skills as an important goal in his life, but he does not appear to be very interested in indulging further in the English language and culture. What is particularly striking is the fact that he shows a low level of concern about his own pronunciation. Although he claims that he would like to improve this particular skill, he does not feel the need to sound like an NS and definitely does not want others to think that he is in fact one.

When asked about his own assessment of his English language skills, David was rather careful and rated his grammar skills as good, pronunciation as average but his vocabulary and fluency as rather weak (Table 4.11).

Table 4.11 David: Self-assessment of English language skills at T1

	1	2	3	4	5
Grammar		x			
Vocabulary				x	
Pronunciation			x		
Fluency				x	

Note: 1 = excellent; 5 = very poor.

Table 4.12 shows the scores when comparing the answers he gave at T1 and the answers to the same question at T2.

Table 4.12 David: Self-assessment of English language skills at T1 as reported in Q2

	1	2	3	4	5
Grammar		x			
Vocabulary			x		
Pronunciation			x		
Fluency			x		

Note: 1 = excellent; 5 = very poor.

Retrospectively, he now rates his vocabulary and fluency as higher at the beginning of his studies than three years previously. Overall, he feels that apart from grammar (which stayed the same), he improved in all three areas of vocabulary, pronunciation and fluency in the course of his studies (Table 4.13).

Table 4.13 David: Self-assessment of English language skills at T2

	1	2	3	4	5
Grammar		x			
Vocabulary		x			
Pronunciation		x			
Fluency		x			

Note: 1 = excellent; 5 = very poor.

Interestingly, the data gathered in Q2 revealed that David had spent a semester at a South Korean university where he spoke predominantly English. Of course, this may also have influenced the perception of his own language skills.

Observed differences between Anna and David

Drawing on the information presented above, which sketches the high achiever Anna and the low achiever David, it appears that the main distinguishing features are the following:

- slight difference in AOL: six versus eight years;
- concern about own pronunciation;
- interest in English language and culture;
- SA in South Korea vs internship in the United States;
- gender;
- amount of media exposure;
- perception of own English language skills;

This clearly shows that the two learners compared here differ regarding a number of variables that are undoubtedly interrelated and combine to create a vague picture of a HP learner and a low-potential (LP) learner. Whereas it could be argued that (slightly) earlier AOL, a positive attitude and higher motivation observed in the HP learner have reinforced the experience the student had in the course of an internship in the United States, a later onset of learning together with a lower interest in the English language and culture paired with a lower degree of concern about his own accent resulted in the LP learner's negative development after a stay in a Korean university. Of course, great care needs to be taken to generalise the claims made here based on the analysis of only two admittedly opposing learner profiles. However, it is fascinating to see that the qualitative analysis of these two learners greatly supports the findings discussed in Chapter 3, according to which it is difficult if not impossible to identify the most important factor that is responsible for the success or failure of a language learner. Instead, it is more appropriate to see these ID variables as part of an intricate and complex web of factors that are unique in every single learner.

A further interesting observation concerns the fact that both the learner with the highest development (Anna) and the learner with the lowest development (David) are members of the control group and not the EMI group. This clearly lends support to the finding presented above according to which the control group is much more heterogeneous in its linguistic abilities than the focus group.

Factors accounting for group differences

Although one of the main concerns of this project was to identify those variables that play a key role in the pronunciation development of the individual learners, it was also considered a worthwhile endeavour to compare the two groups with regard to the mean values of the variables under consideration. In order to discover whether there are any significant group differences, the factors that were found to be decisive players in the pronunciation development of the learners (most notably motivation, attitude, musicality and exposure) were statistically evaluated based on group affiliation.

As some of the variables were represented in the form of an ordinal scale and others on a nominal scale and because normal distribution was not given, the consulted statistician suggested carrying out a Mann–Whitney U-test to see the extent to which the mean values of the variables in the two groups differ. Table 4.14 provides the statistical analysis of ID variables according to groups.

As can be seen from Table 4.14, there is overwhelming evidence corroborating the notion that the two groups are profoundly different with regard to the variables investigated. Accordingly, the learners in the focus group are significantly more motivated, generally have a more positive

Table 4.14 ID variables according to groups

Mann–Whitney *U*-test	Focus group	Control group	*p*
Variable	Mean		
Motivation to improve pronunciation	1.24	1.88	0.001
Motivation to improve English	1.62	2.58	0.000
Anxiety	5.67	4.97	0.029
Attitude	1.77	2.27	0.003
Musicality	4.00	4.10	0.884

attitude towards the English language and culture and they are also less inhibited by anxiety to speak the language. The variable that has yielded the most noticeable differences ($p = 0.000$) is motivation to improve their English language skills. The only variable that has not produced any significant results is musicality, which seems to be similar in both groups.

This result is further substantiated by empirical studies in the secondary school context, which compared Content and Language Integrated Learning (CLIL) and EFL classes. In the majority of the cases, a clear superiority of CLIL groups over non-CLIL groups was revealed. More specifically, it has been claimed that CLIL students hold more positive attitudes towards language learning (e.g. Lasagabaster & Sierra, 2009; Seikkula-Leino, 2007) and they also report lower anxiety levels (e.g. Maillat, 2010; Nikula, 2007) and a higher degree of motivation to improve their English language skills (e.g. Lasagabaster, 2011; Seikkula-Leino, 2007).

As far as I know, very few contrastive studies so far have taken account of the university context, which could be traced back to the fact that hardly any EMI degree programmes are in parallel offered in English and in the L1. Therefore, finding comparable groups is undoubtedly difficult. One exception in this respect is a study conducted by Dafouz *et al.* (2014) at the University of Madrid. In an attempt to measure the impact of EMI on students' academic performance, they compared an EMI group with a group of students studying the same content in Spanish. Their findings show that both cohorts obtained similar results, which leads the authors to conclude that the language of instruction does not appear to compromise the learning of academic content. To the best of my knowledge, no study to date has looked at the linguistic gains of tertiary EMI from a contrastive point of view.

4.2.2 The factor 'exposure to the target language'

Despite the fact that 'exposure to the L2' has not been identified as the most reliable predictor in the language learning process, it is still interesting to explore it in more detail in order to capture any possible implications that might otherwise be overlooked in the present context.

Factors Influencing L2 Pronunciation Mastery 123

As discussed in Section 4.1.7, this variable is commonly researched in the form of different sub-variables. For the current project, it seemed sensible to investigate four sub-variables, namely exchange semester abroad, internship abroad, media exposure and exposure to the English language in the English-medium classroom. In the following, data derived from Q1 and Q2 exploring these sub-variables will be presented to provide an informed view of the differences that can be discerned between the two groups.

Exchange semester abroad

As explained in Chapter 2: Section 2.4, students at the UAS Vienna are generally encouraged to study abroad. In the case of the degree programme Entrepreneurship, this occurs in the third semester (i.e. the winter term 2012/2013). In this endeavour, they are largely supported by the Centre for International Education and Mobility (CIEM) located on the UAS campus. The information in Figure 4.1 is based on data gathered in Q2 and contrasts the two groups in relation to the number of students who decided to study for one semester in a foreign country.

The English-speaking countries where the students studied were the United States, Canada, Australia, New Zealand, South Africa and Ireland and the non-English-speaking countries were France, Spain, Estonia, South Korea, the Netherlands, Argentina, Chile and Romania. Clearly, the students in the focus group show a considerably greater

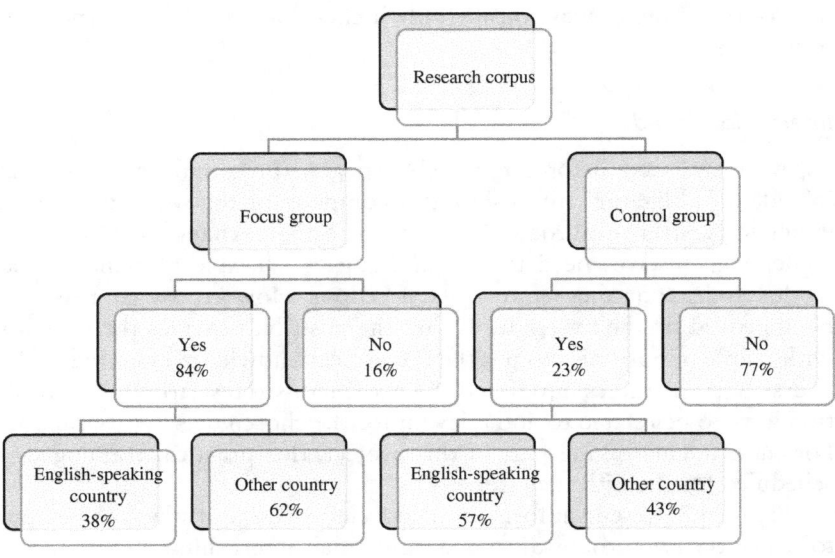

Figure 4.1 Exchange semester abroad

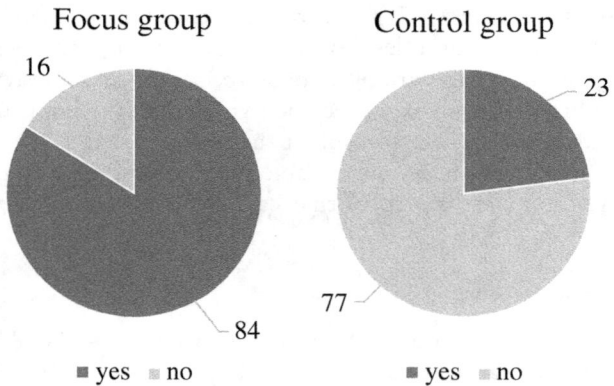

Figure 4.2 Exchange semester – comparison

willingness to study abroad. Figure 4.2 visualises the striking difference between the two groups.

As can be seen from Figure 4.2, at T2 it turned out that of the 25 informants in the bilingual programme, 84% had studied abroad for one semester and only 16% had not. For the 30 students in the control group, the ratio is almost reversed with 23% going abroad and 77% staying. Interestingly, in Q1, 100% of the focus group said they were considering a stay abroad, whereas in the control group this number was significantly lower at only 66%. In both cases, the desire to go abroad at the beginning of their studies was considerably higher than what later turned out to be reality.

Internship abroad

As mentioned before, most UAS degree programmes in Austria include an obligatory internship at a company of the student's choice, either in Austria or abroad. As opposed to the exchange semester, the students themselves need to find and suggest suitable placements and in this endeavour they enjoy great freedom. However, what needs to be approved by the university is that the position provides the students with ample opportunity to put the theoretical knowledge acquired in the course of their studies into practice, i.e. the industrial sector and the position have to be related to and relevant for the chosen degree programme. For the students taking part in this project, this practical training was scheduled for the fifth semester.

Figure 4.3 presents information collected in Q2 and shows the extent to which the two groups differ regarding their internship abroad.

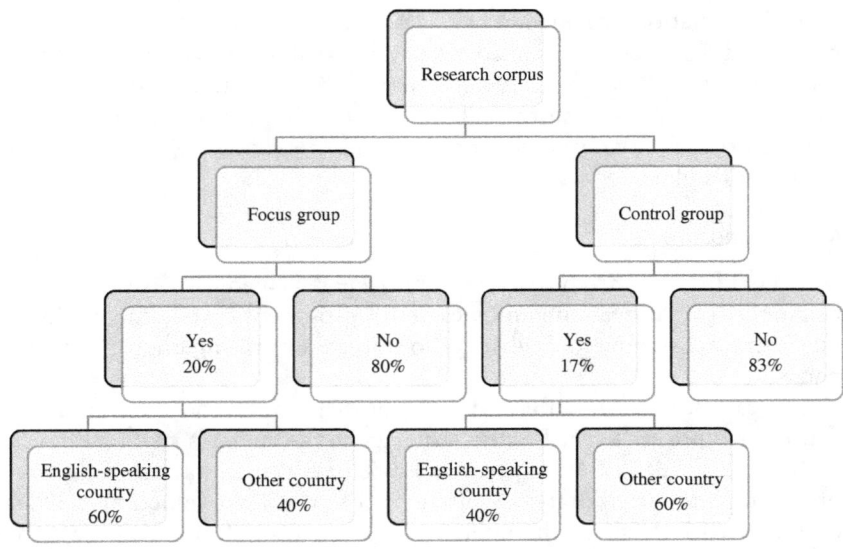

Figure 4.3 Internship abroad

The English-speaking countries the students selected were the United States and the UK; the non-English-speaking countries were Mexico, Italy, Germany and Spain. In contrast to the exchange semester, Figure 4.4 – 'internship abroad' – shows a much less diverse picture.

Accordingly, 20% of the students in the focus group and 17% of the students in the control group did their internship abroad. When looking

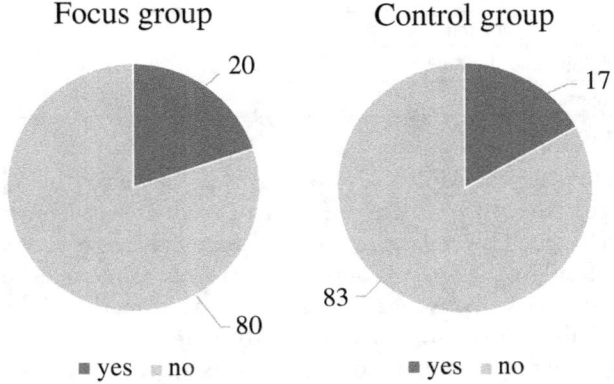

Figure 4.4 Internship abroad – comparison

at the information provided in Q1, 72% of the learners in the focus group had stated that they were considering an internship abroad. In the control group, this figure was much lower at only 47%. Again, for both groups it can be said that many more students had initially expressed the wish to work abroad and two years later only a small percentage of them actually realised this plan.

Media exposure

The third sub-variable to be examined here is media exposure to English in the form of watching movies or TV programmes, reading books or newspapers, listening to English radio stations or visiting English internet pages.

As can be seen in Table 4.15, the most popular and most frequent source of exposure to the English language in the media is visiting English internet pages (68%). An impressive 100% of the students in the bilingual programme reported that they often (68%) or at least sometimes (32%) encountered English on the internet. This is closely followed by watching movies (60%) or TV programmes (60%) in English. The item with the lowest response rate was listening to English radio stations with only 12% claiming that they often and 32% sometimes tuned in. Interestingly, more than half of the learners in this group said they never listened to English radio stations.

Table 4.15 Media exposure: Focus group

How often do you...	Often (%)	Sometimes (%)	Never (%)
... watch movies in English?	60	36	4
... read English books?	40	40	20
... read English newspapers or magazines?	20	52	28
... watch English TV programmes?	60	28	12
... listen to English radio stations?	12	32	56
... visit English internet pages?	68	32	0

The figures for the control group, however, yielded a diverging picture that is largely shaped by a general shift of student answers towards the right of the scale. This means that those items that were overwhelmingly ticked as 'often' by the focus group, were rated as 'sometimes' by the control group and those items that were classified as 'sometimes' turned out to be 'never'. Table 4.16 shows the results of the control group in more detail.

Clearly, the most popular source by far is again the internet with the students from the control group reporting that 33% of them often and 60% sometimes visited English internet pages; 7% of them said that they never looked at English websites. The least popular medium is again the radio; 23% of the respondents claimed that they sometimes and 77% that

Table 4.16 Media exposure: Control group

How often do you...	Often (%)	Sometimes (%)	Never (%)
... watch movies in English?	7	67	26
... read English books?	0	63	37
... read English newspapers or magazines?	7	33	60
... watch English TV programmes?	13	67	20
... listen to English radio stations?	0	23	77
... visit English internet pages?	33	60	7

they never listened to English radio stations. A similar trend, although less drastic, can be seen when it comes to reading books in English. Two thirds (67%) sometimes read a book in the English language, one third (37%) never did.

Media exposure and group affiliation

The investigation of the sub-variable media exposure has shown that the students in the bilingual programme are clearly exposed to a larger amount of English through the media than the control group. The most popular source in both groups appears to be the internet and the least frequently used is English radio stations.

In order to find out whether the differences between the groups as reported above are significant, the data were subjected to appropriate statistical methods. As some of the variables were coded with yes/no (i.e. exchange semester abroad and internship abroad), a Chi^2-test was carried out, which is particularly suitable for nominal data. For ordinal variables, however, the Mann–Whitney U-test was considered more suitable. Both tests use frequency data from a sample in order to test hypotheses about population proportions (cf. Carver & Gradwohl Nash, 2012). Table 4.17 shows the results obtained from those two statistical methods.

Again, in the majority of cases, the differences between the two test groups are statistically significant (books, TV, newspapers, internet) or even highly significant (cinema, exchange semester abroad). One might therefore argue that the factor 'exposure to the target language' has been substantiated as a differentiating factor that clearly sets the EMI group apart from the control group. The only factor that seems to be fairly similar across both groups is internship abroad where differences could not be observed.

In summary, it can be said that although the ID variable 'exposure to the target language' has not yielded a significant influence on the learners' pronunciation development, major differences between the two groups could be confirmed. A close examination of the sub-variables 'exchange semester abroad', 'internship abroad' and 'media exposure' has shown that the students in the focus group are more likely to study abroad than

Table 4.17 Exposure according to groups

Mann–Whitney U-test	Control group (%)	Focus group (%)	p
	Frequency (often) mean		
Cinema	60.0	6.7	0.000
Books	40.0	0.0	0.003
Newspapers	20.0	6.7	0.014
TV	60.0	13.3	0.002
Radio	12.0	0.0	0.070
Internet	68.0	33.3	0.008
Chi^2-test	Frequency (yes/no)		
Exchange semester abroad	84.0	23.3	0.000
Internship abroad	20.0	20.0	1.000

their peers in the control group (84% as opposed to 23%). The ratio regarding an internship abroad, however, is very similar with 20% and 17%, respectively. In terms of media exposure, it was found that the learners in the bilingual programme were considerably more exposed to the English language with the internet being the most frequently mentioned source reported by both groups.

For the UAS Vienna, several far-reaching implications arise from these trends. Firstly, the extremely high number of students in the bilingual programme who study abroad for one semester necessitates organisational, financial and staff-related reconsiderations of existing practices. In order to deal with the temporary but drastic reduction in student numbers (from 25 to 4 in the case of the participants in the present project), the UAS decided to fill the class with incoming exchange students from all over the world. If the current trend continues and more students from this programme go abroad, the management will have to contemplate extensive adaptations to the existing BA curriculum. This could, for instance, mean introducing an obligatory stay abroad with no classes offered in the third semester.

Secondly, the increasing popularity of internships abroad is bound to impact on the UAS' commitment to internationalisation and globalisation processes. Recognising the growing interest of their students not only to study abroad but also to do their internship in a foreign country, the UAS might want to consider expanding its services and networks and also provide assistance in finding adequate work placements abroad. Attempts in this direction have already been undertaken in the form of small cross-cultural projects.

A third and final implication arising from the exploration of the variable 'exposure to the target language' concerns media exposure. As has been seen in the figures presented above, all the learners in the focus group (100%) and the overwhelming majority of the learners in the control group (93%) visit English internet pages either often or sometimes. More precisely, of all the 55 participants in this project, only one learner stated that he/she never encountered English on the internet. This largely confirms what the management has already suspected and therefore further measures will have to be taken to integrate the learning of content and language with the help of e-learning tools and educational software in English, not only in the bilingual programme but also in the German programme. Thus, it is hoped that the students are encouraged to use English through a medium they are familiar with and enjoy.

4.2.3 Conclusion

In this chapter, I have shown that no single individual variable could be identified as the main driver for change in the present project. Instead, a number of interconnected factors, namely motivation, lack of language learning anxiety, musicality and exposure to English in the form of EMI turned out to be significant parameters affecting the pronunciation development of the learners in the present project. However, a close look at the profile of high performer Anna and low performer David revealed that it is difficult if not impossible to generalise these findings as each and every learner seems to bring along a set of individual propensities that shape the learning process: neither of the students considered themselves musically talented nor did they benefit from additional L1 exposure to the English language in the classroom as both of them were students in the regular – German – programme. Regarding the variable exposure to the TL, which I have explored in great detail, it was found that generally the students in the EMI programme are more likely to embark on an exchange semester abroad or an internship abroad than the regular students from the control group. The importance of doing an internship in a foreign country is an intriguing aspect that I believe is currently gaining in popularity among students and also programme designers who are slowly realising the value of work experience outside the home country. Without doubt, the issue of internships abroad can be a crucial factor when researching variables influencing FL learning that should not be neglected in future SLA research.

5 The Development of the Austrian Accent in the EMI Classroom

The preceding chapters have sought to contextualise the question of how the second language (L2) in general and pronunciation in particular is learned in the English-medium instruction (EMI) classroom and which individual difference (ID) variables might influence the learning process. This chapter now sets out to describe the specific features of the pronunciation of English in Austria in order to find out which aspects of pronunciation are least likely to change over time despite the increased amount of exposure to first language (L1) English in the EMI classroom.

As already discussed in Chapter 3: Section 3.2.2, researchers commonly agree that the learner's L1 exerts a considerable influence on the pronunciation of the target language and is thus a significant factor in accounting for FA. Accordingly, an Austrian learner's (AL) English is bound to carry – to some degree – the signature of his/her L1, which means that the sounds, features and rules of the L1 are internalised to such an extent that in many cases a clear tendency to transfer those sounds, features and rules to the L2 can be observed. In this context, Trubetzkoy (1969: 51) claims that the phonological system of a learner's L1 is 'like a sieve through which everything that is said passes'. Accordingly, learners first acquire the system of their L1 and later when they are exposed to another language being spoken, they intuitively apply this phonological sieve of their L1 to analyse what they have heard. However, as this sieve is not always appropriate for the L2, the sounds receive an incorrect phonological interpretation (as discussed in Chapter 3: Section 3.2.2). For the present study, this means that the sounds of the English language are strained through the phonological sieve of Austrian German, the learners' L1.

This chapter first looks at the phonological inventory of both English and German from a contrastive perspective, thereby seeking to identify the most crucial differences and similarities of the two systems that are frequently assumed to be challenging for German learners of English. As most of the literature on those differences is based on Standard German, it will then also be necessary to outline a number of features that distinguish Standard (German) German from Standard Austrian

German, the accent this study seeks to explore in more detail. Next, an overview of empirical studies into the pronunciation of English in Austria will be given. Here, the large-scale study carried out by Wieden and Nemser in the early 1990s in the primary and secondary school context is still the largest and most influential to date. Grosser (1993) focused on suprasegmental features of learner utterances in terms of stress and accentuation, attempting to classify the accentual preferences of young learners. In contrast to Wieden and Nemser (1991) and Grosser (1993), Hrubes (2008) and Mende (2009) were the first to look at adult English pronunciation. By and large, their explorative studies confirm the findings of earlier studies. Finally, Tatzl (2011) evaluated the pronunciation problems of Austrian students at a University of Applied Sciences (UAS) in Graz. He mainly focused on segmental aspects in the learners' final presentations. Drawing on these studies, the chapter closes by presenting a list of potential problems for ALs of English. This list then serves as the basis for the qualitative part of this project, which seeks to identify those features of Austrian English that are least susceptible to change over time. The features listed are then empirically validated using the data collected here to determine if and to what degree learning takes place.

5.1 Contrasting German and English Phonology

Both German and English have their roots in the Germanic language group, which means that they share a number of features, whether it be in syntax, vocabulary or phonology. For this reason, German speakers generally find it easy to learn English and they tend to make rapid progress (Swan & Smith, 2001: 37).

In the following, significant segmental features (i.e. the vowels and the consonants) of the two languages as well as suprasegmental aspects (i.e. features that transcend the sound level), most notably word stress, intonation, linking and weak forms of English and German, will be compared. It should be noted here that most of the research that has been carried out in this particular field of contrastive phonology uses British received pronunciation (RP) as its frame of reference. This view, however, seems to be too narrow a focus for the present project as it can be assumed that the speakers will not only be influenced by British English (BE) but also by American English. For this reason, I considered it useful to include the most distinctive aspects of General American (GA) pronunciation in the following discussion to account for a broader perspective regarding the varieties of English my respondents may have encountered in their EMI classes.

5.1.1 Segmentals in RP

Without doubt, a crucial feature in describing the sound system of any language is its repertoire of sounds (i.e. consonants and vowels).

In their comprehensive account of learner English, Swan and Smith (2001) attempted to provide a practical reference guide for teachers of (British) English as a foreign language (EFL). Above all, their main intention was to assist instructors in anticipating the typical problems of learners of English who speak a particular L1. Broadly speaking, their research is based on the assumption that those phonemes that have equivalents or near-equivalents in German should be articulated without great difficulty, conceding though that some confusion might still arise. In contrast, those phonemes that are different are likely to cause problems (as discussed in detail in Chapter 3: Section 3.2.2.).

As far as vowels are concerned, Swan and Smith point out that the RP vowels which are potentially difficult for German learners are /æ/, /ɔː/, /ʌ/ and the diphthongs /ei/, /əu/. They claim that /æ/ and /e/ are often confused, therefore *sat* and *set* would be pronounced the same. Further, central /ʌ/ tends to be realised as /a/. Regarding diphthongs, they find that both /əu/ and /eɪ/ tend to be monophthongised as /ɔː/ and /eː/, respectively. What is – rather surprisingly – missing in their discussion is the long central vowel /ɜː/, which also needs to be mentioned in this context. Foreign learners of English often have difficulty copying the long central vowel /ɜː/ (Roach, 1991). Its short counterpart /ə/, which does exist in German but is used differently, is a special case as it plays a crucial role in the prosodic shortening of polysyllabic words. This means that, for example, a two-syllable English word like *flower* has its primary stress on the first syllable and consequently the vowel in the second (unstressed) syllable is reduced to /ə/.

Adding the long central vowel would result in the overview of vowels shown in Table 5.1 that are likely to cause difficulties for German learners of English. Shaded phonemes can result in errors. Thus, a negative transfer regarding vowels will be most likely in the following areas: /ə/, /ɜː/, /ʌ/, /ɔː/, /ə/ and the diphthongs /ei/ and /əu/.

Table 5.1 Difficult English vowels for German learners

iː	ɪ	e	æ	ei	ɑi	oi
ɑː	o	ɔː	uː	au	əu	/iə/
ʊ	ʌ	ɜː	ə	eə	uə	aiə/əuə

Turning now to the consonants that will most probably cause problems for German learners of English, Swan and Smith (2001) list the following:

- fortis/lenis distinction esp. lenis /z/, /dʒ/, /ʒ/, /b/, /d/, /g/;
- the dental fricatives /ð/ and /θ/;
- /v/, /w/;
- /r /;
- /ɫ/.

As far as the distinction between fortis and lenis (voiceless/voiced) sounds is concerned, German learners tend to carry over L1 phonemic habits into the target language by pronouncing lenis obstruents (i.e. plosives, fricatives, affricates) in word-final position like fortis sounds. This could be due to German Auslautverhärtung, which essentially means that final obstruents are devoiced. Therefore, *Rad* is generally pronounced the same as *Rat* in German. In English, however, the distinction between the two in final position is retained, as in *bad* and *bat*. These two examples further illustrate a phenomenon related to the change in vowel quantity if followed by fortis consonants within the same syllable. Thus, the vowel /æ/ in *bad* is pronounced longer (i.e. pre-lenis-lengthening) as it is followed by a lenis consonant compared to the shorter /æ/ in *bat* where it is followed by a fortis consonant (pre-fortis clipping). Accordingly, failing to produce a lenis consonant in word-final position may also affect vowel length negatively.

A second group of consonant sounds that often causes problems is the group of dental fricatives /θ/ and /ð/, which is not part of the German sound system. In this respect, German students frequently mispronounce the unfamiliar English fricative /θ/ as /s/, which can lead to misunderstandings as in the frequently quoted ‹I think› or ‹I sink›. On the other hand, lenis /ð/ is often replaced by the lenis alveolar plosive /d/, resulting in *father* being pronounced as[ˈfɑːdə].

Similarly, the lenis fricative /ʒ/ as in *measure*, which is also an essential component of the affricate /dʒ/ as in *joke* or *religion* is also difficult to articulate for Germans because of its voicing. Conceivably, with /ʃ/ and /tʃ/ as in *ship* or *child*, however, they have fewer problems as they also exist in German.

A further challenge regarding consonants is the example of the unfamiliar English sound /w/, which tends to be replaced with the familiar /v/, which is also supported by the orthography of the phoneme /w/. Therefore, words like ‹vet› and ‹wet› are often pronounced the same.

As opposed to GA, British RP is commonly known as a variety of English that does not realise the post-vocalic /r/. This means that the letter r in *car* would not be pronounced. There is one exception, however, when it is retained, namely as the 'linking-/r/' as in *car‿in the street* where it serves to link the two words.

Table 5.2 gives an overview of the most commonly mispronounced consonants by German learners of English. Shaded phonemes tend to be problematic.

Table 5.2 Difficult English consonants for German learners

p	b	f	v	θ	ð	t	d
s	z	ʃ	ʒ	tʃ	dʒ	k	g
m	n	ŋ	l/ɫ	r	j	w	h

Thus, negative transfer seems likely regarding the lenis consonants /b/, /d/, /z/, /ʒ/, /dʒ/, /g/, the dental fricatives /θ/ and /ð/, the liquids /r/ and 'dark l' [ɫ].

5.1.2 Segmentals in GA

To account for a broader view regarding the contrast between German and English pronunciation, in the following a few selected aspects concerning segmental differences between RP and GA will be outlined.

A comparison of the RP vowel chart with the GA vowel chart reveals the most significant differences as follows:

(1) The shift from the RP diphthong [əu] to GA [ou] consists in the change of the reduced vowel /ə/ to the close-mid back rounded vowel /o/ in the first part of the diphthong. This shift is commonly seen as systematic and renders words like ‹go› as [gou].
(2) In GA, the vowel sound /o/ is missing and is generally replaced with /ɑ:/. Consequently, ‹not› would be pronounced [not] in RP and [nɑ:t] in GA.
(3) The long back vowel /ɔ:/, which in BE occurs in words such as ‹taught› or ‹walk›, is usually more open and less rounded in GA. In some regional varieties, it can either be realised as /ɑ:/ or /ɔ:/.

Turning to consonants, a number of salient features of GA stand out as clearly non-British. Among those, the most prominent ones include post-vocalic [ɹ], dark [ɫ] and the flapped [ṱ]:

(1) The /r/ sound is probably one of the most noticeable features of GA. Unlike RP speakers, speakers of GA pronounce the post-vocalic /r/. As a consequence the word *form* would be pronounced ['foɹm] by a GA speaker and ['fɔ:m] by an RP speaker (Wells, 1982: 125–126).
(2) The use of the dark [ɫ] wherever the phoneme /l/ occurs is also widespread in American English, i.e. also before vowels where RP has clear [l]
(Cruttenden, 1994: 84).
(3) In GA flapping is common; this means that either /t/ or /d/ occurs between a sonorant phoneme and an unstressed vowel. In this case, the allophone /ṱ/ is commonly used (e.g. *better*).

5.1.3 Suprasegmentals

Apart from segmental foreign accent (FA), a selected number of suprasegmental features that go beyond the level of sound (such as word stress, intonation, weak forms) also deserve due notice.

Both German and English are said to be stress-timed languages (cf. Pompino-Marschall, 1995: 236), which means that there is a general tendency to favour a sequence of accentuated syllables at regular intervals (Kohler, 1977: 117). As Scherer and Wollmann (1986: 53) note, this means that there are two to four unaccented syllables between two accented ones.

Whereas Northern German intonation is similar to English intonation, Southern German intonation tends to have long rising glides in mid-sentence positions. Also, wh-questions are often pronounced by German learners with a rising tone at the end based on their L1 equivalent. Most notably, German has a so-called 'Sägeblattintonation' or 'sawtooth intonation', which according to Schuderer (2002: 16), is caused by unaccented syllables which seem to descend too sharply between stressed syllables or at the end of a phrase. This phenomenon is often held responsible for the general perception of German as a harsh-sounding language.

An area that many German speakers find difficult when learning English is the principle of linking. As Kufner (1971: 134) notes, within a tone unit final consonants or vowels need to be linked to the following word or syllable in English. In striking contrast to German, this is particularly the case when the following word starts with a vowel. The following example serves to illustrate this observation:

German: Anna aß ein Ei.
English: Anna ate an egg.

Produced by an L1 speaker of German and English, respectively, this utterance would be transcribed as follows:

German: [ʔana ʔaːs ʔain ʔai]
English: [ænər‿eit‿ən‿eg]

The difference is obvious and hints at a crucial distinguishing feature of the two languages. In German, the lack of the principle of linking together with 'Sägeblattintonation' can be held responsible for the commonly held belief that the German accent sounds harsh and staccato-like.

In English, structure words (e.g. articles, pronouns, prepositions and auxiliaries) have two different kinds of realisation, namely a strong form and a weak form (Biersack, 2002: 69). The use of one or the other hinges on the phonetic context, pacing and style. As Gimson (1994: 229) notes, in spoken English, the weak form is the unmarked form and the strong form is marked. In contrast to that, weak forms in German are rare and not even part of the Standard variety (Scherer & Wollmann, 1986: 229). This is further enforced by the fact that, in general, German pronunciation dictionaries do not feature weak forms. Accordingly, German L1 speakers of English tend to give structure words such as *and*, *but*, *than* or *as* their strong pronunciation regardless of the context.

5.1.4 The specifics of Austrian German

Austrian German or Austrian Standard German is the variety of the German language written and spoken in Austria. Owing to a number of sociocultural, geographical and historical reasons, it has come to be clearly distinguished from the rest of the German-speaking area. In fact, Austrian Standard German is a formally recognised national variety of German that deviates sufficiently enough from the Standard German spoken in Germany to be considered a variety in its own right, but not different enough to be acknowledged as a separate language (Ammon, 1997; Wiesinger, 2000). In 1951, the establishment of the Österreichisches Wörterbuch, a comprehensive cataloguing of the Austrian variety of German, was a significant step in codifying the national variety and fusing this variety with Austrian identity. Although clearly noticeable features of this variety can be made out at all the various levels of the language, they are most salient in the words that are commonly referred to as 'Austriazismen' (Ebner, 1998). A typical example in this respect would be the Austrian German word for tomato 'Paradeiser' which is 'Tomate' in German German.

As far as pronunciation is concerned, the vast majority of Austrians strongly believe that an independent standard exists for Austria, and they are also fairly consistent in what this standard variety sounds like (Moosmüller, 1991). Tests carried out by Moosmüller (1991) revealed that the phonology of Standard Austrian German is largely based on the Middle Bavarian varieties and is generally spoken by educated Austrians coming from the upper and middle social classes. However, in his account of the features of Austrian English, Wiesinger (2000) points out that a specific feature of Austrian German is dialect colouring, which most Austrians would be able to recognise and locate correctly.

This range of variation within the country may also be closely related to the fact that it appears to be difficult to define a Standard variety. As Ehrlich (2009) in her dissertation on the pronunciation of Standard Austrian German notes, there is still a clear lack of generally agreed on prescriptive norm, despite the fact that in 2007 the Austrian pronunciation dictionary 'Österreichische Aussprachewörterbuch' with its Austrian pronunciation database marked a decisive but certainly not final step in this direction.

Regarding segmentals, the most interesting and far-reaching difference to be heard in large parts of Southern Germany and Austria is that lenis plosives and lenis fricatives are not voiced (e.g. in *beben, geben, bringen*). Similarly, fortis plosives in initial position are not aspirated, rendering words like *dank* the same as *tank*. The exception in this respect is k/g but only before vowels, which would result in a clear difference between *Garten/Karten* but not in *Greis/Kreis*. Interestingly, in striking contrast to Southern and Central German, /d, t/ in medial position are in fact pronounced differently (e.g. *leiden/leiten*).

In general, Austrian German vowels are much closer than in Central and Northern Germany. The umlaut ‹ä› is pronounced /e/ and the pronunciation of the letter ‹a› misses the dark quality that it has, for example, in Bavaria. In addition, a number of diphthongs tend to be monophthongised, particularly in the Viennese region, thus turning, for example, /au/ as in *Haus* into /ɔː/. As far as vowel length is concerned, Iivonen (1987) investigated the difference in vowel duration between speakers of Austrian (Standard) German and speakers of German (more specifically East Central) German and discovered that in general, vowel duration was 32% higher for the Austrian speakers as opposed to the German speakers.

On the suprasegmental level, the most striking difference between Austrian German and German German is to be found in word stress and intonation. In German German, a clear tendency to stress the first syllable of a word prevails, whereas Austrian German prefers the second syllable in words like *Abteil, unmöglich, Tabak* or *Kaffee* (Schmidt, 2009).

5.2 Empirical Research into the Austrian Accent in English

Although only a handful of empirical studies on the Austrian accent in English exist, they do give some indication as to the specifics of this particular domain. In the following, I will discuss the most significant findings these studies have yielded. By far the most influential and far-reaching work titled 'Pronunciation of English in Austria' was carried out by Wieden and Nemser in the early 1990s. On a much smaller scale, Grosser's (1997) seminal article 'On the Acquisition of Tonal and Accentual Features of English by Austrian Learners' focused on the intonational structures and the assignment of sentence accents. Then, in 2008 a short bachelor's (BA) paper by Hrubes and in 2009 Mende's diploma thesis 'The pronunciation of Austrian students of English at university-level' attempted a descriptive account of adult students' English. And finally, Tatzl (2012) investigated pronunciation problems in aeronautical engineering students' final presentations.

5.2.1 Wieden and Nemser (1991)

The pioneering work by Wieden and Nemser (1991) is the first database to analyse what mistakes ALs of English make over a certain period of time. They investigated the acquisition of English phonology by 384 Austrian school children in Grades 3–11 (two classes in four regions at each age) to determine the stages of development and the typical problems of ALs. To gain a comprehensive view of the phonological resources of the learners, they administered four different tests, namely a questionnaire, a perception test, an imitation test and a production test.

The sound file recordings were analysed by four listeners and yielded a detailed phonetic specification. The pronunciation model underlying their study was RP, other regional varieties or accents were not included.

Overall, Wieden and Nemser claim that the accurate production of English vowels seems to be more challenging for ALs than the production of consonants. In their presentation of the correct scores for vowels, /iː/ with 57% and /i/ with 44.1%, respectively, head the table, whereas /ʊə/ and /ɜː/ with 8% and 5.6%, respectively, are located at the other end. In the higher ranks, a large proportion of close vowels as well as diphthongs can be found, while central and open vowels and diphthongs score lowest. This seems to confirm that Austrian vowels in general are closer than English vowels and therefore learners find it more challenging to produce open vowel sounds.

According to the authors, the deviant pronunciation of RP vowels by ALs can be attributed to two main reasons. Firstly, vowel quantity (i.e. vowel length) seems to play a major role as ALs tend to have problems with the shortening and lengthening of vowel sounds, which Wieden and Nemser (1991: 56) have mainly detected in the high categories of the international phonetic alphabet (IPA) vowel chart, i.e. /iː/, /ɪ/, /uː/ and /ʊ/. Secondly, a number of problems can be attributed to L1 transfer, for instance high vowels tend to be raised even further because their position in Austrian German is generally higher than in RP.

To a certain extent, potential problems with the low central vowels /ɜː/, /ʌ/, /ə/ and /ɑː/ are also related to the notion of L1 transfer, which can be held responsible for a general tendency towards lowering. A particularly noteworthy case is the long central vowel /ɜː/, which is not only shortened but also diphthongised producing /əə/. In terms of vowel length, Wieden and Nemser (1991: 57) even discovered a tendency towards merger, a phenomenon that becomes apparent in the observed lengthening of /ə/ and the shortening of /ɜː/.

Further significant observations regarding vowels as observed by Wieden and Nemser (1991: 56–58) include the raising of /æ/ (64%), a shifting of /e/ towards /æ/ (37%) and a lowering of /ɔː/ (50%), which often goes hand in hand with diphthongisation when orthographically followed by r (as in *sports*).

Regarding consonants, Wieden and Nemser (1991: 54) point out that the percentages of convergence for the consonants /m/, /h/ and /j/ are very high with 99.3%, 98.7% and 98.0%, respectively. At the bottom of the league, however, convergence patterns for /ʒ/, /v/, /z/ and /dʒ/ only range from 18.2% to 4.2%, which are attributed to the fact that those sounds are either not part of the Austrian German consonant system, or they are realised differently. As expected, Wieden and Nemser (1991: 63) also discovered a clear tendency for obstruents to abandon the fortis/lenis (unvoiced/voiced) distinction, with fortis sounds being the preferred choice. The difference between /v/ and /w/ is essentially characterised by the polar opposites of opening/closing and rounding/unrounding, which are bound to cause problems. In addition, pronouncing /θ/ and /ð/ correctly also seems to be difficult. In Austrian English, the pronunciation of /θ/ seems to be characterised by backing, whereas /ð/ is marked by closing and backing. Therefore, ALs often replace /θ/ and /ð/ with /s/ and /d/, respectively. Overall, these findings confirm the results of the discussion on the differences between German and English phonology in Section 5.2.6.

In their study, Wieden and Nemser also looked beyond the level of sounds and investigated the development of prosodic features of young ALs' accent in English. By and large, they found that short rudimentary rhythmic units tend to be frequently interrupted by pauses (Wieden & Nemser, 1991: 231).

As far as the *learning stages* are concerned, the authors identified a developmental sequence consisting of four different stages in the development of L2 phonology, namely 'pre-systemic' (learner basically imitates L2 input), 'transfer' (L2 phonological elements are systematically represented in L1 terms), 'approximation' (influence of L1 declines, new phonological categories are introduced) and 'consolidation'. Interestingly, these stages vary for the two different aspects of speech, namely sounds/segments and prosody.

Accordingly, in the case of sounds, the pre-systemic/transfer stages overlap, followed by later approximation and consolidation, whereas for prosody, transfer follows the sequence pre-systemic, transfer, approximation (Wieden & Nemser, 1991: 230). As can be seen, the prosodic features clearly lag behind and never reach the phase of consolidation (Figure 5.1).

As far as the early stages of learning English are concerned, the use of word stress tends to be pre-systemic and imitative and largely characterised by memorised stress patterns for individual words (Wieden & Nemser, 1991: 233). Also, rhythm and intonation exhibit pre-systemic features. In other words, rhythmic units are void of clear nuclei, contracted or reduced forms and stress timing (Wieden & Nemser, 1991: 233). At intermediate level, word stress appears to be governed partly by stress rules transferred from German and an over-generalisation of target

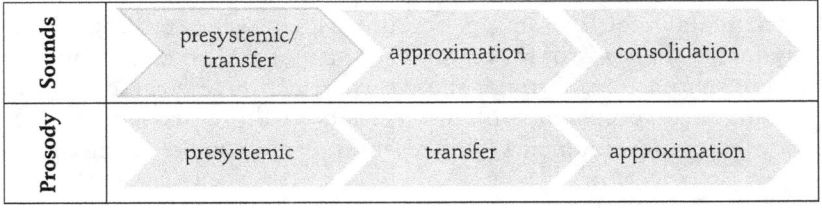

Figure 5.1 Learning stages (adapted from Wieden & Nemser, 1991: 230)

language rules (as in ['həʊtel], for example). Furthermore, the number of utterances the informants produced was found to be systematically but not imitatively correct. This systematic acquisition of rhythm and stress typically starts in the intermediate stage of learning, giving rise to the development of coherent rhythmic groups that sound 'like typical Austrian English' (Wieden & Nemser, 1991: 234). At the advanced level, word stress sub-rules appear and a fairly high degree of target-like productions was reported. In terms of rhythm and stress, prominence only occasionally tends to be used as a rhythmic principle and infrequent reductions and contractions may occur. In addition, stress timing emerges as the prosodic domain is generally extended, which can be observed by learners beginning to pay attention to rhythm, stress and intonation in longer utterances.

The data analysed by Wieden and Nemser show that the young ALs in this large-scale project were more successful and faster in their acquisition of L2 segmentals than suprasegmentals. Clearly, this study suggests that suprasegmental features should not be left aside in English language teaching (ELT) in Austria. Rather than focusing on the correct pronunciation of individual vowels and consonants from the early stages of learning, suprasegmental aspects of the language also deserve due attention. Apparently, both aspects rightly deserve a place in the curriculum and in textbooks and should be addressed in the foreign language (FL) classroom in order to enable students to speak intelligibly.

One interesting finding concerned the receptive processing of the diphthong /əʊ/ as in *boat*, which improved with increasing exposure time, and other phonemes such as the final schwa /ə/ in *folder* and the dark /ɫ/ in *ball*, which did not change after eight years of schooling (Wieden & Nemser, 1991: 145–155). That is to say, some phonemes develop more easily than others. It will be interesting to see whether the findings of the present project confirm these observations.

Without doubt, the pioneering work carried out by Wieden and Nemser in the early 1990s marks a crucial point of departure for any exploration into the pronunciation of English in Austria. However, more than two decades have passed and a great number of sociocultural, political, economic and educational changes have left their imprint on the way English is taught and learned in the 21st century. In particular, the increasing amount of exposure to English not only inside the classroom (e.g. in the form of EMI courses) but also outside school (e.g. through the internet) can be expected to affect the language competence of the learners. Taking account of these far-reaching developments, this research project makes a significant step towards fleshing out the present-day features of the Austrian accent in English.

5.2.2 Grosser

In his longitudinal study on the acquisition of intonation and sentence stress by young ALs of English, Grosser (1993) looked at five female and three male students aged 10–12 over their first two years of learning. His description of accentual patterns is based on the reading of a short text, telling a story and free conversation.

In his article on aspects of intonational L2 acquisition of ALs, Grosser (1993: 81–92) classifies four categories in which his informants make mistakes with regard to the use of stress patterns:

(a) *Cumulative accentuation* (i.e. more words or syllables are given prominence without the intention of giving special emphasis). This essentially means that the learner does not distinguish between known and unknown information and does not know how to reduce vowels in unaccented words to produce weak forms. In his data, for example, Grosser found that in many cases the young learners stressed every single word (e.g. WHAT'S YOUR NAME?).

(b) *Alternating accentuation* (i.e. an overuse of tonal accents characterised by an alternating principle). This means that both lexical content words as well as grammatical items or structure words are tonally accented (Grosser, 1993: 84), suggesting that the learner cannot distinguish between content and structure words. Although there seems to be a general awareness that stress can be employed as a cohesive device, it is mainly used in a rhythmic rather than a semantic way (e.g. The Lion TOLD him).

(c) *Backshifting of accentuation* (i.e. a tendency to shift accentuation towards the end of an utterance). In an attempt to explain this phenomenon, Grosser argues that these learner utterances call for a contrastive interpretation, which is not appropriate in the given context. Bearing in mind that for both English as well as German, the tonal accentuation on the final position is 'unmarked', this failure to move the tonal accent from the final position to an item on the left may be attributed to what Grosser (1993: 85) calls a 'dominance of over-productivity of the final accentuation or end-focus rule'.

(d) *Fronting of accentuation* (i.e. the opposite of backshifting, causing a word at the beginning of an utterance to be stressed in order to give emphasis). For Grosser, this signals a marked focus on the word whereas the context would have called for an accent further to the right.

To sum up, Grosser's findings suggest that the young learners in his sample clearly struggle with the basic concept of stress as a means to accentuate important information in an utterance. They use accentuation ambiguously and inappropriately, resulting in a general overuse of stress placement (which Grosser claims to be typical of the early stages of learning), the use of stress with the mere intention to create rhythm rather than meaning, and the general misplacement of stress (too far front or too far back) which are said to frequently occur in later stages of learning. What is of importance for the present project is the observation that ALs of English tend to cumulate accentuation by stressing words that need not be stressed.

5.2.3 Hrubes

In his BA thesis on the typical problems of German speakers of English, Hrubes (2008) analysed the pronunciation of six adult ALs of English whose language competence was supposed to correspond to B2 in the Common European Framework of Reference (CEFR). He analysed the reading of a text and the description of a picture and found that the most outstanding pronunciation problems of his speakers were threefold:

- *Auslautverhärtung* caused lenis consonants to be devoiced.
- The lenis dental fricative /ð/ was frequently mispronounced as /d/.
- /æ/ was pronounced as /e/.

5.2.4 Mende

In her descriptive analysis, Mende (2009) attempted to shed light on the pronunciation of Austrian students of English at the Karl-Franzens University in Graz. The aim of her master's (MA) paper was to identify pronunciation errors that these advanced learners make at the segmental level. In addition, she looked at the consistency of those students who had chosen a particular target variety such as BE or American English. Interviews with 10 Austrian students were recorded, transcribed and subsequently analysed. Regarding consonants, she found that devoicing was a major challenge for her informants:

- /dʒ/: devoiced by 99%.
- /z/: devoiced by 87%.
- /ʒ/: devoiced by 74%.
- /v/: devoiced in word-final position by 92%.
- /ð/ turned into a plosive (51%), which was particularly true in the case of structure words, such as *the*, *that*, *these* and so on.

- /w/ substituted by /v/.
- clear [l] instead of dark [ɫ].

Interestingly, she also noted a highly inconsistent use of the post-vocalic /r/ no matter whether the speakers claimed GA or BE as their model. For vowels, she pointed out the following deviant pronunciations:

- /æ/ was substituted for /a/ or /e/;
- diphthongs were monophthongised, especially /əu/;
- /ə/ was substituted by a full vowel (mostly in content words).

As far as the choice of model (GA or RP) is concerned, she observed that the speakers of RP hardly ever used GA sounds; the speakers of GA, however, frequently resorted to the articulation of RP sounds. Additionally, Mende observed that in those speakers who did not claim to pursue a particular target variety, a tendency to use RP sounds more than GA sounds could be detected.

5.2.5 Tatzl

In his study on students' pronunciation at a technical UAS in Graz, Tatzl (2011) looked into the main pronunciation problems that learners encountered in their final presentations. His findings again support the general view that vowels and diphthongs more than consonants seem to cause problems. Top of this list is the schwa. As for consonants, the greatest difficulties were recorded with /s/, /ʤ/, /l/. The author claims that the mispronunciation of /s/ in his sample might be attributed to the fact that in the words they recorded (i.e. process, certification), these sounds would be pronounced /ts/ in German. Interestingly, lenis /z/ is not named as troublesome, neither is /ð/.

5.2.6 Conclusion

Tables 5.1 and provide an overview of the most common problems for ALs of English based on the literature discussed in this chapter. The items provided here are taken from the text 'The North Wind and the Sun' that the participants in the present project were asked to read. For each phoneme (for segmentals) or category (for suprasegmentals), one representative item was chosen. The only exception in this respect is the phoneme /ʒ/ which only occurs in combination with the affricate /ʤ/ in this text. For this reason, the item *vision* as a typical example is added in parentheses. Table 5.3 covers the segmental features and Table 5.4 shows the suprasegmental aspects of the pronunciation of English that are bound to be difficult for ALs.

Table 5.3 Segmental features likely to cause problems for ALs of English

Category	Phoneme	Item	Explanation
Vowels and diphthongs	æ	tr<u>a</u>veller	• Does not exist in German • Is often confused with /e/ and vice versa
	ɜː	f<u>i</u>rst	• Long central vowel does not exist in German • Often diphthongised and substituted with /øɐ/
	ə	travell<u>er</u>	• Fewer weak vowels in German • Often full vowel is pronounced
	ɔː	m<u>o</u>re	• Less lip rounding in German • Often too short • Often diphthongised /oə/
	əu	cl<u>o</u>sely	• Does not exist in Standard German • Failure to produce second vowel resulting in o: • In GA: /ou/
	ei	c<u>a</u>me	• Failure to produce second vowel resulting in /e:/
Consonants	w	<u>w</u>ind	• Letter ‹w› exists in German, but is pronounced differently • Insufficient lip rounding of AL results in /v/
	v	ga<u>v</u>e up	• Often confused with /w/ • Lack of vibration
	ð	<u>th</u>ey	• Does not exist in German • Substituted with /d/
	θ	Nor<u>th</u>	• Does not exist in German • Substituted with /f/ or /s/
	z ʤ ʒ	a<u>s</u> hard a<u>s</u> obli<u>g</u>ed (vision)	• These lenis sounds do not exist in Austrian German • Preference of ALs for fortis sound
	p t k	wra<u>pp</u>ed <u>t</u>ake <u>c</u>oat	• Frequent lack of differentiation between p/b, t/d, k/g in Austrian German • /p, t, k/ need to be fully aspirated when at the beginning of a stressed syllable
	r	ha<u>r</u>d	• In British English r after a vowel is not pronounced (except for linking) • In American English /r/ is a rhotic consonant sound
	ɫ	fo<u>l</u>d	• Only clear l exists in Standard German • AL tend to prefer clear l

5.3 Insights from the UAS Vienna

In order to put the findings of the literature as provided in Chapter 4 to the test, I chose to scrutinise the sound files of those 10 informants who were perceived by the raters as having made the most noticeable progress in the development of their FA. The decision to focus on those 10 students was prompted by the assumption that a repeated acoustic analysis of two sound files collected from each informant (one at T1

Table 5.4 Suprasegmental features likely to cause problems for ALs of English

Category	Item	Explanation
Word stress and vowel reduction	trav<u>e</u>ller	• In English the vowel in unstressed syllables is often reduced to /ə/ (schwa sound) • In German this is not always the case
Sentence stress	And so the North <u>Wind</u> was <u>obliged</u> to <u>confess</u> that the <u>Sun</u> was the <u>stronger</u> of the two.	• In English only 'content words' (nouns, verbs, adjectives) are normally stressed; structure words tend to be unstressed and reduced to a 'weak form' (see below): The result is a fairly regular rhythm.
Weak forms	<u>as</u> hard <u>as</u>	• In English 'structure words' prepositions, conjunctions, pronouns, etc.) are normally not stressed and therefore reduced to 'weak forms'
Linking	when‿a traveller came along	• No principle of linking in German resulting in ALs pronouncing every word individually

and one at T2) would reveal developmental patterns of speech sounds that tend to be more salient in high performers than in low performers. Table 5.5 gives an overview of the informants chosen for a detailed acoustic analysis.

As can be seen, my research corpus for the qualitative phonetic analysis comprised five female and five male speakers of whom six came from the focus group (FG) and four from the control group (CG). The difference in terms of their development over the given time period ranged from an average of +3.5 to +1.9.

With the detailed phonetic specification of the recordings, I was hoping to be able to reveal potential markers of the Austrian accent that are least susceptible to change. For the close qualitative scrutiny of the sound files, Tables 5.1 through 5.4 compiled for the segmental and suprasegmental features of the Austrian accent as described in the literature were drawn upon. For each phoneme, one representative word or item from 'The North Wind and the Sun' containing this particular feature was selected and subjected to repeated acoustic analysis. As mentioned before, one of the crucial advantages of this short text is that it features all of the most important phonemes of the English language and therefore output can be controlled. However, due to the text's brevity, there is in some cases only one instance of a particular phoneme. In order to guarantee a balanced approach to the data, I decided to focus merely on one item even if the text contained a second or third one. For suprasegmentals, on the other hand, at least two examples of the production of the respective category could be identified and subsequently analysed.

5.3.1 Segmental features of the Austrian accent in English

The students in this project were asked to read the fable 'The North Wind and the Sun' and to narrate a picture story by Gary Larson. For the

Table 5.5 Overview of informants for phonetic analysis

Rank	File #	Group	Gender	Average score overall at T1	Average score at T1	Difference
1.	61	CG	f	4.7	8.2	+3.5
2.	50	CG	f	5.4	8.3	+2.9
3.	15	FG	m	5.2	8.0	+2.8
4.	40	CG	m	5.2	7.6	+2.4
4.	12	FG	f	6.3	8.7	+2.4
6.	1	FG	m	5.9	8.0	+2.1
6.	29	FG	f	6.9	9.0	+2.1
6.	35	FG	f	4.8	6.9	+2.1
9.	48	CG	m	3.1	5.1	+2
10.	31	FG	m	7.4	9.3	+1.9

qualitative part of my research, I decided to focus only on the reading of the text and not on the narration of the cartoon as the output produced in the reading was considerably more controllable and hence did not bear the risk of respondents consciously avoiding or not producing the features that I was interested in.

Tables 5.6 and 5.7 show the results of the acoustic analysis of the realisations of those phonemes that were considered relevant for the present study. Further detailed information is provided as to whether correct productions are considered to be closer to GA (i.e. GA-like) or RP (i.e. RP-like).

As can be seen, the most problematic phonemes at T1 were the consonant /ð/ (0% correct) and the diphthong /ei/ (20% correct). At the other end of the scale, /æ/ and /ə/ for vowels and /t/, /k/ and /r/ for consonants were located with 100% correct realisations.

Three years later, all instances of /æ/, /ɜː/, /ə/ and /ɔː/ were produced correctly, as were /ə/, /p/, /t/, /k/, /r/ and /ɬ/. The phonemes that seemed to be most difficult were again /ei/ (50% correct) and /ð/ (0% correct).

The results detailed above lead to the ranking of the vowels and diphthongs at T1 and T2, respectively, as shown in Table 5.8.

Generally speaking, more correct pronunciations for all the phonemes investigated were found at T2 than at T1, an observation that supports the results of the sound file ratings by expert raters as presented in Chapter 3: Section 3.4.2, according to which both groups managed to ameliorate their FA. Clearly, the most problematic sounds in this category are the diphthongs /ei/ and /əu/, which were frequently monophthongised. Particularly /ei/ as in *making* proved to be problematic, even for those who otherwise showed a remarkable improvement in many areas. At T2, only 50% of the respondents managed to produce the diphthong correctly, which has to be seen in contrast to an initial failure rate of 80%. For consonants, the findings shown in Table 5.9 were observed.

Table 5.6 Segmental features of the Austrian accent in English at T1

Category	Phoneme	Item(s)	Production			
			Flawed (%)	Correct (%)	GA-like (%)	RP-like (%)
Vowels and diphthongs	/æ/	tr<u>a</u>veller	–	100	60	40
	/ɜ/ː	f<u>i</u>rst	20	80	70	10
	/ə/	travell<u>e</u>r	–	100		
	/ɔː/	m<u>o</u>re	20	80	50	30
	/əu/	f<u>o</u>ld	20	80	60	20
	/ei/	m<u>a</u>king	80	20		
Consonants	/w/	<u>w</u>ind	70	30		
	/v/	ga<u>v</u>e up	80	20		
	/ð/	<u>th</u>ey	100	–		
	/θ/	Nor<u>th</u>	20	80		
	/z/ /dʒ/ /ʒ/	a<u>s</u> hard a<u>s</u> obli<u>g</u>ed	90 90	10 10		
	/p/ /t/ /k/	wra<u>pp</u>ed <u>t</u>ake dispu<u>t</u>ing <u>c</u>oat	10 – – –	90 100 100 100	30	70
	/r/	ha<u>r</u>d	–	100	80	20
	/l/	fo<u>l</u>d	20	80		

Here again, a general tendency to produce consonants more accurately at T2 can be detected as almost every single phoneme saw a gradual progression towards a more standardised variety. What clearly stands out as the phoneme least susceptible to change is the lenis dental fricative /ð/. In this case, no change could be observed. In all the recorded instances of the item *they* both at T1 and T2, the informants consistently produced /d/ instead of /ð/.

Despite the fact that many English language teachers see /ð/ and /θ/ as typical features of the pronunciation of English, the two dental fricatives are not part of the sound system of certain native speaker varieties of English, such as Irish English or Jamaican English (cf. Walker, 2010: 29). Furthermore, these two phonemes are not part of the sound system of a large number of languages in the world, including German, which renders their target-like production a great challenge for many learners. It has also been found that L1 English-speaking children seem to struggle in this respect as studies suggest that the last phonemes to acquire in childhood are in fact /ð/ and /θ/ (e.g. Jackson & Stockwell, 2011: 138). This notable difficulty in learning the English phonological system as experienced by both L1 and L2 speakers together with the frequent absence of the two sounds in a great number of languages often results

Table 5.7 Segmental features of the Austrian accent in English at T2

Category	Phoneme	Word item	Production			
			Flawed (%)	Correct (%)	GA-like (%)	RP-like (%)
Vowels and diphthongs	/æ/	tr<u>a</u>veller	–	100	70	30
	/ɜː/	f<u>i</u>rst	–	100	90	10
	/ə/	travell<u>e</u>r	–	100		
	/ɔː/	m<u>o</u>re	–	100	80	20
	/əʊ/	f<u>o</u>ld	20	80	40	40
	/eɪ/	m<u>a</u>king	50	50		
Consonants	/w/	<u>w</u>ind	60	40		
	/v/	ga<u>v</u>e up	50	50		
	/ð/	<u>th</u>ey	100	–		
	/θ/	Nor<u>th</u>	–	100		
	/z/ /ʤ/ /ʒ/	a<u>s</u> hard a<u>s</u> obli<u>g</u>ed	80 60	20 40		
	/p/ /t/ /k/	wra<u>pp</u>ed <u>t</u>ake dispu<u>t</u>ing <u>c</u>oat	– – – –	100 100 100 100	80	20
	/r/	ha<u>r</u>d	–	100	90	10
	/l/	fo<u>l</u>d	–	100		

in the learners substituting the phonemes with similar sounds 'they find easier' (cf. Walker, 2010: 30).

What seems striking in this context is that in the sample analysed in the present study, the fortis variant /θ/ reached 100% correctness in the second rating with an increase between T1 and T2 of +20%, whereas its lenis counterpart did not experience any development at all (0% correct at T1 and 0% correct at T2). A possible explanation for the difficulty observed with the production of lenis /ð/ can be related to the distribution of the phoneme. As a matter of fact, the lenis dental fricative most frequently occurs in word-initial position in function words such as pronouns (e.g. *they*), articles (e.g. *the*) and conjunctions (e.g. *than*) rather than in content words such as nouns, verbs and adjectives (cf. Collins & Mees, 2013: 92) where /θ/ (as in *threat, think, thirsty*) is more common. As these function words do not carry lexical meaning, it could be argued that learners in their attempt to construct meaning seemingly focus more on content words, thereby neglecting function words. In other words, an L2 learner who pays more attention to the accurate production of content words in the target language is likely to disregard features of function words of which the /ð/ is a crucial phonological component. This disregard can be assumed to take place not only on the level of production but

Table 5.8 Frequencies of vowels and diphthongs ranked

Correct (%)	T1	T2
100	/æ/	/æ/
	/ə/	/ə/
		/ɜː/
		/ɔː/
80	/ɜː/	/əu/
	/ɔː/	
	/əu/	
50		/ei/
20	/ei/	

also on the level of perception, which can be seen in relation to Flege's Speech Learning Model (as discussed in Chapter 3: Section 3.2.2), according to which accurate L2 production cannot take place unless there is accurate L2 perception.

As can be seen in Table 5.9, a further difficulty for the participants alveolar fricative /z/ (+10% change between T1 and T2) and the palato-alveolar fricative /ʤ/ (+20% change between T1 and T2), where little progress could be noted as the learners tended to produce fortis sounds instead. /v/ and /w/ also seemed difficult: /v/ as in ‹give up› was realised as /f/ and /w/ often showed no or too little lip-rounding resulting in /v/. This shows again that those sounds that have no equivalent counterpart in German appear to be troublesome for the learners.

By and large, the findings presented here confirm the results discussed in the review of empirical research into the pronunciation of Austrian English in Section 5.2.6. With the exception of Tatzl (2011), all other scholars agreed that the lenis consonants /ð/, /z/, /ʤ/, /v/ were bound to cause difficulties. This observation also largely confirms the tenets of the Contrastive Analysis Hypothesis, as outlined in Chapter 3: Section 3.2.2, which purports that an L2 sound that does not exist in the L1 (such as /ð/, /z/ or /ʤ/) or is used differently (such as /v/) will be difficult for a learner.

A final – and rather unexpected – finding in the course of my acoustic analysis of the sound files concerns the increasing tendency of the learners to produce GA variants of a number of phonemes. This development seems to result in the overall impression that the Austrian accent in English is highly influenced by GA. In this regard, Table 5.10 provides an overview of a few selected segmental features with a focus on the difference in choice regarding GA or RP at T1 and T2.

Table 5.9 Frequencies of consonants ranked

Correct (%)	T1	T2
100	/t/	/t/
	/k/	/k/
	/r/	/p/
		/θ/
		/l/
90	/p/	/r/
80	/l/	
	/θ/	
50		/v/
40		/w/
		/dʒ/
30	/w/	
20	/v/	/z/
10	/z/	
	/dʒ/	
0	/ð/	/ð/

Table 5.10 Development of GA phonemes

GA phoneme	Word item	T1 (%)	T2 (%)	Difference (%)
/æ/	tr<u>a</u>veller	60	70	+10
/ɜː/	F<u>i</u>rst	70	90	+20
/ɔː/	m<u>o</u>re	50	80	+30
/əʊ/	F<u>o</u>ld	60	40	−20
/t̬/	dispu<u>t</u>ing	30	80	+50
/ɹ/	ha<u>r</u>d	80	90	+10

Accordingly, the most popular GA phoneme is /ɹ/ with 90% of the items produced at T2, particularly in combination with the vowel /ɜ/ as in *first* but also /ɔː/ as in *more*. Also quite remarkable is the production of the flapped /t̬/ as in ‹disputing›, which saw an increase of 50%.

Based on these observations, two questions arise:

(1) Where does this influence come from?
(2) Are the students aware of the GA features in their accent?

Whereas the latter question can be addressed by retrieving information gathered in the questionnaires of this study, the former calls for a different project which would certainly be worth pertaining to in the future. The fact that the overwhelming majority of the EMI lecturers at the UAS Vienna spoke with an American accent can only be assumed to have played a role. Data confirming this suspicion are unfortunately not yet available.

Putting this general tendency to opt for GA variants into a broader perspective, it would be interesting to see whether this is a context-specific and regional phenomenon or whether there are similar trends to be observed in other European countries. Very recently, a study conducted by Brekelmans (2015) in the Netherlands supports the view that the influence of GA phonemes on learners of English appears to be on the rise. Although the author was mainly interested in the effects of the discontinuation of explicit pronunciation instruction on undergraduate students, she also found that L1 Dutch learners of English preferred GA allophones to those of RP. She claims that this could possibly be explained by the students' 'seeking out more American media and even wanting to sound more American' (Brekelmans, 2015: 88). Clearly, further empirical data are necessary to explore what seems to be an emerging trend not only among learners at the UAS Vienna but possibly also in other European educational institutions.

As far as learner awareness is concerned, in Q1 and Q2 the respondents were asked to rate their own accent. Table 5.11 shows the answers provided at T1 and T2.

Interestingly, the figures shown in Table 5.11 do not support the view that the students themselves feel that their own accent has moved towards GA. When looking at the FG, very few changes can be observed with the exception that at T2 more learners (+8%) felt that they could

Table 5.11 How would you rate your own accent?

	Focus group (%)		Control group (%)	
	T1	T2	T1	T2
More British	24	20	7	13
More American	36	36	13	27
More Austrian		12	53	37
Other	8	4	0	0
I don't know	20	28	27	23

no longer place their accent. One possible explanation for this might be that of those students who studied abroad for a semester, more than two thirds (62%) were located in a non-English-speaking country and of those who did an internship abroad almost half (40%) were posted in a country where English was not spoken as an L1. In the CG, however, a clearer tendency to rate their own accent as 'more American' (from 13% at T1 to 27% at T2) could be observed together with the fact that the number of students judging their own accent as 'more Austrian' decreased remarkably from 53% at T1 to 37% at T2. Overall, the most frequently provided answer was 'more American' in the FG and 'more Austrian' in the CG both at T1 and T2.

5.3.2 Suprasegmental features of the Austrian accent in English

Table 5.12 presents the findings derived from the phonetic analysis of the suprasegmental features of the Austrian accent in English at T1 and T2, respectively. For each category, two representative items were selected from the text 'The North Wind and the Sun'.

Accordingly, the aspect that was found to be least difficult at T1 with an accuracy rate of 100% was word stress and vowel reduction as in *traveller*, followed by linking in *when a traveller* with 90%. At the end, we find weak forms in a sequence of two as in *stronger of the two* with 10%, followed by linking as in *took off his coat* (30%). Three years later, at T2, it is still those two features that seem to cause most problems. The correct production of the weak form in *as hard as* only increased by 10% and the scores for linking in *took off* even saw a deterioration of 10%. In contrast, the production of linking in the item *when a traveller* reached 100% correctness at T2. It appears that for the suprasegemental features of Austrian English investigated in this project, the correct pronunciation of weak forms seems to be least susceptible to change over time. Both items *as hard as* and *stronger of the two* were found to be most problematic.

Table 5.12 Suprasegmental features of Austrian-accented English at T1 and T2

Problem	Item(s)/chunks	T1 Flawed (%)	T1 Correct (%)	T2 Flawed (%)	T2 Correct (%)
Word stress and vowel reduction	• 'trave<u>ll</u>er • a'roun<u>d</u>	0 20	100 80	0 0	100 100
Sentence stress	And so the North Wind was <u>obliged</u> to <u>confess</u> that the <u>Sun</u> was the <u>stronger</u> of the two.	30	70	0	100
Weak forms	• <u>as</u> hard <u>as</u> • stronger <u>of the</u> two	70 90	30 10	40 80	60 20
Linking	• when a traveller • took off his coat	10 70	90 30	0 40	100 60

Two possible reasons behind this phenomenon can be assumed, which largely correspond to what has been said above about the lenis dental fricative being the most challenging phoneme for the ALs in the present project. Firstly, as discussed in Section 5.1.3. weak forms are not part of Standard German (cf. Scherer & Wollmann, 1986: 229). This is further reinforced by the fact that German pronunciation dictionaries generally do not feature weak forms. Secondly, weak forms are mostly associated with function words such as articles, pronouns and auxiliaries. By nature, these function words play a minor role in conveying lexical meaning (as opposed to content words) and thus they are given less attention by learners. This lack of attention may also be responsible for the potential link between inaccurate production as a consequence of insufficient perception. Those learners who do not perceive the difference between the marked (i.e. strong form) and the unmarked (i.e. weak form) form will struggle with accurate production. In addition, the pronunciation of function words is often neglected in many Austrian EFL classrooms. These aspects taken together – the practical non-existence of weak forms in the L1, their subordinated role in constructing meaning and their general negligence on the part of FL teachers – tend to result in ALs of English producing strong rather than weak forms. Clearly, these findings support the view expressed by Hasenberger (2012: 38) that suprasegmental features should not be left aside in ELT in Austria. Rather than focusing on individual vowels and consonants from the start of the learning process, suprasegmental aspects such as weak forms and linking also need to be considered.

I would like to add here that the features that have been identified as the most prominent aspects of Austrian-accented English in the present study can of course only reflect a tendency that is based on a clearly defined sample. Naturally, this does not mean that all ALs of English share the same characteristics. A much larger sample would in fact be necessary to generalise the findings and describe the Austrian accent in more detail.

6 Conclusion

In this book, I have explored the role of English-medium instruction (EMI) in adult foreign language learning in general and pronunciation learning in particular. My research has been guided by the main question which asks if and to what extent the students at the University of Applied Sciences (UAS) Vienna develop their pronunciation skills in the course of their studies. More specifically, I have examined how my participants' degree of foreign accent changed over time, why it changed and what exactly changed. This concluding chapter will first draw together the main findings presented in Chapters 2 through 5 and then present the limitations of the study as well as suggestions for further research. Finally, a number of implications will be elucidated.

6.1 Synopsis

For the present project, two groups of adult students from the bachelor's (BA) programme Entrepreneurship at the UAS Vienna were selected: firstly, a focus group from the bilingual programme (with up to 50% of the content classes taught in English by native speakers [NSs] of the language) and secondly, a control group from the German programme (with regular English for specific purposes [ESP] classes only). To track the development of the learners' pronunciation, all the participants were recorded twice, once at the beginning of their studies and then again at the end. The elicitation techniques that were utilised in this case study consisted of two different tasks, the reading of the text 'The North Wind and the Sun' and the narration of a picture story by Gary Larson. In addition, questionnaires were given to the participants with the aim of gathering data regarding factors that are commonly associated with the level of pronunciation mastery (e.g. attitude, motivation, anxiety and exposure to the second language [L2]). With the help of a purposefully designed online rating tool, these sound files were then rated by expert listeners. For a closer investigation of those features of the Austrian accent that appear to be least likely to change over time, a selected number of sound files were subjected to repeated acoustic analysis.

The results obtained in this study have provided convincing evidence that the learners in both groups, the EMI focus group and the German control group, managed to ameliorate their foreign accent. However, the difference in the degree of development of the two groups is highly significant as the EMI students decidedly outperformed their peers in the control group at the beginning of their studies as well as at the end. Over a period of almost three academic years, the focus group ameliorated their foreign accent by an average of 1.1 points, whereas the control group in the German programme scored significantly lower at 0.6 points. This means that the advancement observed in the pronunciation of the EMI group was almost twice as high as that for the control group. Regarding the factors that may have contributed to the changes in the students' foreign accent, no single variable could be identified as the driving force in the language learning process. Although the most outstanding feature of the EMI programme Entrepreneurship is exacerbated in the form of increased amounts of exposure to NS input, the success of the focus group could not be traced to this factor alone. Instead, it appears that a dynamic combination of interrelated factors such as strong motivation to learn the language and to improve one's pronunciation, a certain musical talent, a notable lack of language learning anxiety as well as increased exposure to first language (L1) English can have a beneficial effect on the development of the students' foreign-accented speech.

In addition, this study explored those features of the Austrian accent in English that are least susceptible to change over time. A close phonetic specification of the recordings of a selected number of learners revealed that on the segmental level, the production of the lenis consonant /ð/ together with the diphthongs /ei/ and /əu/ showed no or only little change. As far as suprasegmental features are concerned, the informants in the present project struggled most with accurate pronunciation of weak forms and linking. Furthermore, a general tendency of the learners to produce General American phonemes rather than British variants was detected. This development seems to result in the overall impression that the Austrian accent in English is increasingly influenced by General American phonology.

All in all, it can be said that this empirical study demonstrates that in the long run EMI can have a measurable effect on learners' phonological development. The degree programme described and analysed here clearly sets favourable conditions for advancing the learners' pronunciation skills, thereby rejecting the widely held view that the language learning process of adult students is barred with the almost unsurmountable barrier of a critical period for phonological acquisition.

6.2 Limitations of the Study

The findings presented in this book naturally have to be seen in the light of a number of limitations, which can be assigned to three main categories, namely contextual, conceptual and methodological.

As far as contextual parameters are concerned, perhaps the most important limitation refers to the setting. Here, a very specific EMI classroom at an Austrian UAS is described, analysed and interpreted. Whereas this educational institution provides the perfect context for a longitudinal research project in terms of the comparability of the two cohorts and also the trackability of the changes in the learners' pronunciation, it also has to be noted that the findings are closely tied to the peculiarities of this type of tertiary education. As outlined in Chapter 2: Section 2.4, at a UAS, student groups are considerably smaller and there is in general more interaction between lecturers and teachers than at a regular university. This also means that the learners engage in the target language more actively than at a university which is characterised largely by teacher-fronted classrooms. Consequently, care should be taken to transfer the findings to other, less student-centred tertiary educational institutions where different situational factors shape the learning experience of the students. Thus, generalising the findings beyond this small sample should only be done with great care. Yet, it would, of course, be interesting to scrutinise the impact that EMI has on learners' pronunciation development in other academic environments.

In terms of conceptual considerations, perhaps the most important limitation refers to the nature of the degree of foreign accent reflected in this study. As has been pointed out by a number of scholars, defining foreign accent is no easy task as it encompasses the notion of inherent variability. Moyer (2014), for instance, postulates that no two members of a speech community sound exactly the same, nor does a learner speak in acoustically identical ways across a number of different situations, even if the words are the same. Without doubt, we continuously adjust our pronunciation to changing circumstances, rendering it a context-related expression of our personal and social identity. It, therefore, has to be taken into account that the ratings gathered here in this study can only capture two moments in time of a student's language learning process. Keeping in mind that the major aim here was to track the development of the learners' degree of foreign accent over a period of three years, the methodology employed was indeed able to determine the extent to which the foreign accent in the learner utterances changed. Further complicating this conceptual limitation, the results presented here rest on the raters' subjective perceptions of foreign accent. For this study, utmost care was taken to ensure that all the raters shared a homogeneous view of what exactly constitutes the notion of foreign accent. This implicitly shared knowledge is grounded in many years of assessing the pronunciation of

Austrian learners of English. Although it is reasonable to assume that the linguistic features of foreign-accented speech are transferable, different groups of raters (expert and non-expert) are bound to define and judge pronunciation skills in diverging ways. As a consequence, the ratings are likely to yield different results if carried out by different judges.

This study also presents a number of limitations in terms of its methodological approach. One of the major cautions that must be taken refers to sample size both in terms of listeners and speakers. The group of listeners was by nature very small. The closely defined requirements for the judges to act as listeners meant that only a select few could be considered suitable. In total, I was very fortunate to recruit seven raters with the necessary pedagogical background and long-standing experience as pronunciation teachers and examiners who committed themselves to spending several hours of their valuable time rating as many as 300 sound files. The same is naturally true of the fact that there was only one expert judging the productions of the learners in the qualitative segment of the study. Needless to say, a larger sample of listeners could have produced more accurate results. It has to be noted, however, that the high degree of intra-rater reliability inherent in the repeated acoustic analysis carried out by one researcher also adds to the validity of the categorisation.

Not only more listeners could have been employed, but also more informants could have been used. As there is no clear-cut suggestion as to how large a sample size should be, it can be assumed that the larger the sample, the better. Although at the beginning of the project, each cohort consisted of more than 30 participants, the final number of speakers to be used in the analytical stage saw a moderate decline, which is of course due to the longitudinal nature of the research and an inherent disadvantage of any long-term study. Clearly, the scarcity of longitudinal studies in language learning is often associated with high attrition rates related to the need to test and re-test the same individuals over an extended period of time. Therefore, the longer the follow-up period, the higher the chances are for dropout and the lower statistical power. In the present project, however, this attrition rate could be kept to a minimum, a fortunate circumstance that can be attributed to the fact that in Austria UAS are organised in a school-like manner with fixed time schedules and a rigidly set curriculum which makes it easier for a researcher to procure participants, to keep track of their progress and to compare parallel groups.

These potential imprecisions and limitations clearly open up room for further discussion and empirical research to refine and improve the conceptual understanding of how pronunciation is learned in the tertiary EMI classroom.

6.3 Suggestions for Further Research

Suggestions for further research can be deduced from the limitations of the study identified above. For instance, the rather unexpected finding showing the large extent of positive development in the advanced learners' pronunciation skills, which could not be anticipated, definitely leads to entirely new avenues to explore in future studies. Although the results presented in this case study have to be seen within the given context, namely a business degree programme at an Austrian UAS, it would certainly be worth revisiting the research questions in a different setting. A replication of this study involving EMI courses in other European tertiary educational settings would not only be desirable but essentially needed to provide further support for the generalisability of the findings. In particular, investigating potential differences in teaching styles and learning experiences between a UAS and a regular university seems to be a promising path to take when looking into the linguistic gains of EMI students. No matter what specifics L1 future studies with a similar design might investigate, the results will contribute to the exploration of a scientific field that deserves tribute and due attention. It is therefore hoped that researchers with a keen interest in pronunciation learning and teaching will shift their focus away from initial learning stages in children towards a more advanced and more experienced age group of learners.

This study has shown that increased exposure to the target language in the form of exchange semesters abroad, internships abroad and media exposure can play a crucial role in the development of the learners' pronunciation. These days an increasing number of undergraduate as well as post-graduate degree programmes are building an optional or obligatory internship abroad into their courses to prepare their students for the global workplace (cf. Taft, 2015). As this type of practical training in a foreign country is often seen as a distinct asset in the learner's curriculum vitae that greatly enhances his/her employability, it could also be assumed that this variable has a potential impact on the student's language competence. So far, research has predominantly focused on the linguistic gains of studying abroad, thereby leaving aside that spending a semester working abroad may be worth exploring as a separate variable. Future researchers might thus want to gain greater insights into this aspect, in particular by exploring the precise differences in linguistic gains between working abroad and studying abroad.

Another question certainly worth investigating pertains to the effects of Austrian-accented speech on intelligibility and comprehensibility. Empirical studies actually measuring intelligibility are rare and do not seem to provide evidence that non-native speaker (NNS) speech is generally less intelligible than NS speech. Especially with regard to the role of English as a lingua franca, the question of how these features impact on the communicative aims in conversation needs to be explored further.

For the present project, this means that an empirical study into how intelligible the speakers in the present project are would probably yield enlightening results that could trigger new ideas in pronunciation teaching and learning.

Lastly, this research has also brought to the fore a general tendency of Austrian students to produce General American rather than British phonological variants. This observation naturally raises a number of questions. Perhaps the most probing issue in this respect is related to the reasons for this trend. Follow-up projects could, for example, elaborate on the subject of exposure to specific types of accent in English (most notably British and American) in the media that could further help our understanding of what causes this preference and what this might eventually entail for the English as a foreign language (EFL) classroom.

6.4 Implications

Despite the fact that further research is both necessary and desirable to substantiate the results presented here, the study breaks new ground in pronunciation research and forges ahead into EMI, a teaching approach that is currently sweeping European higher education institutions. Thus, the findings also have a number of potential implications for EMI programme designers as well as EFL teachers.

Perhaps the most salient topic that runs through this book like a red thread is also the most important implication for the EFL classroom. The findings that mature EFL learners are indeed capable of improving their foreign accent, even if their attention is on content rather than language, calls for a radical change in the mind of many teachers and students alike. Pronunciation should no longer be viewed as a lost cause, an essential but often neglected skill hardly worth spending valuable class time on since improvement will only be minimal or not likely at all. Instead, educators need to recognise and embrace the phonological capacities of all their learners, no matter what age. This study provides convincing evidence that individual aspects other than age play a pivotal role in determining the success or failure of a learner. Clearly, the biological constraints of the aging brain should not be used as an excuse for a general neglect or intentional absence of pronunciation teaching in the adult EFL classroom. Hence, creating an anxiety-free learning environment that is committed to fostering motivation in every student by cherishing diversity and individual differences is essential to success.

The results derived from my study can be interpreted as a clear sign that the bilingual BA degree programme Entrepreneurship is a highly attractive offer amid the myriad of business-oriented undergraduate programmes that the Viennese tertiary landscape presents. For the programme designers at the UAS Vienna, important ramifications arise in relation to student population and quality assurance. Firstly, the data gathered here clearly revealed that the learners in the bilingual programme differ considerably from those in the German programme, not only regarding their English language competence but also concerning affective variables like attitude, motivation and desire to spend a semester abroad (either in the form of an internship or a study abroad). In fact, this largely confirms what department heads and teachers have already suspected but never had empirical proof of. Thus, the subjective observations of a great number of lecturers shared in many informal in-house conversations according to which the students in the bilingual programme are more challenging to teach and more demanding in their expectations of the programme are clearly confirmed. This highlights the need for the programme designers at the UAS Vienna to reconsider the decision that the two cohorts, the bilingual group and the German group, largely share the same curriculum with the same classes and the same learning aims. Based on the admittedly narrow focus of my research (i.e. the development of the students' foreign accent in English), the clear superiority of the learners in the EMI group already at the time of admission calls for a more pronounced differentiation and perhaps modification of existing course outlines and teaching practices so as to ensure that all students realise their full potential. Despite the fact that the phonological gains as recorded in the focus group are of central concern in my project, the improvements noted in the control group should not be overlooked. It appears that the study environment created by the UAS fosters and promotes incidental pronunciation acquisition although the focus of the EMI and the ESP courses lies elsewhere. What this perhaps means for other universities offering EMI programmes is that effective instructional practices such as small groups and interactive teaching and increased exposure to L1 English can give their graduates a much-desired competitive edge.

Moreover, the present study also has implications for EFL teachers in general, and EFL teachers in Austria in particular. This book pioneers a comprehensive account of the features of the Austrian accent in English with which most learners, including those who are widely experienced speakers or highly proficient speakers of the language, seem to struggle. I would argue that especially in teacher training, as for example provided by the English Department at the University of Vienna, pronunciation specialists should draw upon this list as a highly useful resource in order to provide prospective teachers and other English language learners with an up-to-date descriptive account of what constitutes the Austrian accent in English. The results of the present project have also reconfirmed the current debate on pedagogical priorities in the pronunciation classroom which seems to be characterised by a general shift of attention from individual phonemes or sounds to suprasegmentals and other features of the larger context of utterances. Thus, prosodic aspects such as weak forms or linking should not be left aside in English language teaching.

Clearly, both of these levels of phonology have their rightful place and need to be taken into consideration to reach the goals of communicative language teaching. Of course, owing to time shortage, teachers are often forced to set priorities and need to be selective from an abundance of materials. Nevertheless, they need to be aware that both parameters should be taught. Rather than drilling sound discrimination from the very beginning of the learning process, a more balanced approach epitomising the integration of segmentals and suprasegmental features seems advisable.

In conclusion, I would like to reaffirm my sincere hope that the insights into pronunciation learning in a bilingual EMI programme as granted in this book will give new impetus to the advance of English-medium teaching in European higher education. Thus, the findings could be seen as another relevant piece that fits into the much larger jigsaw puzzle of L2 acquisition.

Source: Clker

Appendix

Questionnaire 1

Liebe Studierende!..Wien, im Oktober 2011

Dieser Fragebogen ist Teil eines wissenschaftlichen Projekts des Studiengangs Unternehmensführung zum Thema **Sprachbegabung** und **Entwicklung der englischen Sprachkompetenz** im Laufe des 3jährigen Studiums.

Ich ersuche Sie nun, diesen Fragebogen **nach bestem Wissen und Gewissen** auszufüllen. Ich kann Ihnen versichern, dass Ihre Angaben **anonymisiert** und nur für **wissenschaftliche Zwecke** verarbeitet werden.

Für Fragen stehe ich Ihnen selbstverständlich jederzeit gerne zur Verfügung!

Vielen Dank für Ihre Teilnahme!...........................Karin Richter

Um eine leichtere Lesbarkeit zu gewährleisten, wurde auf geschlechtsspezifische Endungen („-Innen") verzichtet. Es sind an allen Textstellen, wo natürliche Personen bzw. Personengruppen erwähnt werden, immer Menschen beiderlei Geschlechts angesprochen.

_____

Einverstanden:

_____........................._____

Ort, Datum   Unterschrift

_____

Teil 1 – Persönliche Daten

1. Name: _____
2. Geschlecht:

M	W
☐	☐

1. Geburtsdatum: _____
2. Wann haben Sie begonnen Englisch zu lernen?

   ☐ ab meiner Geburt

   ☐ Kindergarten   Alter: ca._____

   ☐ Volksschule   Alter: ca._____

   ☐ Unterstufe Gymnasium/Hauptschule   Alter: ca._____

   ☐ Sonstiges: _____   Alter: ca._____

3. Welche Muttersprache(n) sprechen Ihre Eltern?

   Mutter: _____

   Vater: _____

4. Welche Fremdsprachen sprechen Ihre Eltern?

   Mutter: _____

   Vater: _____

5. Welche Sprache/n wird/werden bei Ihnen zu Hause/in ihrem privaten Umfeld gesprochen?

   _____

6. Haben Sie Freunde/Verwandte mit englischer Muttersprache, mit denen Sie regelmäßig (mindestens 3 x pro Jahr) Kontakt haben?

Ja	Nein
☐	☐

7. Welche anderen Fremdsprachen sprechen Sie? (*bitte in der Reihenfolge des Beherrschungsgrades angeben*):

   _____

   _____

   _____

   _____

8. Wie viele und welche Dialekte sprechen Sie?

Wie viele Dialekte?		Welche?
keine	☐	
1	☐	
2 oder mehr	☐	

9. **Höchste bisher abgeschlossene Schulausbildung**
   (bitte kreuzen Sie an bzw. geben Sie das Jahr des Abschlusses an):

Institution		Jahr des Abschlusses
Lehre/Fachschule	☐	
Matura	☐	
Universität, FH	☐	

10. Haben Sie in Ihrer bisherigen Schullaufbahn eine rein englischsprachige Schule besucht?

Ja	Nein
☐	☐

Wenn nein, bitte weiter zu Frage 11.

Wenn ja:

Schultyp/Ort: _____

Wie lange? _____

11. Haben Sie in Ihrer bisherigen Schullaufbahn eine bilinguale Schule besucht?

Ja	Nein
☐	☐

Wenn nein, bitte weiter zu Frage 12.

Wenn ja:

Schultyp/Ort:_____

Wie lange? _____

Wie viele Fächer wurden auf Englisch unterrichtet?

☐ 1–2 Fächer pro Jahr

☐ 3–4 Fächer pro Jahr

☐ bis 50%

☐ mehr als 50%

12. Waren Sie schon einmal in einem englischsprachigen Land?

Ja	Nein
☐	☐

Wenn nein, bitte weiter zu Frage 13.

Wenn ja, bitte geben Sie Details an:

	Großbritannien/ Irland	USA/ Kanada	Australien/ Neuseeland	Südafrika
Wo?	☐	☐	☐	☐
Wann?				
Wie lange?				

13. Hatten Sie beruflich schon mit Englisch zu tun?

Ja	Nein
☐	☐

Wenn nein, bitte weiter zu Frage 14.

Wenn ja, bitte kreuzen Sie an:

Schriftlich	Mündlich
☐	☐

Teil 2 – Englisch in der Freizeit

Wie oft …

	oft	manchmal	nie
16. … sehen Sie sich Kinofilme auf Englisch an?	☐	☐	☐
17. … lesen Sie englischsprachige Bücher?	☐	☐	☐
18. … lesen Sie englischsprachige Zeitungen/ Zeitschriften?	☐	☐	☐
19. … sehen Sie englischsprachiges Fernsehen?	☐	☐	☐
20. … hören Sie englischsprachige Radiosender?	☐	☐	☐
21. … besuchen Sie englischsprachige Internetseiten?	☐	☐	☐

Teil 3 – Begabungen

Bitte kreuzen Sie an.

....1 = *sehr gerne* .... 7 = *überhaupt nicht gerne*

		1	2	3	4	5	6	7
22.	Singen Sie gerne?	☐	☐	☐	☐	☐	☐	☐
23.	Schauspielern Sie gerne?	☐	☐	☐	☐	☐	☐	☐
24.	Imitieren Sie gerne Stimmen?	☐	☐	☐	☐	☐	☐	☐
25.	Imitieren Sie gerne Dialekte?	☐	☐	☐	☐	☐	☐	☐

26. Spielen Sie ein Musikinstrument?

Ja	Nein
☐	☐

Wenn nein, bitte weiter zu Frage 27.

Wenn ja, welche/s: _____

Wie lange schon? _____

		ja	eher ja	weder/noch	eher nein	nein
27.	Halten Sie gerne Präsentationen in Ihrer Muttersprache?	☐	☐	☐	☐	☐
28.	Sind Sie ein guter Redner (in Ihrer Muttersprache)?	☐	☐	☐	☐	☐
29.	Hören Sie manchmal von Ihren Freunden, dass Sie viel reden?	☐	☐	☐	☐	☐
30.	Hören Sie manchmal von Ihren Freunden, dass Sie gut Dialekte und Akzente nachmachen können?	☐	☐	☐	☐	☐
31.	Haben Sie generell ein gutes Gehör?	☐	☐	☐	☐	☐
32.	Passen Sie sich beim Sprechen mit anderen Menschen Ihrer Muttersprache leicht dem Akzent/Dialekt an?	☐	☐	☐	☐	☐
33.	Fühlen Sie sich als Sprachtalent?	☐	☐	☐	☐	☐

Teil 4 – Sprachenlernen/Sprachkompetenz

34. **Wie schätzen Sie Ihre Englischkenntnisse ein?**
    (Schulnotensystem 1 = Sehr gut, 5 = Nicht genügend)

	1	2	3	4	5
Grammatik	☐	☐	☐	☐	☐
Vokabular/Ausdruck	☐	☐	☐	☐	☐
Aussprache	☐	☐	☐	☐	☐
Flüssiges Sprechen	☐	☐	☐	☐	☐

35. **Wie schätzen Sie Ihre Deutschkenntnisse ein?**
    (Schulnotensystem 1 = Sehr gut, 5 = Nicht genügend)

	1	2	3	4	5
Grammatik	☐	☐	☐	☐	☐
Vokabular/Ausdruck	☐	☐	☐	☐	☐
Aussprache	☐	☐	☐	☐	☐
Flüssiges Sprechen	☐	☐	☐	☐	☐

36. **Was würden Sie gerne an Ihrem Englisch verbessen?**
    (Bitte ankreuzen. Mehrfachantworten möglich).

    ☐ Grammatik

    ☐ Vokabular/Ausdruck

    ☐ Aussprache

    ☐ Flüssiges Sprechen

    ☐ Eigentlich gar nichts

    ☐ Sonstiges: _____

37. **Was ist für Sie an einer Fremdsprache das Wichtigste?**

	sehr wichtig	eher wichtig	weder/noch	eher nicht wichtig	nicht wichtig
Grammatik	☐	☐	☐	☐	☐
Vokabular/Ausdruck	☐	☐	☐	☐	☐
Aussprache	☐	☐	☐	☐	☐
Flüssiges Sprechen	☐	☐	☐	☐	☐

38. Wenn Sie Englisch sprechen, ist Ihr Akzent Ihrer Einschätzung nach eher
   - ☐ britisch
   - ☐ amerikanisch
   - ☐ österreichisch
   - ☐ sonstige: _____
   - ☐ weiß ich nicht

Teil 5 – Ihre Meinung/Erfahrungen zum Thema Sprachen/Sprachenlernen

Inwieweit stimmen Sie folgenden Aussagen zu?

.... = *stimme völlig zu* 7 = *stimme überhaupt nicht zu*

	1	2	3	4	5	6	7
39. Ich würde gerne mehrere Fremdsprachen fließend sprechen	☐	☐	☐	☐	☐	☐	☐
40. Ich würde gerne so klingen wie ein Native Speaker.	☐	☐	☐	☐	☐	☐	☐
41. Ich mag die englische Sprache	☐	☐	☐	☐	☐	☐	☐
42. Ich lerne sehr gerne Fremdsprachen	☐	☐	☐	☐	☐	☐	☐
43. Wenn ich englische Musik höre, versuche ich den Text zu verstehen.	☐	☐	☐	☐	☐	☐	☐
44. Ich finde, die englische Sprache klingt gut.	☐	☐	☐	☐	☐	☐	☐
45. Ich möchte gerne alles, was mit der englischen Sprache und Kultur zu tun hat kennenlernen.	☐	☐	☐	☐	☐	☐	☐
46. Ehrlich gesagt ist der Englischunterricht für mich Zeitverschwendung.	☐	☐	☐	☐	☐	☐	☐
47. Ich werde nervös, wenn mich ein Tourist auf Englisch anspricht.	☐	☐	☐	☐	☐	☐	☐
48. Ich fühle mich unsicher, wenn ich in der Klasse Englisch sprechen muss.	☐	☐	☐	☐	☐	☐	☐

		1	2	3	4	5	6	7
49.	Gut Englisch zu sprechen ist ein wichtiges Ziel in meinem Leben.	☐	☐	☐	☐	☐	☐	☐
50.	Ich spreche sehr gerne Englisch.	☐	☐	☐	☐	☐	☐	☐
51.	Ich hätte gerne mehr Englisch/ mehr englischsprachige Lehrveranstaltungen auf der FH.	☐	☐	☐	☐	☐	☐	☐
52.	Meine Eltern glauben, dass es wichtig für mich ist Englisch zu lernen.	☐	☐	☐	☐	☐	☐	☐
53.	Ich bin sehr ehrgeizig.	☐	☐	☐	☐	☐	☐	☐

..............................1 = stimme **völlig** zu 7 = stimme **überhaupt nicht** zu

		1	2	3	4	5	6	7
54.	Ich habe kein Problem damit im Unterricht Englisch zu sprechen.	☐	☐	☐	☐	☐	☐	☐
55.	Mich interessieren Fremdsprachen einfach nicht.	☐	☐	☐	☐	☐	☐	☐
56.	Ich versuche jeden Tag mein Englisch zu verbessern.	☐	☐	☐	☐	☐	☐	☐
57.	Ich würde gerne ein Austauschsemester in einem anderen Land machen.	☐	☐	☐	☐	☐	☐	☐
58.	Ich hatte bisher sehr kompetente Englischlehrer.	☐	☐	☐	☐	☐	☐	☐
59.	Englisch ist ein wichtiger Teil eines Wirtschaftsstudiums.	☐	☐	☐	☐	☐	☐	☐
60.	Ich habe Angst davor ein Telefonat auf Englisch zu führen.	☐	☐	☐	☐	☐	☐	☐
61.	Es beunruhigt mich, dass andere Studierende meiner Klasse besser Englisch können als ich.	☐	☐	☐	☐	☐	☐	☐
62.	Meine bisherigen Englischlehrer haben Aussprachefehler ausgebessert.	☐	☐	☐	☐	☐	☐	☐
63.	Wenn jemand einen starken fremdsprachlichen Akzent hat, dann glaubt man automatisch, dass er schlecht Englisch spricht, auch wenn er kaum Grammatikfehler macht.	☐	☐	☐	☐	☐	☐	☐

64.	Um seine Aussprache zu verbessern, muss man in einem englischsprachigen Land leben.	☐	☐	☐	☐	☐	☐	☐
65.	Ich würde gerne mein Praktikum im Ausland machen.	☐	☐	☐	☐	☐	☐	☐
66.	Ich freue mich schon auf die nächste Englischstunde/englischsprachige Lehrveranstaltung.	☐	☐	☐	☐	☐	☐	☐
67.	Ich würde gerne meine englische Aussprache verbessern.	☐	☐	☐	☐	☐	☐	☐
68.	Sehr gute Englischkenntnisse sind wichtig für meine berufliche Zukunft.	☐	☐	☐	☐	☐	☐	☐
69.	Ich habe nie einen Zugang zu Englisch gefunden, weil ich Probleme mit meinem/meinen Englischlehrer/n hatte.	☐	☐	☐	☐	☐	☐	☐
70.	Eine gute Aussprache in einer Fremdsprache ist grundsätzlich wichtiger als grammatikalische Korrektheit.	☐	☐	☐	☐	☐	☐	☐
71.	Gutes Englisch gehört zur Allgemeinbildung.	☐	☐	☐	☐	☐	☐	☐

.............................1 = stimme **völlig** zu 7 = stimme **überhaupt nicht** zu

		1	2	3	4	5	6	7
72.	Es macht mir nichts aus, wenn man sofort hört, dass ich kein Native Speaker bin.	☐	☐	☐	☐	☐	☐	☐
73.	Ich hoffe, dass ich nach dem Studium einen Job bekomme, in dem ich möglichst viel Englisch sprechen kann.	☐	☐	☐	☐	☐	☐	☐
74.	Ich unterhalte mich gerne mit anderen Menschen.	☐	☐	☐	☐	☐	☐	☐
75.	Ich habe vor, nach meinem Studium eine gewisse Zeit in einem anderen Land zu leben und zu arbeiten.	☐	☐	☐	☐	☐	☐	☐

Vielen Dank für Ihre Mitarbeit!

Questionnaire 2

Liebe Studierende! ....Wien, im März 2014

Dieser Fragebogen ist der 2. **Teil** eines wissenschaftlichen Projekts des Studiengangs Unternehmensführung zum Thema **Sprachbegabung** und **Entwicklung der englischen Sprachkompetenz** im Laufe des 3jährigen Studiums.

Ich ersuche Sie nun, auch diesen Teil **nach bestem Wissen und Gewissen** auszufüllen. Ich kann Ihnen versichern, dass Ihre Angaben **anonymisiert** und nur für **wissenschaftliche Zwecke** verarbeitet werden.

Für Fragen stehe ich Ihnen selbstverständlich jederzeit gerne zur Verfügung!

Vielen Dank für Ihre Teilnahme! Karin Richter

Um eine leichtere Lesbarkeit zu gewährleisten, wurde auf geschlechtsspezifische Endungen („-Innen") verzichtet. Es sind an allen Textstellen, wo natürliche Personen bzw. Personengruppen erwähnt werden, immer Menschen beiderlei Geschlechts angesprochen.

Einverstanden:

_____....................._____

Ort, Datum   Unterschrift

1. Name: _____

2. Während Ihres Studiums hier an der FH, haben Sie ein **Auslandssemester** gemacht

Ja	Nein
☐	☐

   Wenn nein, bitte weiter zu Frage 3.

   Wenn ja:

   Wo? _____

   Welche **Sprache(n)** haben Sie dort überwiegend gesprochen?

   _____

3. Während Ihres Studiums hier an der FH, haben Sie das **Berufspraktikum im Ausland** gemacht

Ja	Nein
☐	☐

   Wenn nein, bitte weiter zu Frage 4.

   Wenn ja:

   Wo? _____

   Wie lange? _____

   Welche Sprache(n) haben Sie dort überwiegend gesprochen?

   _____

   _____

4. Gab es andere **Auslandsaufenthalte** (länger als 1 Woche) während Ihres Studiums:

Ja	Nein
☐	☐

   Wenn nein, bitte weiter zu Frage 5.

   Wenn ja:

   Wann? Wo? Wie lange? _____

   _____

   _____

Welche Sprache(n) haben Sie dort überwiegend gesprochen:

_____

_____

5. Fällt Ihnen noch etwas ein, das während Ihres Studiums außerhalb des Unterrichts zur Verbesserung Ihrer Englischkenntnisse beigetragen hat?

_____

_____

6. Rückblickend, wie schätzen Sie Ihre **Englischkenntnisse im 1. Semester** (2011) Ihres Studiums ein:

(Schulnotensystem 1 = Sehr gut, 5 = Nicht genügend)

	1	2	3	4	5
Grammatik	☐	☐	☐	☐	☐
Vokabular/Ausdruck	☐	☐	☐	☐	☐
Aussprache	☐	☐	☐	☐	☐
Flüssiges Sprechen	☐	☐	☐	☐	☐

7. Wie schätzen Sie Ihre **Englischkenntnisse jetzt (2014)** am Ende Ihres Studiums ein:

(Schulnotensystem 1 = Sehr gut, 5 = Nicht genügend)

	1	2	3	4	5
Grammatik	☐	☐	☐	☐	☐
Vokabular/Ausdruck	☐	☐	☐	☐	☐
Aussprache	☐	☐	☐	☐	☐
Flüssiges Sprechen	☐	☐	☐	☐	☐

8. Wenn Sie jetzt Englisch sprechen, ist Ihr **Akzent** Ihrer Einschätzung nach eher

☐ britisch

☐ amerikanisch

☐ österreichisch

☐ sonstige: _____

☐ weiß ich nicht

9. Würden Sie sich wieder für das bilinguale Programm entscheiden?

Ja	Nein
☐	☐

Warum?_____
_____
_____

10. Was könnte man am bilingualen Programm verbessern?
_____
_____

Vielen Dank!

References

Abrahamsson, N. and Hyltenstam, K. (2009) Age of L2 acquisition and nativelikeness: Listener perception versus linguistic scrutiny. *Language Learning* 59, 249–306.
Acton, W. (1984) Changing fossilized pronunciation. *TESOL Quarterly* 18 (1), 71–85.
Adjemian, C. (1976) On the nature of interlanguage systems. *Language Learning* 26 (2), 297–320.
Airey, J. (2004) Can you teach it in English? Aspects of the language choice debate in Swedish higher education. In R. Wilkinson (ed.) *Integrating Content and Language: Meeting the Challenge of a Multilingual Higher Education* (pp. 97–108). Maastricht: Maastricht University Press.
Al-Issa, A. (2003) Sociocultural transfer in L2 speech behaviours: Evidence and motivating factors. *International Journal of Intercultural Relations* 27, 581–601.
Altenberg, E.P. (2005) The perception of word boundaries in a second language. *Second Language Research* 21, 325–358.
Ament, J.R. and Pérez-Vidal, C. (2015) Linguistic outcomes of English medium instruction programmes in higher education: A study on economics undergraduates at a Catalan university. *Higher Learning Research Communications* 5 (1), 47–67.
Ammon, U. (1997) Nationale Varietäten des Deutschen. Studienbibliographien. *Sprachwissenschaft* 19. Heidelberg: Julius Groos.
Ammon, U. and McConnell, G. (2002) *English as an Academic Language in Europe: A Survey of Its Use in Teaching*. Frankfurt am Main/Berlin/Bern: Peter Lang.
Anderson-Hsieh, J. and Koehler, K. (1988) The effect of foreign accent and speaking rate on native speaker comprehension. *Language Learning* 38 (4), 561–613.
Ard, J. (1990) A constructivist perspective on non-native phonology. In S. Gass and J. Schachter (eds) *Linguistic Perspectives on Second Language Acquisition* (2nd edn; pp. 243–260). New York: Cambridge University Press.
Asher, J. and Price, B. (1967) The learning strategy of total physical response: Some age differences. *Child Development* 38, 1219–1227.
Asher, J. and Garcia, R. (1969) The optimal age to learn a foreign accent. *The Modern Language Journal* 53, 3–17.
Avello, P., Mora, J.C. and Perez-Vidal, C. (2012) Perception of FA by non-native listeners in a study abroad context. *Research in Language* 1 (1), 63–77.
Badran, A.H. (2001) Extraversion/Introversion and Gender in Relation to the English Pronunciation Accuracy of Arabic Speaking College Students. See https://eric.ed.gov/?id=ED454740 (accessed 22 February 2016).
Baker, S.C. and MacIntyre, P. (2000) The role of gender and immersion in communication and second language orientations. *Language Learning* 50 (2), 311–341.
Ball, P. and Lindsay, D. (2013) Language demands and support for English-medium instruction in tertiary education. Learning from a specific context. In A. Doiz, D. Lasagabaster and J.M. Sierra (eds) *English-Medium Instruction at Universities: Global Challenges* (pp. 3–24). Bristol: Multilingual Matters.

Bamkin, S. (2010) How not to x a problem: Misapplications of pronunciation theory. Gateway Papers. *A Journal for Pedagogic Research in Higher Education* 1, 163–174.

Bassetti, B. and Atkinson, N. (2015) Effects of orthographic forms on pronunciation in experienced instructed second language learners. *Applied Psycholinguistics* 36 (1), 67–91.

Beebe, L. (1984) Myths about interlanguage phonology. In S. Eliasson (ed.) *Studies in Descriptive Linguistics: Theoretical Issues in Contrastive Phonology* (pp. 51–62). Heidelberg: Julius Groos Verlag.

Bent, T. and Bradlow, A.R. (2003) The interlanguage speech intelligibility benefit. *Journal of the Acoustical Society of America* 114, 1600–1610.

Bernaus, M., Masgoret, A., Gardner, R. and Reyes, E. (2004) Motivation and attitudes towards learning language in multicultural classrooms. *International Journal of Multilingualism* 1 (2), 75–89.

Best, C. (1994) The emergence of native-language phonological influences in infants: A perceptual assimilation model. In C. Goodman and H. Nusbaum (eds) *The Development of Speech Perception* (pp. 167–224). Cambridge, MA: MIT Press.

Best, C. (1995) *Speech Perception and Linguistic Experience: Theoretical and Methodological Issues*. Timonium, MD: York Press.

Best, C. and Strange, W. (1992) Effects of phonological and phonetic factors on cross-language perception of approximants. *Journal of Phonetics* 20, 305–330.

Best, C.T., McRoberts, G.W. and Sithole, N.M. (1988) Examination of perceptual reorganization for nonnative speech contrasts: Zulu click discrimination by English-speaking adults and infants. *Journal of Experimental Psychology: Human Perception and Performance* 14, 45–60.

Best, C.T., McRoberts, G. and Goodell, E. (2001) American listeners' perception of nonnative consonant contrasts varying in perceptual assimilation to English phonology. *Journal of the Acoustical Society of America* 1097, 775–794.

Biersack, S. (2002) Systematische Aussprachefehler deutscher Muttersprachler im Englischen. Eine phonetisch-phonologische Bestandsaufnahme. In *Forschungsberichte des Instituts für Phonetik und Sprachliche Kommunikation der Universität München (FIPKM)* 39, 37–130. See http://www.phonetik.uni-muenchen.de/forschung/FIPKM/vol39/f39_biersack.pdf (accessed 27 February 2016).

Birdsong, D. (2005) Interpreting age effects in second language acquisition. In J.F. Kroll and A.M.B. DeGroot (eds) *Handbook of Bilingualism: Psycholinguistic Approaches* (pp. 109–127). New York: Oxford University Press.

Blankenship, B. (1991) Second language vowel perception. *Journal of the Acoustical Society of America* 90, 22–52.

Bleyhl, W. (2009) The hidden paradox of foreign language instruction. Or: Which are the real foreign language learning processes? In T. Piske and M. Young-Scholten (eds) *Input Matters in SLA* (pp. 137–155). Bristol: Multilingual Matters.

Bohn, O.S. and Flege, J.E. (1990) Interlingual identification and the role of foreign language experience in L2 vowel perception. *Applied Psycholinguistics* 11, 303–328.

Bohn, O.S. and Flege, J.E. (1992) The production of new and similar vowels by adult German learners of English. *Studies in Second Language Acquisition* 14, 131–158.

Bohn, O.S. and Flege, J.E. (1997) Perception and production of a new vowel category by adult second language learners. In J. Leather and A. James (eds) *Second Language Speech: Structure and Process* (pp. 51–71). Berlin: de Gruyter.

Bolton, K. and Kuteeva, M. (2012) English as an academic language at a Swedish University: Parallel language use and the 'threat' of English. *Journal of Multilingual and Multicultural Development* 33 (5), 429–447.

Bongaerts, T. (1999) Ultimate attainment in L2 pronunciation: The case of very advanced late L2 learners. In D. Birdsong (ed.) *Second Language Acquisition and the Critical Period Hypothesis* (pp. 133–159). Mahwah, NJ: Lawrence Erlbaum Associates.

Bongaerts, T., Planken, B. and Schils, E. (1995) Can late learners attain a native accent in a foreign language? A test of the critical period hypothesis. In D. Singleton and Z. Lengyel (eds) *The Age Factor in Second Language Acquisition* (pp. 30–50). Clevedon: Multilingual Matters.

Bongaerts, T., van Summeren, C., Planken, B. and Schils, E. (1997) Age and ultimate attainment in the pronunciation of a foreign language. *Studies in Second Language Acquisition* 19, 447–465.

Bongaerts, T., Mennen, S. and van der Slik, S. (2000) Authenticity of pronunciation in naturalistic second language acquisition: The case of very advanced late learners of Dutch as a second language. *Studia Linguistica* 54, 298–308.

Bonnet, A. (2012) Towards an evidence base for CLIL: How to integrate qualitative and quantitative as well as process, product and participant perspectives in CLIL research. *International CLIL Research Journal* 1 (4), 65–78.

Brantmeier, C., Schueller, J., Wilde, J. and Kinginger, C. (2007) Gender equity in foreign and second language learning. In S. Klein (ed.) *Handbook for Achieving Gender Equity through Education* (pp. 305–334). Mahwah, NJ: Lawrence Erlbaum Associates.

Brekelmans, G. (2015) L2 English pronunciation stability. The effect of a discontinuation of pronunciation coaching. MA thesis, Radboud University Nijmegen.

Brière, E. (1966) An investigation of phonological interference. *Language* 42 (4), 768–796.

Broeders, A. (1982) English in Dutch ears. Pronunciation preference in Dutch students of English. *Toegepaste Taalkunde in Artikelen* 9, 127–128.

Broselow, E. (1984) An investigation of transfer in second language phonology. *International Review of Applied Linguistics* 22, 253–269.

Broselow, E. (1988) Prosodic phonology and the acquisition of a second language. In S. Flynn and W. O'Neil (eds) *Linguistic Theory in Second Language Acquisition* (pp. 295–308). Dordrecht: Kluwer Press.

Brown, A. (ed.) (1992) *Approaches to Pronunciation Teaching*. London: Macmillan.

Brown, C. (2000) The interrelation between speech perception and phonological acquisition from infant to adult. In J. Archibald (ed.) *Second Language Acquisition and Linguistic Theory* (pp. 4–63). Malden, MA/Oxford: Blackwell.

Brumfit, C.J. (2004) Language and higher education: Two current challenges. *Arts and Humanities in Higher Education* 3 (2), 163–173.

Bruner, J.S. (1978) The role of dialogue in language acquisition. In A. Sinclair, R.J. Jarvelle and W.J.M. Levelt (eds) *The Child's Concept of Language* (pp. 241–256). New York: Springer.

Byrd, D. (1992) Preliminary results on speaker-dependent variation in the TIMIT database. *Journal of the Acoustical Society of America* 92 (1), 593–596.

Calloway, D.R. (1980) Accent and the evaluation of ESL oral proficiency. In J. Oller and K. Perkins (eds) *Research in Language Testing* (pp. 102–115). Rowley, MA: Newbury House.

Campbell, C. and Ortiz, J. (1991) Helping students overcome foreign anxiety: A foreign language anxiety workshop. In E. Horwitz and D. Young (eds) *Language Anxiety: From Theory and Research to Classroom Implications* (pp. 153–168). Englewood Cliffs, NJ: Prentice Hall.

Carey, M.D., Mannell, R. and Dunn, P. (2011) Does a rater's familiarity with a candidate's pronunciation affect the rating in oral proficiency interviews? *Language Testing* 28 (2), 201–219.

Carver, R. and Gradwohl Nash, J. (2012) *Doing Data Analysis with SPSS Version 18*. Boston, MA: Cengage Learning.

Cenoz, J., and García Lecumberri, M. (1999) The effect of training on the discrimination of English vowels. *International Review of Applied Linguistics* 37 (4), 261–275.

Cheng, J. (2005) The relationship to foreign language anxiety of oral performance achievement, teacher characteristics and in-class activities. MA thesis, Ming Chuan University, Taiwan.

Coleman, J.A. (2006) English-medium teaching in European Higher Education. *Language Teaching* 39 (1), 1–14.
Collentine, J. (2004) The effects of learning contexts on morphosyntactic and lexical development. *Studies in Second Language Acquisition* 26 (2), 227–248.
Collins, B. and Mees, I. (2013) *Practical Phonetics and Phonology. A Resource Book for Students*. New York: Routledge.
Corder, S.P. (1971) Idiosyncratic dialects and error analysis. *IRAL* 9 (2), 147–160.
Corder, S.P. (1978) Language-learner language. In J.C. Richards (ed.) *Understanding Second and Foreign Language Learning* (pp. 71–92). Rowley, MA: Newbury House.
Couper, G. (2003) The value of an explicit pronunciation syllabus in ESOL teaching. *Prospect* 18 (3), 53–70.
Couper, G. (2006) The short and long-term effects of pronunciation instruction. *Prospect* 21 (1), 46–66.
Coyle, D., Hood, P. and Marsh, D. (2010) *CLIL: Content and Language Integrated Learning*. New York: Cambridge University Press.
Crandall, J. (1992) Content-centered learning in the United States. *Annual Review of Applied Linguistics* 13, 111–127.
Cruttenden, A. (1994) Rises in English. In J. Windsor-Lewis (ed.) *Studies in General and English Phonetics: Essays in Honour of Professor J.D. O'Connor* (pp. 155–173). London: Routledge.
Cucchiarini, C., Strik, H., Binnenpoorte, D. and Boves, L. (2002) Pronunciation evaluation in read and spontaneous speech: A comparison between human ratings and automatic scores. In *Proceedings of the Fourth International Symposium on the Acquisition of Second-Language Speech* (New Sounds 2000) (pp. 72–99). Klagenfurt: University of Klagenfurt.
Cutler, A. and Butterfield, S. (1992) Rhythmic cues to speech segmentation: Evidence from juncture misperception. *Journal of Memory and Language* 31, 218–236.
Dafouz, E. and Sánchez, D. (2013) Does everybody understand? Teacher questions across disciplines in English-mediated university lectures: An exploratory study. *Language Value* 5 (1), 129–151.
Dafouz, E., Camacho, M. and Urquía, E. (2014) 'Surely they can't do as well': A comparison of business students' academic performance in English-medium and Spanish-as-first-language-medium programmes. *Language and Education* 28 (3), 223–236.
Dalton-Puffer, C. (2007) *Discourse in Content and Language Integrated Learning (CLIL) Classrooms*. Amsterdam: John Benjamins.
Dalton-Puffer, C. (2008) Outcomes and processes in Content and Language Integrated Learning (CLIL): Current research from Europe. In W. Delanoy and S. Volkmann (eds) *Future Perspectives for English Language Teaching* (pp. 139–157). Heidelberg: Carl Winter.
Dalton-Puffer, C. (2011) Content and Language Integrated Learning: From practice to principle? *Annual Review of Applied Linguistics* 2011 (31), 182–204.
Dalton-Puffer, C. and Nikula, T. (2006) Pragmatics of content-based instruction: teacher and student directives in Finnish and Austrian classrooms. *Applied Linguistics* 27, 241–267.
Dalton-Puffer, C. and Smit, U. (2007) Introduction. In C. Dalton-Puffer and U. Smit (eds) *Empirical Perspectives on CLIL Classroom Discourse* (pp. 7–23). Frankfurt am Main/Wien: Peter Lang.
Dalton-Puffer, C., Kaltenboeck, G. and Smit, U. (1997) Learner attitudes and L2 pronunciation in Austria. *World Englishes* 16 (1), 115–128.
Day, R.R., Omura, C. and Hiramatsu, M. (1991) Incidental EFL vocabulary learning and reading. *Reading in a Foreign Language* 7, 541–551.
de Bot, K. (1983) Visual feedback of intonation 1: Effectiveness and induced practice behaviour. *Language and Speech* 26, 331–350.
de Bot, K. and Mailfert, K. (1982) The teaching of intonation: Fundamental research and classroom applications. *TESOL Quarterly* 16, 71–77.

de Bot, K., Lowie, W. and Verspoor, M. (2007) A dynamic systems theory approach to second language acquisition. Bilingualism: *Language and Cognition* 10 (1), 7–21.
De Cillia R. and Schweiger, T. (2001) English as a language of instruction at Austrian universities. In U. Ammon (ed.) *The Dominance of English as a Language of Science. Effects on Other Languages and Language Communities* (pp. 363–387). Berlin/New York: Mouton de Gruyter.
Dearden, J. (2014) English as a Medium of Instruction – A Growing Global Phenomenon: Phase 1 (Interim report. British Council/University of Oxford). See http://www.britishcouncil.org/sites/britishcouncil.uk2/files/english_as_a_medium_of_instruction.pdf (accessed 14 March 2016).
Deci, E.L. and Ryan, R. (1985) *Intrinsic Motivation and Self-Determination in Human Behavior.* New York: Plenum.
DeKeyser, R.M. (2000) The robustness of critical period effects in second language acquisition. *Studies in Second Language Acquisition* 22 (4), 493–533.
Derwing, T.M. and Rossiter, M.J. (2002) ESL learners' perceptions of their pronunciation needs and strategies. *System* 30, 155–166.
Derwing, T.M. and Munro, M. (2005) Second language accent and pronunciation teaching: A research-based approach. *TESOL Quarterly* 39, 379–397.
Derwing, T.M., Munro, M. and Wiebe, G. (1997) Pronunciation instruction for fossilized learners: Can it help? *Applied Language Learning* 8 (2), 217–235.
DesBrisay, M. (1984) Who knows best? A comparison of two placement procedures. *Institut des Langues Vivantes Journal* 29, 162–165.
Díaz-Campos, M. (2004) Context of learning in the acquisition of Spanish second language phonology. *Studies in Second Language Acquisition* 26 (2), 249–273.
Díaz-Campos, M. (2006) The effect of style in second language phonology: An analysis of segmental acquisition in study abroad and regular-classroom students. In C.A. Klee and T.L. Face (eds) *Selected Proceedings of the 7th Conference on the Acquisition of Spanish and Portuguese as First and Second Languages* (pp. 26–39). Somerville, MA: Cascadilla Press.
Dimova, S. and Kling, J. (2015) Lecturers' English proficiency and university language polices for quality assurance. In R. Wilkinson and M. Walsh (eds) *Integrating Content and Language in Higher Education: From Theory to Practice Selected Papers from the 2013 ICLHE Conference* (pp. 50–65). Frankfurt: Peter Lang.
Dogil, G. and Reiterer, S.M. (eds) (2009) *Language Talent and Brain Activity. Trends in Applied Linguistics 1.* Berlin/New York: Mouton de Gruyter.
Dorfberger, S., Adi-Japha, E. and Karni, A. (2009) Sex differences in motor performance and motor learning in children and adolescents: An increasing male advantage in motor learning and consolidation phase gains. *Behavioural Brain Research* 198, 165–171.
Dörnyei, Z. (1990) Conceptualizing motivation in foreign language learning. *Language Learning* 4 (1), 45–78.
Dörnyei, Z. (1994) Understanding L2 motivation: on with the challenge. *Modern Language Journal* 78 (4), 515–523.
Dörnyei, Z. (2001) New themes and approaches in L2 motivation research. *Annual Review of Applied Linguistics* 21, 43–59.
Dörnyei, Z. (2005) *The Psychology of the Language Learner: Individual Differences in Second Language Acquisition.* Mahwah, NJ: Lawrence Erlbaum.
Dörnyei, Z. (2006) Creating a motivating classroom environment. In J. Cummins and C. Davison (eds) *The Handbook of English Language Teaching* (pp. 719–731). New York: Springer.
Dunn, W. and Lantolf, J. (1998) Vygotsky's zone of proximal development and Krashen's i+1: Incommensurable constructs; incommensurable theories. *Language Learning* 48, 411–442.
Ebner, J. (1998) *Wie sagt man in Österreich? Wörterbuch des österreichischen Deutsch.* Mannheim/Wien/Zürich: Bibliographisches Institut.

Eckman, F.R. (1977) Markedness and the contrastive analysis hypothesis. *Language Learning* 27, 315–330.
Eckman, F.R. (1987) Markedness and the contrastive analysis hypothesis. In G. Ioup and S.H. Weinberger (eds) *Interlanguage Phonology: The Acquisition of a Second Language Sound System* (pp. 55–69). Cambridge, MA: Newbury House.
Egron-Polak, E. and Hudson, R. (2010) *Internationalization of Higher Education: Global Trends, Regional Perspectives: IAU 3rd Global Survey Report*. Paris: International Association of Universities.
Ehrlich, K. (2009) Die Aussprache des österreichischen Standarddeutsch. PhD thesis, University of Vienna.
Ekstrand, L. (1976) Age and length of residence as variables related to the adjustment of migrant children, with special reference to second language learning. In G. Nickel (ed.) *Proceedings of the Fourth International Congress of Applied Linguistics* (Vol. 3; pp. 179–197). Stuttgart: Hochschulverlag.
Elkhafaifi, H. (2005) Listening comprehension and anxiety in the Arabic language classroom. *The Modern Language Journal* 89 (2), 206–220.
Elliot, A.R. (1995) Foreign language phonology: Field independence, attitude, and the success of formal instruction in Spanish pronunciation. *The Modern Language Journal* 79 (4), 530–542.
Ellis, G. (1996) How culturally appropriate is the communicative approach? *ELT Journal* 50 (3), 213–218.
Ellis, N. (ed.) (1994) *Implicit and Explicit Learning of Languages*. San Diego, CA: Academic Press.
Ellis, R. (1990) *Instructed Second Language Acquisition*. Oxford: Blackwell Publishers Ltd.
Ellis, R. (1994) *The Study of Second Language Acquisition*. New York: Oxford University Press.
Ellis, R. (1997) *Second Language Acquisition*. Oxford: Oxford University Press.
Ellis, R. (2004) The definition and measurement of explicit knowledge. *Language Learning* 54, 227-275.
Ellis, R., Tanaka, Y. and Yamazaki, A. (1994) Classroom interaction, comprehension, and the acquisition of L2 word meanings. *Language Learning* 44, 449–491.
Elyan, O. (1978) Sex differences in speech style. *Women Speaking* 4, 4–8.
Ericsdotter, C. and Ericsson, A. (2001) Gender differences in vowel duration in read Swedish: Preliminary results. In *Proceedings of Fonetik 2001, XIVth Swedish Phonetics Conference. Working Papers of the Department of Linguistics* (pp. 34–37). Lund: Lund University.
Eurodyce Report (2015) See https://webgate.ec.europa.eu/fpfis/mwikis/eurydice/index.php/Austria:Secondary_and_Post-Secondary_Non-Tertiary_Education (accessed 14 March 2016).
European Ministers of Education (1999) The Bologna declaration of 19 June 1999: Joint declaration of the European ministers of education. See https://www.eurashe.eu/library/modernising-phe/Bologna_1999_Bologna-Declaration.pdf (accessed 14 March 2016).
Eveyik, E. (1999) Development of an attitude scale to investigate Turkish EFL teachers' attitudes. Boğaziçi Üniversitesi Sosyal Bilimler Enstitüsü. Basılmamış Yüksek Lisans Tezi. İstanbul. See http://dergiler.ankara.edu.tr (accessed 22 June 2016).
Fathman, A. (1975) The relationship between age and second language productive ability. *Language Learning* 25, 245–253.
Feigenbaum, E.J. (2007) The role of language anxiety in teacher-fronted and small-group interaction in Spanish as a foreign language: How is pronunciation accuracy affected? MA thesis, University of Pittsburgh.
Figl, B. (2013) Lehrerausbildung neu. Alle Lehrer werden Akademiker. Wiener Zeitung. See http://www.wienerzeitung.at/themen_channel/bildung/schule/536654_Alle-Lehrer-werden-Akademiker.html (accessed 14 March 2016.

Fiske, S.T. and Taylor, S.E. (1991) *Social Cognition* (2nd edn). New York: McGraw-Hill.
Flege, J.E. (1987) A critical period for learning to pronounce foreign languages? *Applied Linguistics* 8, 162–177.
Flege, J.E. (1988a) Factors affecting degree of perceived foreign accent in English sentences. *Journal of the Acoustical Society of America* 84, 70–79.
Flege, J.E. (1988b) The production and perception of foreign language speech sounds. In H. Winitz (ed.) *Human Communication and Its Disorders. A Review* (pp. 224–401). Norwood, NJ: Ablex.
Flege, J.E. (1992a) The intelligibility of English vowels spoken by British and Dutch talkers. In R. Kent (ed.) *Intelligibility in Speech Disorders: Theory, Measurement and Management* (pp. 157–232). Amsterdam: John Benjamins.
Flege, J.E. (1992b) Speech learning in second language. In C. Ferguson; I. Menn and C. Stoel-Gammon (eds) *Phonological Development: Models, Research, Implications* (pp. 565–604). Timonium, MD: York Press.
Flege, J.E. (1995) Second language speech learning. Theory, findings, and problems. In W. Strange (ed.) *Speech Perception and Linguistic Experience* (pp. 233–277). Timonium. MD: York Press.
Flege, J.E. and Hillenbrand, J. (1987) Differential use of closure voicing and release burst as cue to stop voicing by native speakers of French and English. *Journal of Phonetics* 15, 203–208.
Flege, J.E. and Fletcher, K.L. (1992) Talker and listener effects on degree of perceived foreign accent. *Journal of the Acoustical Society of America* 91, 370–389.
Flege, J.E. and Liu, S. (2001) The effect of experience on adults' acquisition of a second language. *Studies in Second Language Acquisition* 23, 527–552.
Flege, J.E., Munro, M. and MacKay, I. (1995) Factors affecting strength of perceived foreign accent in a second language. *Journal of the Acoustical Society of America* 97, 3125–3134.
Flege, J.E., Bohn, O. and Jang, S. (1997a) Effects of experience on non-native speakers' production and perception of English vowels. *Journal of Phonetics* 25, 437–470.
Flege, J., Frieda, E. and Nozawa, T. (1997b) Amount of native-language (L1) use affects the pronunciation of an L2. *Journal of Phonetics* 25, 169–186.
Flege, J.E., MacKay, I. and Meador, D. (1999a) Native Italian speakers' production and perception of English vowels. *Journal of the Acoustical Society of America* 106, 2973–2987.
Flege, J.E., Yeni-Komshian, G. and Liu, H. (1999b) Age constraints on second language acquisition. *Journal of Memory and Language* 41, 78–104.
Flege, J.E., MacKay, I.R.A. and Piske, T. (2002) Assessing bilingual dominance. *Applied Psycholinguistics* 23, 567–598.
Flege, J.E., Birdsong, D., Bialystok, E., Mack, M., Sung, H. and Tsukada, K. (2006) Degree of foreign accent in English sentences produced by Korean children and adults. *Journal of Phonetics* 34, 153–175.
Fortanet-Gomez, I. and Räisänen, C.A. (eds) (2008) *ESP in European Higher Education: Integrating Language and Content*. Amsterdam/Philadelphia, PA: John Benjamins.
Freed, B.F. (1995) What makes us think that students who study abroad become fluent? In B. Freed (ed.) *Second Language Acquisition in a Study Abroad Context* (pp. 123–148). Amsterdam: John Benjamins.
Freed, B.F. (1998) An overview of issues and research in language learning in a study abroad setting. *Frontiers* 4, 31–60.
Freed, B.F., Segalowitz, N. and Dewey, D.P. (2004) Context of learning and second language fluency in French: Comparing regular classroom, study abroad, and intensive domestic immersion programs. *Studies in Second Language Acquisition* 26 (2), 275–301.
Gallardo del Puerto, F. and García-Lecumberri, M.L. (2006) Age effects on single phoneme perception for learners of English as a foreign language. In C. Abello-Contesse, R.

Chacón-Beltrán, M.D. López-Jiménez and M.M. Torreblanca-López (eds) *Age in L2 Acquisition and Teaching* (pp. 15–131). Bern: Peter Lang.
Gallardo del Puerto, F. and Lacabex, E. (2013) The impact of additional CLIL exposure on oral English production. *Journal of English Studies* 11, 113–131.
Gallardo del Puerto, F., Gomez, E., Lacabex, E. and Garcia Lecumberri, M. (2007) The assessment of foreign accent by native and non-native judges. In J. Maidment (ed.) *Phonetics Training and Learning Conference 2007*. London: University College London. See www.phon.ucl.ac.uk/ptlc/proceedings/ptlcpaper_20e.pdf (accessed 13 May 2016).
Gallardo del Puerto, F., Garcia Lecumberri, M. and Gomez Lacabex, E. (2009) Testing the effectiveness of content and language integrated learning in foreign language contexts: Assessment of English pronunciation. In Y. Ruiz de Zarobe and R.M. Jimenez Catalan (eds) *Content and Language Integrated Learning: Evidence from Research in Europe* (pp. 215–234). Bristol: Multilingual Matters.
Gardner, R.C. (1985) *Social Psychology and Language Learning: The Role of Attitudes and Motivation*. London: Edward Arnold.
Gardner, R.C. (1988) Attitudes and motivation. *Annual Review of Applied Linguistics* 9, 135–148.
Gardner, R.C. (1993) Language learning. *Language Learning* 43, 157–194.
Gardner, R.C. and Lambert, W. (1959) Motivational variables in second-language acquisition. *Canadian Journal of Psychology* 13, 266–272.
Gardner, R.C. and Lambert, W. (1972a) Motivational variables in second language acquisition. In R.C. Gardner and W. Lambert (eds) *Attitudes and Motivation in Second Language Learning* (pp. 119–216). Rowley, MA: Newbury House.
Gardner, R.C. and Lambert, W. (1972b) *Attitudes and Motivation in Second Language Learning*. Rowley, MA: Newbury House.
Gardner, R.C. and Smythe, P. (1975) Motivation and second language acquisition. *Canadian Modern Language Review* 31 (3), 218–230.
Gardner, R.C. and MacIntyre, P. (1991) An instrumental motivation in language study: Who says it isn't effective. *Studies in Second Language Acquisition* 13, 57–72.
Gardner, R. and Tremblay, P.F. (1994) On motivation, research agendas, and theoretical frameworks. *The Modern Language Journal* 78 (3), 359–368.
Gass, S. and Varonis, E. (1994) Input, interaction, and second language production. *Studies in Second Language Acquisition* 16, 283–302.
Gass, S. and Selinker, L. (2008) *Second Language Acquisition: An Introductory Course*. New York: Routledge.
Gatbonton, E., Trofimovich, P. and Magid, M. (2005) Learners' ethnic group affiliation and L2 pronunciation accuracy: A sociolinguistic investigation. *TESOL Quarterly* 39 (3), 489–511.
Gibbons, P. (2002) *Scaffolding Language, Scaffolding Learning: Teaching Second Language Learners in the Mainstream Classroom*. Portsmouth, NH: Heinemann.
Gibson, S. (2008) Reading aloud: A useful learning tool? *ELT Journal* 62/1, 29–36.
Gilakjani, A., Ahmadi, S. and Adhmadi, M. (2011) Why is pronunciation so difficult to learn? *English Language Teaching* 4 (3), 74–81.
Giles, H. (1970) Evaluative reactions to accents. *Educational Review* 22, 211-227.
Gimson, A.C. (1994) *Gimson's Pronunciation of English* (revised by Alan Cruttenden). London: Arnold.
Goffman, E. (1981) *Forms of Talk*. Philadelphia, PA: University of Pennsylvania Press.
Golestani, N. and Pallier, C. (2007) Anatomical correlates of foreign speech sound production. *Cerebral Cortex* 17 (4), 929–934.
Golestani, N. and Zatorre, R. (2009) Individual differences in the acquisition of second language phonology. *Brain and Language* 109, 55–67.
Gottfried, T. (2008) Music and language learning. Effects of musical training on learning L2 speech contrasts. In O. Bohn and M. Munro (eds) *Language Experience in Second Language Speech Learning* (pp. 221–237). Amsterdam: John Benjamins.

Greere, A. and Räsänen, C. (2008) Year One Report: LANQUA Subproject on Content and Language Integrated Learning – Redefining 'CLIL' towards Multilingual Competence. See https://www.unifg.it/sites/default/files/allegatiparagrafo/20-01-2014/lanqua_subproject_on_clil.pdf (accessed 5 June 2015).
Grosser, W. (1993) Aspects of intonation L2 acquisition. In B. Kettemann and W. Wieden (eds) *Current Issues in European Second Language Acquisition Research* (pp. 81–94). Tübingen: Gunter Narr Verlag.
Grosser, W. (1997) On the acquisition of tonal and accentual features of English by Austrian learners. In A. James and J. Leather (eds) *Second Language Speech – Structure and Process* (pp. 211–228). Berlin/New York: Mouton de Gruyter.
Gregg, K. (1984) Krashen's monitor and Occam's razor. *Applied Linguistics* 5, 79–100.
Guiora, A., Beit-Hallami, B., Brannon, R., Dull, C. and Scovel, T. (1972a) The effects of experimentally induced changes in ego states on pronunciation ability in second language: An exploratory study. *Comprehensive Psychiatry* 13, 421–428.
Guiora, A., Brannon, R. and Dull, C.Y. (1972b) Empathy and second language learning. *Language Learning* 22, 111–130.
Gussenhoven, C. (1979) Pronunciation preference among Dutch students. Paper presented at the Second International conference on the Teaching of Spoken English, University of Leeds.
Gussmann, E. (1984) Contrastive analysis. Substantive evidence and the abstractness issue. In S. Eliasson (ed.) *Studies in Descriptive Linguistics: Theoretical Issues in Contrastive Phonology* (pp. 27–36). Heidelberg: Julius Groos Verlag.
Gustafsson, M. and Jacobs, C. (2013) Student learning and ICLHE: Frameworks and contexts. *Journal of Academic Writing* 3 (1), ii–xii.
Han, Z. (2004) To be a native speaker means not to be a non-native speaker. *Second Language Research* 20, 166–187.
Harnsberger, J.D. (2001) The perception of Malayalam nasal consonants by Marathi, Punjabi, Tamil, Oriya, Bengali, and American English listeners: A multidimensional scaling analysis. *Journal of Phonetics* 29, 303–327.
Hasenberger, T. (2012) The role of pronunciation in secondary-school TEFL: Current views and an evaluation of teaching materials. MA thesis, University of Vienna.
Hellekjær, G. (2010) Language matters: Assessing lecture comprehension in English-medium higher education. In C. Dalton-Puffer, T. Nikula and U. Smit (eds) *Language Use and Language Learning in CLIL Classrooms* (pp. 233–258). Amsterdam: John Benjamins.
Hellekjær, G. and Westergaard, M. (2003) An exploratory survey of content learning through English at Nordic universities. In C. Van Leeuwen and R. Wilkinson (eds) *Multilingual Approaches in University Education: Challenges and Practices* (pp. 56–80). Nijmegen: Uitgeverij Valkhof Pers and Talencentrum Universiteit Maastricht.
Henton, C. (1995) Cross-language variation in the vowels of female and male speakers. In K. Elenius and P. Braderud (eds) *Proceedings of the XIIIth International Congress of Phonetic Sciences ICPhS 95* (pp. 420–423). Stockholm: Congress organisers at KTH and Stockholm University.
Hermann, G. (1980) Attitudes and success in children's learning of English as a second language: The motivational vs. resultative hypothesis. *English Language Teaching Journal* 34, 247–254.
Herschensohn, J.R. (2007) *Language Development and Age*. Cambridge: Cambridge University Press.
Hiang, T.C. and Gupta, A.F. (1992) Postvocalic /r/ in Singapore English. *York Papers in Linguistics* 16, 139–152.
Hillenbrand, J.M., Getty, L.A., Clark, M. and Wheeler, K. (1995) Acoustic characteristics of American English vowels. *The Journal of the Acoustical Society of America* 97, 3099–3111.

Hirata, Y. (2005) Effects of speaking rate on the single/geminate stop distinction in Japanese. *Journal of the Acoustical Society of America* 118 (3), 1647–1660.

Holdaway, D. (1979) *The Foundations of Literacy*. Sydney: Ashton Scholastic.

Hopp, H. and Schmid, M. (2013) Perceived foreign accent in first language attrition and second language acquisition: The impact of age of acquisition and bilingualism. *Applied Psycholinguistics* 34, 361–394.

Horgues, C. and Scheuer, S. (2014) 'I understood you, but there was this pronunciation thing...' L2 pronunciation feedback in English/French tandem interactions. Research in language. *The Journal of the University of Lodz* 12 (2), 145–161.

Horwitz, E.K. (2010) Foreign and second language anxiety. *Language Teaching* 43 (2), 154–167.

Horwitz, E.K. and Young, D.J. (eds) (1991) *Language Anxiety: From Theory and Research to Classroom Implications*. Englewood Cliffs, NJ: Prentice Hall.

Horwitz, E.K., Horwitz, M. and Cope, J. (1986) Foreign language classroom anxiety. *The Modern Language Journal* 70 (2), 125–132.

Howard, D.M. and Angus, J. (1998) A comparison between singing pitching strategies of 8 to 11 year olds and trained adult singers. *Logopedics Phoniatrics Vocology* 22, 169–176.

Howard, M. (2005) Second language acquisition in a study abroad context: A comparative investigation of the effects of study abroad and foreign language instruction on the L2 learner's grammatical development. In A. Housen and M. Pierrard (eds) *Investigations in Instructed Second Language Acquisition* (pp. 495–530). Berlin: Mouton deGruyter.

Hrubes, P. (2008) Some problems with the pronunciation of English typical of native speakers of German (a tentative case study). BA thesis, Masaryk University, Brno.

Huang, B.H. (2013) The effects of accent familiarity and language teaching experience on raters' judgments of non-native speech. *System* 41 (3), 770–785.

Humphreys, G. and Spratt, M. (2008) Many languages, many motivations: A study of Hong Kong students' motivation to learn different target languages. *System* 36, 313–335.

Hüttner, J. and Rieder-Bünemann, A. (2010) A cross-sectional analysis of oral narratives by children with CLIL and non-CLIL instruction. In C. Dalton-Puffer, T. Nikula and U. Smit (eds) *Language Use and Language Learning in CLIL Classrooms* (pp. 61–80). Amsterdam: John Benjamins.

Hultgren, A.K. (2017) The drive towards English as a medium of instruction in non-English-dominant European higher education: The role of university rankings. In. E. Macaro (ed.) *English Medium Instruction: Global Views and Countries in Focus: Introduction to the Symposium held at the Department of Education, University of Oxford on Wednesday 4 November 2015. Language Teaching*, 1–18.

Hyltenstam, K. and Abrahamsson, N. (2003) Maturational constraints in SLA. In C. Doughty and M.H. Long (eds) *The Handbook of Second Language Acquisition* (pp. 539–588). Oxford: Blackwell.

Iivonen, A. (1987) Monophthonge des gehobenen Wienerdeutsch. *Folia Linguistica* 21, 293–336.

Ioup, G., Boustagui, E., Tigi, M. and Moselle, M. (1994) Re-examining the critical period hypothesis: A case study in a naturalistic environment. *Studies in Second Language Acquisition* 16, 73–98.

Isabelli, C.A. (2007). Development of the Spanish subjunctive by advanced learners: Study abroad followed by at-home instruction. *Foreign Language Annals* 40 (2), 330–341.

Isabelli, C.A. and Nishida, C. (2005) Development of the Spanish subjunctive in a nine month study-abroad setting. In D. Eddington (ed.) *Selected Proceedings of the 6th Conference on the Acquisition of Spanish and Portuguese as First and Second Languages* (pp. 78–91). Somerville, MA: Cascadilla Press.

Iverson, P. and Kuhl, P. (1996) Influences of phonetic identification and category goodness on American listeners' perception of /r/ and /l/. *Journal of the Acoustical Society of America* 99, 1130–1140.

Iverson, P., Kuhl, P., Reiko, A., Diesch, E., Tohkura, Y., Kettermann, A. and Siebert, C. (2003) A perceptual interference account of acquisition difficulties for non-native phonemes. *Cognition* 87, B47–B57.
Jackson, H. and Stockwell, P. (2011) *An Introduction to the Nature and Functions of Language* (2nd edn). London: Continuum International Publishing.
Jahandar, S., Hodabandehlou, M., Seyedi, G. and Mousavi Dolat Abadi (2012) A gender-based approach to pronunciation accuracy of advanced EFL learners. *International Journal of Scientific and Engineering Research* 3. See http://www.ijser.org (accessed 22 March 2016).
Jakobson, R. (1969) *Kindersprache, Aphasie und allgemeine Lautgesetze.* Frankfurt: Suhrkamp.
Järvinen, H.M. (2008) Learning contextualized language: Implications for tertiary foreign-medium education. In E. Rauto and L. Saarikallio (eds) *Foreign Language Medium Studies in Tertiary Education: Principles and Practices.* Tutkimuksia 1/2008. Vaasa: Vaasa University of Applied Sciences.
Jenkins, J. (2014) *English as a Lingua Franca in the International University: The Politics of Academic English Language Policy.* Abingdon: Routledge.
Jenner, B. (1976) Interlanguage and foreign accent. *Interlanguage Studies Bulletin* 1 (2–3), 166–195.
Jensen, C., Denver, L., Mees, I.M. and Werther, C. (2011) Students' and teachers' self-assessment of English language proficiency in English-medium higher education in Denmark – A questionnaire study. In B. Preisler, I. Klitgård and A. Fabricius (eds) *Language and Learning in the International University: From English Uniformity to Diversity and Hybridity* (pp. 19–38). Bristol: Multilingual Matters.
Jilka, M. (2000) The contribution of intonation to the perception of foreign accent. *Arbeitspapiere des Instituts für Maschinelle Sprachverarbeitung* 6 (3), University of Stuttgart.
Jilka, M. (2009) Assessment of phonetic ability. In G. Dogil and S. Reiterer (eds) *Language Talent and Brain Activity. Trends in Applied Linguistics 1* (pp. 17–48). Berlin/New York: Mouton de Gruyter.
Jilka, M., Anufryk, V., Baumotte, H., Lewandowski, N., Rota, G. and Reiterer, S. (2007) Assessing individual talent in second language production and perception. In A.S. Rauber, M.A. Watkins and B.O. Baptista (eds) *New Sounds 2007: Proceedings of the Fifth International Symposium on the Acquisition of Second Language Speech* (pp. 243–258). Florianópolis: Federal University of Santa Catarina.
Johnson, J. and Newport, E. (1989) Critical period effects in second language learning: The influence of maturational state on the acquisition of English as a second language. *Cognitive Psychology* 21, 60–99.
Johnson, J.S. and Lim, G. (2009) The influence of rater language background on writing performance assessment. *Language Testing* 26 (4), 485–505.
Kennedy, S. and Trofimovich, P. (2008) Intelligibility, comprehensibility, and accentedness of L2 speech: The role of listener experience and semantic context. *Canadian Modern Language Review* 64, 459–490.
Kenworthy, J. (1987) *Teaching English Pronunciation.* Harlow: Longman.
Khamkhien, A. (2010) Factors affecting language learning strategy reported usage by Thai and Vietnamese EFL learners. *Electronic Journal of Foreign Language Teaching* 7 (1), 66–85.
Kinginger, C. (2008) Language learning in study abroad: Case studies of Americans in France. *Modern Language Journal* 92 (Suppl), 1–124.
Kinginger, C. (2009) *Language Learning and Study Abroad: A Critical Reading of Research.* Basingstoke: Palgrave Macmillan.
Kirkpatrick, A. (2006) Which model of English: Native-speaker, nativized or lingua franca? In R. Rubdy and M. Saraceni (eds) *English in the World. Global Rules, Global Roles* (pp. 71–83). London/New York: Continuum.

Kissau, S. (2006) Gender differences in motivation to learn French. *Canadian Modern Language Review* 62 (3), 401–422.

Klaassen, R.G. and Graaff, E. (2001) Facing innovation: Preparing lecturers for English-medium instruction in a non-native context. *European Journal of Engineering Education* 26 (3), 281–289.

Klaassen, R.G., and Bos, M. (2010) English language screening for scientific staff at Delft University of Technology. *Hermes–Journal of Language and Communication Studies* 45, 61–75.

Klein, W. (1995) Language acquisition at different ages. In D. Magnusson (ed.) *The Lifespan Development of Individuals: Behavioral, Neurobiological, and Psychosocial Perspectives. A Synthesis* (pp. 244–274). New York: Cambridge University Press.

Kleinmann, H. (1977) Avoidance behaviour in adult second language acquisition. *Language Learning* 27, 93–107.

Knight, J. (2008) *Higher Education in Turmoil: The Changing World of Internationalization*. Rotterdam: Sense Publishing.

Kohler, K. (1977) *Einführung in die Phonetik des Deutschen*. Berlin: Erich Schmidt.

Kouritzin, S., Piquemal, N. and Renaud, R. (2009) An international comparison of socially constructed language learning motivation and beliefs. *Foreign Language Annals* 42 (2), 287–317.

Krashen, S. (1977) Some issues relating to the Monitor Model. In H. Brown, C. Yorio and R. Crymes (eds) *On TESOL '77* (pp. 144–158). Washington DC: Teachers of English to Speakers of Other Languages.

Krashen, S.D. (1981) *Second Language Acquisition and Second Language Learning*. Oxford: Pergamon Press.

Krashen, S.D. (1982) Accounting for child–adult differences in second language rate and attainment. In S. Krashen, R. Scarcella and M. Long (eds) *Child-Adult-Differences in Second Language Acquisition*. Rowley, MA: Newbury House.

Krashen, S.D. (1985) *The Input Hypothesis*. Harlow: Longman.

Krashen, S.D. (1989) We acquire vocabulary and spelling by reading: Additional evidence for the input hypothesis. *The Modern Language Journal* 73 (4), 440-464.

Krashen, S.D. (1998) Comprehensible output. *System* 26, 175–182.

Kufner, H. (1971) *Kontrastive Phonologie Deutsch Englisch*. Stuttgart: Ernst Klett.

Kuhl, P.K. (1991) Human adults and human infants show a 'perceptual magnet effect' for the prototypes of speech categories, monkeys do not. *Perception and Psychophysics* 50, 93–107.

Kuhl, P.K. and Iverson, P. (1995) Linguistic experience and the 'Perceptual Magnet Effect'. In W. Strange (ed.) *Speech Perception and Linguistic Experience* (pp. 121–154). Timonium, MD: York Press.

Kuhl, P.K., Williams, K., Lacerda, F., Stevens, K. and Lindblom, B. (1992) Language experience alters phonetic perception in infants by 6 months of age. *Science* 255, 606–608.

Kyriacou, C. and Zhu, D. (2008) Shanghai pupils' motivation towards learning English and the perceived influence of important others. *Educational Studies* 34 (2), 97–104.

Ladegaard, H. and Sachdev, I. (2006) I like the Americans… but I certainly don't aim for an American accent: Language attitudes, vitality and foreign language learning in Denmark. *Journal of Multilingual and Multicultural Development* 27 (2), 91–108.

Ladefoged, P. (1999) Illustrations of the IPA: American English. *International Phonetic Association* 42–44.

Lado, R. (1957) *Linguistics across Cultures*. Ann Arbor MI: University of Michigan Press.

Lafford, B.A. (2006) The effects of study abroad vs. classroom contexts on Spanish SLA: Old assumptions, new insights and future research directions. In C.A. Klee and T.L. Face (eds) *Selected Proceedings of the 7th Conference on the Acquisition of Spanish and Portuguese as First and Second Languages* (pp. 26–39). Somerville, MA: Cascadilla Press.

Lafford, B. and Collentine, J. (2006) The effects of study abroad and classroom contexts on the acquisition of Spanish as a second language: From research to application. In B. Lafford and R. Salaberry (eds) *Spanish Second Language Acquisition: From Research Findings to Teaching Applications* (pp. 103–126). Washington, DC: Georgetown University Press.

Lamb, M. (2004) Integrative motivation in a globalizing world. *System* 32, 3–19.

Lantolf, J.P. and Thorne, S.L. (2006) *Sociocultural Theory and the Genesis of Second Language Development*. Oxford: Oxford University Press.

Larsen-Freeman, D. (1997) Chaos/complexity science and second language acquisition. *Applied Linguistics* 18 (2), 141–165.

Larsen-Freeman, D. (1983) Second language acquisition: Setting the whole picture. In K. Bailey, M. Long and S. Peck (eds) *Second Language Acquisition Research* (pp. 3–24). Rowley, MA: Newbury House.

Larsen-Freeman, D. and Long, M. (1991) *An Introduction to Second Language Acquisition Research*. New York: Longman Press.

Lasagabaster, D. (2008) Foreign language competence in content and language integrated courses. *The Open Applied Linguistics Journal* 1 (11), 30–41.

Lasagabaster, D. (2011) English achievement and student motivation in CLIL and EFL settings. *Innovation in Language Learning and Teaching* 5 (1), 3–18.

Lasagabaster, D. and Sierra, J. (2009) Language attitudes in CLIL and traditional EFL classes. *International CLIL Research Journal* 1 (2), 4–17.

LeBlanc, R. and Painchaud, G. (1985) Self-assessment as a second language placement instrument. *TESOL Quarterly* 19 (4), 673–687.

Lee, B., Guion, S. and Harada, T. (2006) Acoustic analysis of the production of unstressed English vowels by early and late Korean and Japanese bilinguals. *Studies in Second Language Acquisition* 28, 476–513.

Lenneberg, E.H. (1967) *Biological Foundations of Language*. New York: John Wiley & Sons.

Levis, J. (2005) Changing contexts and shifting paradigms in pronunciation teaching. *TESOL Quarterly* 39, 369–377.

Levitin, D.J. and Menon, V. (2003) Musical structure is processed in language areas of the brain: A possible role for Brodmann Area 47 in temporal coherence. *Neuro Image* 20, 2142–2152.

Lightbown, P. and Spada, N. (2006) *How Languages Are Learned*. Oxford: Oxford University Press.

Liu, M.L. (2006) Anxiety in Chinese EFL students at different proficiency levels. *System* 34, 301–316.

Liu, M. and Huang, W. (2011) An exploration of foreign language anxiety and English motivation. *Education Research International* 1 (8).

Livingstone, S. (2002) *Young People and New Media*. Thousand Oaks, CA: Sage.

Long, M.H. (1990) Maturational constraints on language development. *Studies in Second Language Acquisition* 12 (3), 251–281.

Long, M.H. (1996) The role of the linguistic environment in second language acquisition. In W.C. Ritchie and T.K. Bhatia (eds) *Handbook of Second Language Acquisition* (pp. 413–468). New York: Academic Press.

Long, M.H. (2003) Stabilization and fossilization. In C. Doughty and M. Long (eds) *The Handbook of Second Language Acquisition* (pp. 487–535). Malden, MA: Blackwell.

Loranc-Paszylk, B. (2006) Evaluation of foreign language achievement based upon a CLIL programme in tertiary education: A Polish perspective. In R. Wilkinson and V. Zegers (eds) *Integrating Content and Language in Higher Education*. Maastricht: Maastricht University Language Centre.

Lord, G. (2006) Defining the indefinable: Study abroad and phonological memory abilities. In C. Klee and T. Face (eds) *Selected Proceedings of the 7th Conference on the Acquisition of Spanish and Portuguese as First and Second Languages* (pp. 40–46). Somerville, MA: Cascadilla Proceedings Project.

Lu, Z. and Liu, M. (2011) Foreign language anxiety and strategy use: A study with Chinese undergraduate EFL learners. *Journal of Language Teaching and Research* 2 (6), 1298–1305.

Ludwig, J. (1982) Native-speaker judgments of second language learners' efforts at communication: A review. *Modern Language Journal* 66, 274–283.

Macaro, E., Curle, S., Pun, J., Jiangshan, A. and Dearden, J. (2018) A systematic review of English medium instruction in higher education. *Language Teaching* 51 (1), 36–76.

MacDonald, D., Yule, G. and Powers, M. (1994) Attempts to improve English L2 pronunciation: The variable effects of different types of instruction. *Language Learning* 44, 75–100.

Mack, M. (1982) Voicing-dependent vowel duration in English and French: Monolingual and bilingual production. *Journal of Acoustical Society of America* 71, 173–178.

Mack, M. (2003) The phonetic systems of bilinguals. In M. Banich and M. Mack (eds) *Mind, Brain, and Language* (pp. 309–349). Mahwah, NJ: Lawrence Erlbaum Associates.

Magen, H.S. (1998) The perception of foreign-accented speech. *Journal of Phonetics* 26 (4), 381–400.

Maier, N. (2010) We are all students: The Bologna Process. *Amsterdam Law Forum* 116–120.

Maillat, D. (2010) The pragmatics of L2 in CLIL. In C. Dalton-Puffer, T. Nikula and U. Smit (eds) *Language Use and Language Learning in CLIL* (pp. 39–60). Amsterdam: John Benjamins.

Mairs, J. (1989) Stress assignment in interlanguage phonology: An analysis of the stress system of Spanish speakers learning English. In S. Gass and J. Schachter (eds) *Linguistic Perspectives on Second Language Acquisition* (pp. 260–283). Cambridge: Cambridge University Press.

Maiworm, F. and Wächter, B. (2002) *English-Language-Taught Degree Programmes in European Higher Education: Trends and Success Factors*. Bonn: Lemmens.

Maiworm, F. and Wächter, B. (2003) *Englischsprachige Studiengänge in Europa: Merkmale, Impulse, Erfolgsfaktoren*. See http://www.stifterverband.info/publikationen_und_podcasts/positionen_dokumentationen /englischsprachige_studiengaenge_in_europa_2003.pdf (accessed 16 August 2016).

Maiz-Arevalo, C. and Dominguez Romero, E. (2013) Students' response to CLIL in tertiary education: The case of business administration and economics at Complutense University. *Revista de Lingüística y Lenguas Aplicadas* 8, 1–12.

Major, R.C. (1987) Measuring pronunciation accuracy using computerized techniques. *Language Testing* 4 (2), 155–169.

Major, R.C. (1998) Interlanguage phonetics and phonology. An introduction. *Studies in Second Language Acquisition* 20 (2), 131–137.

Major, R.C. (2001) *Foreign Accent: The Ontogeny and Phylogeny of Second Language Phonology*. Mahwah, NJ: Lawrence Erlbaum Associates.

Mak, B. (2011) An exploration of speaking-in-class anxiety with Chinese ESL learners. *System* 39, 202–214.

Maljers, A., Marsh, D. and Wolff, D. (eds) (2007) *Windows on CLIL. Content and Language Integrated Learning in the Spotlight*. The Hague: European Platform for Dutch Education.

Marinova-Todd, S., Marshall, D. and Snow, C. (2000) Three misconceptions about age and L2 learning. *TESOL Quarterly* 34 (1), 9–34.

Marques, C., Moreno, S., Castro, S. and Besson, M. (2007) Musicians detect pitch violation in a foreign language better than nonmusicians: Behavioral and electrophysiological evidence. *Journal of Cognitive Neuroscience* 19, 1453–1463.

Marsh, D. (2002) *CLIL/EMILE – The European Dimension. Actions, Trends and Foresight Potential. UniCOM Continuing Education Centre*. Jyväskylä: University of Jyväskylä. See http://ec.europa.eu/education/languages/pdf/doc491_en.pdf (accessed 4 March 2015).

Marsh, D. and Laitinen, J. (2005) *Medium of Instruction in European Higher Education: Summary of Research Outcomes of European Network for Language Learning Amongst Undergraduates (ENLU) Task Group 4*. Jyväskylä: UniCOM University of Jyväskylä.
Martohardjono, G. and Flynn, S. (1995) Is there an age-factor for universal grammar? In D. Singleton and L. Zsolt (eds) *The Age Factor in Second Language Acquisition* (pp. 135–153). Clevedon: Multilingual Matters.
McAllister, R. (2000) Perceptual foreign accent and its relevance for simultaneous interpreting. In K. Hyltenstam and B. Englund-Dimitrova (eds) *Language Processing and Simultaneous Interpreting* (pp. 45–63). Amsterdam: John Benjamins.
McAllister, R. (2001) Experience as a factor in L2 phonological acquisition. *Working Papers* 49, 116–119.
McAllister, R. (2007) Strategies for realization of L2 categories. In O. Bohn and M. Munro (eds) *Language Experience in Second Language Speech Learning. In Honour of James Emil Flege* (pp. 153–166). Amsterdam: John Benjamins.
McAllister, R., Flege, J.E. and Piske, T. (2002) The influence of L1 on the acquisition of Swedish quantity by native speakers of Spanish, English and Estonian. *Journal of Phonetics* 30, 229–258.
McClintock, K. (2014) Acculturation process and its implications for foreign language learners and teachers. *International Journal of Innovative Interdisciplinary Research* (2). See http://auamii.com/jiir/Vol-02/issue-03/1McClintock.pdf (accessed 22 April 2016).
McKenzie, R. (2008) Social factors and non-native attitudes towards varieties of spoken English: A Japanese case study. *International Journal of Applied Linguistics* 18 (1), 63–88.
McLaughlin, B. (1987) *Theories of Second-Language Learning*. London: Arnold.
Meador, D., Flege, J.E. and MacKay, I. (2000) Factors affecting the recognition of words in a second language. *Bilingualism: Language and Cognition* 3, 55–67.
Mehisto, P., Marsh, D. and Frigols, M. (2008) *Uncovering CLIL – Content and Language Integrated Learning in Bilingual and Multilingual Education*. Oxford: Macmillan.
Mende, C. (2009) The pronunciation of Austrian students of English at university level: A descriptive analysis. MA thesis, Universität Graz.
Meng, H., Harrison, A. and Wang, L. (2009) Developing a computer-aided pronunciation system for Chinese-speaking learners of English. *Bulletin of Advanced Technology Research* 3 (2). See http://www1.se.cuhk.edu.hk/~hccl/publications/pub/MengAP-SIPA2010.pdf (accessed 16 April 2015).
Mewald, C. (2007) A comparison of oral language performance of learners in CLIL and mainstream classes at lower secondary level in Lower Austria. In C. Dalton-Puffer and U. Smit (eds) *Empirical Perspectives on CLIL Classroom Discourse* (pp. 139-178). Frankfurt: Peter Lang.
Michaels, E., Handfield-Jones, H. and Axelrod, B. (2001) *The War for Talent*. Boston, MA: Harvard Business School Press.
Milovanov, R., Huotilainen, M., Esquef, P., Alku, P.,Valimaki, V. and Tervaniemi, M. (2009) The role of musical aptitude and language skills in pre-attentive duration processing in school-aged children. *Neuroscience Letters* 460 (2), 161–165.
Mitchell, R. and Myles, F. (1998) *Second Language Learning Theories*. Oxford: Oxford University Press.
Molesworth, M., Nixon, E. and Scullion, R. (2009) Having, being and higher education: The marketisation of the university and the transformation of the student into consumer. *Teaching in Higher Education* 14 (3), 277–287.
Molesworth, M., Scullion, R. and Nixon, E. (eds) (2011) *The Marketisation of Higher Education and the Student as Consumer*. London: Routledge.
Moore, P. (2009) On the emergence of L2 oracy in bilingual education: A comparative analysis of CLIL and mainstream learner talk. PhD thesis, Universidad Pablo de Olavide, Sevilla.

Moosmüller, S. (1991) *Hochsprache und Dialekt in Österreich. Soziophonologische Untersuchungen zu ihrer Abgrenzung in Wien, Graz, Salzburg und Innsbruck.* Wien: Böhlau.
Morell, T. (2007) What enhances EFL students' participation in lecture discourse. *Journal of English for Academic Purposes* 6, 222–237.
Morgan, C. (2003) Musical aptitude and second-language phonetics learning: Implications for teaching methodology. PhD thesis, University of British Columbia.
Moyer, A. (1999) Ultimate attainment in L2 phonology. *Studies in Second Language Acquisition* 21, 81–108.
Moyer, A. (2004) *Age, Accent and Experience in Second Language Acquisition. An Integrated Approach to Critical Period Inquiry.* Clevedon: Multilingual Matters.
Moyer, A. (2007) Do language attitudes determine accent? A study of bilinguals in the USA. *Journal of Multilingual and Multicultural Development* 28 (6), 502–518.
Moyer, A. (2013) *Foreign Accent. The Phenomenon of Non-Native Speech.* New York: Cambridge University Press.
Moyer, A. (2014). Exceptional Outcomes in L2 Phonology: The Critical Factors of Learner Engagement and Self-Regulation. *Applied Linguistics* 35/ 4, 418-440.
Munro, M.J. (1993) Production of English vowels by native speakers of Arabic: Acoustic measurements and accentedness ratings. *Language and Speech* 36, 39–66.
Munro, M.J. (1998) The effects of noise on the intelligibility of foreign-accented speech. *Studies in Second Language Acquisition* 20, 139–154.
Munro, M.J. (2008) Foreign accent and speech intelligibility. In. J. Hansen Edwards and M. Zampini (eds) *Phonology and Second Language Acquisition* (pp. 193–218). Philadelphia, PA: John Benjamins.
Munro, M.J. and Derwing, T.M. (1995) Foreign accent, comprehensibility, and intelligibility in the speech of second language learners. *Language Learning* 45, 73–97.
Munro, M.J. and Derwing, T.M. (2008) Segmental acquisition in adult ESL learners: A longitudinal study of vowel production. *Language Learning* 58, 479–502.
Munro, M.J., Flege, J. and MacKay, I. (1996) The effects of age of second language learning on the production of English vowels. *Applied Psycholinguistics* 17 (3), 13–334.
Munro, M.J., Derwing, T.M. and Morton, S.L. (2006) The mutual intelligibility of L2 speech. *Studies in Second Language Acquisition* 28, 111–131.
Munro, M.J., Derwing, T.M. and Sato, K. (2006) Salient accents, covert attitudes: Consciousness-raising for preservice second language teachers. *Prospect: An Australian Journal of TESOL* 21, 65–77.
Murakawa, H. (1981) Teaching English pronunciation to Japanese adults. PhD thesis, University of Texas, Austin.
Nagao, K., Byung-jin, L. and de Jong, K. (2003) Perceptual Acquisitions of Non-Native Syllable Structures by Native Listeners of Japanese. The 15th International Congress of Phonetic Sciences (ICPhS), Barcelona, Spain.
Nakuma, C. (1998) A new theoretical account of fossilization: Implications for L2 attrition research. *IRAL* 36 (3), 247–256.
Nardo, D. and Reiterer, S. (2009) Musicality and phonetic language aptitude. In G. Dogil and S. Reiterer (eds) *Language Talent and Brain Activity. Trends in Applied Linguistics* (pp. 213–256). Berlin: Mouton De Gruyter.
Nemser, W. (1971) Approximative systems of foreign language learners. *IRAL* 9 (2), 115–124.
Neufeld, G. and Schneiderman, E. (1980) Prosodic and articulatory features in adult language learning. In R.C. Scarcella and S.D. Krashen (eds) *Research in Second Language Acquisition* (pp. 105–109). Rowley, MA: Newbury House.
Newport, E. (1990) Maturational constraints on language learning. *Cognitive Science* 14, 11–28.
Nickel, G. (1998) The role of interlanguage in foreign language teaching. *IRAL* 35 (1), 1–10.

Nikula, T. (2007) Speaking English in Finnish content-based classrooms. *World Englishes* 26, 206–223.
Nikula, T., Llinares, A. and Dalton-Puffer, C. (2013) European research on CLIL classroom discourse. *International Journal of Immersion and Content Based Education* 1 (1), 70–100.
Noels, K.A., Pelletier, L., Clément, R. and Vallerand, R. (2003) Why are you learning a second language? Motivational orientations and self-determination theory. *Language Learning* 50, 57–85.
Nolting, W., Donohue, D., Matherly, C. and Tillman, M. (2013) *Internships, Service Learning, and Volunteering Abroad: Successful Models and Best Practices*. Washington, DC: NAFSA.
Norton, B. and Toohey, K. (eds) (2004) *Critical Pedagogies and Language Learning*. Cambridge: Cambridge University Press.
Norton Peirce, B. (1995) Social identity, investment, and language learning. *TESOL Quarterly* 29 (1), 9–31.
Novoa, L., Fein, D. and Obler, L. (1988) Talent in foreign languages: A case study. In L. Obler and D. Fein (eds) *The Exceptional Brain. Neuropsychology of Talent and Special Abilities* (pp. 294–302). New York: Guildford Press.
ÖAD Österreichischer Akademischer Dienst (2017). Study in Austria – Find your Programme! See http://www.studienwahl.at/Content.Node/homepage.en.php?fl=en (accessed 17 April 2017).
Ohata, K. (2005) Potential sources of anxiety for Japanese learners of English: Preliminary case interviews with five Japanese college students in the US. *TESL-EJ* 9 (3), 1–21.
Olivares-Cuhat, G. (2010) Relative importance of learning variables on L2 performance. *Linguistik Online* 43 (3), 99–116.
Oliver, R. (1998) Negotiation of meaning in child interactions. The relationship between conversational interaction and second language acquisition. *Modern Language Journal* 82, 372–386.
Olson, L.L. and Samuels, S. (1973) The relationship between age and accuracy of foreign language pronunciation. *Journal of Educational Research* 66, 263–268.
Olson, L.L. and Samuels, S. (1982) The relationship between age and accuracy of foreign language pronunciation. In S. Krashen, R. Scarcella and M. Long (eds) *Child–Adult Differences in Second Language Acquisition* (pp. 67–75). Rowley, MA: Newbury House; Oxford: Pergamon Press.
Oxford, R.L. (1998) Anxiety and the language learner: New insights. In J. Arnold (ed.) *Affective Language Learning* (pp. 58–67). Cambridge: Cambridge University Press.
Oxford, R.L. and Shearin, J. (1994) Language learning motivation: Expanding the theoretical framework. *The Modern Language Journal* 78, 12–28.
Oyama, S. (1976) A sensitive period for the acquisition of a non-native phonological system. *Journal of Psycholinguistic Research* 5, 261–283.
Pae, T. (2008) Second language orientation and self-determination theory: A structural analysis of the factors affecting second language achievement. *Journal of Language and Social Psychology* 27, 5–27.
Pastuszek-Lipińska, B. (2004) An overview of a research project and preliminary results of two experiments on perception and production of foreign language sounds by musicians and nonmusicians. *TMH-QPSR* 46 (1), 61–74.
Patel, A. and Daniele, J. (2003) An empirical comparison of rhythm in language and music. *Cognition* 87, 35–45.
Patkowski, M. (1994) The critical age hypothesis and interlanguage phonology. In M. Yavas (ed.) *First and Second Language Phonology* (pp. 205–211). San Diego, CA: Singular Publishing Group.
Penfield, W. and Roberts, L. (1959) *Speech and Brain Mechanisms*. New York: Athenaeum.
Pennington, M. (1994) Recent research in L2 phonology: Implications for practice. In J. Morley (ed.) *Pronunciation Pedagogy and Theory. New Views, New*

Directions (pp. 92–108). Alexandria, VA: Teachers of English to Speakers of Other Languages.
Phillips, E. (1992) The effects of language anxiety on students' oral test performance and attitudes. *The Modern Language Journal* 76 (1), 14–26.
Phillipson, R. (2009) *Linguistic Imperialism Continued*. London: Routledge.
Pica, T. (1994) Research on negotiation: What does it reveal about second-language learning conditions, processes, and outcomes? *Language Learning* 44, 493–527.
Pickard, N. (1996) Out-of-class language learning strategies. *English Teaching Journal* 50, 150–159.
Piller, I. (2002) Passing for a native speaker: Identity and success in second language learning. *Journal of Sociolinguistics* 6, 179–206.
Pincas, A. (1996) Memory in foreign language learning. *Modern English Teacher* 5 (4), 9–17.
Piske, T., MacKay, I. and Flege, J. (2001) Factors affecting degree of foreign accent in an L2: A review. *Journal of Phonetics* 29, 191–215.
Pitts, M., White, H. and Krashen, S. (1989) Acquiring second language vocabulary through reading: A replication of the Clockwork Orange study using second language acquirers. *Reading in a Foreign Language* 5, 271–275.
Polat, N. and Mahalingappa, L. (2010) Gender differences in identity and acculturation patterns and L2 accent attainment. *Journal of Language, Identity and Education* 9 (1), 17–35.
Polka, L. and Werker, J. (1994) Developmental changes in perception of non-native vowel contrasts. *Journal of Experimental Psychology: Human Perception and Performance* 20, 421–435.
Pompino-Marschall, B. (1995) *Einführung in die Phonetik*. Berlin: de Gruyter.
Preckel, F., Goetz, T., Pekrun, R. and Kleine, M. (2008) Gender differences in gifted and average-ability students. *Gift. Child Q* 52, 146–159.
Price, G. (1984) *The Language of Britain*. London: Edward Arnold.
Price, M.L. (1991) The subjective experience of foreign language anxiety: Interviews with highly anxious students. In E. Horwitz and D. Young (eds) *Language Learning Anxiety: From Theory and Research to Classroom Implications* (pp. 101–108). Englewood Cliffs, NJ: Prentice Hall.
Purcell, E. and Suter, R. (1980) Predictors of pronunciation accuracy. *Language Learning* 30, 271–287.
Räisänen, C.A. (2000) *Learning and Teaching through English at the University of Jyvaskyla* (Project Report 4). Jyvaskyla: Jyvaskyla University Language Centre.
Räisänen, C.A. and Fortanet-Gómez, I. (2008b) The state of ESP teaching and learning in Western European higher education after Bologna. In I. Fortanet-Gómez and C. Räisänen (eds) *ESP in European Higher Education: Integrating Language and Content* (pp. 11–51); AILA Applied Linguistics Series 4. Amsterdam/Philadelphia, PA: John Benjamins.
Rallo Fabra, L. and Juan Garau, M. (2011) Assessing FL pronunciation in a semi-immersion setting: The effects of CLIL instruction on Spanish-Catalan learners' perceived comprehensibility and accentedness. *Póznan Studies in Contemporary Linguistics* 47 (1), 96–108.
Reid, J. (1999) *Learning Styles in the ESL/EFL Classroom*. Boston, MA: Heinle and Heinle.
Richard-Amato, P.A. (2003) *Making it Happen: From Interactive to Participatory Language Teaching: Theory and Practice*. White Plains, NY: Pearson Education.
Richter, K. (2016) Exploring English-medium instruction and pronunciation: What's in it for the students? in T. Psonder, A. Casey, D. Tatzl, A. Millward-Sadler and K. Meixner (eds) *Teaching ESP in Higher Education: Examples from Evidence-Based Practice. Proceedings of the 8th Austrian UAS Language Instructors' Conference* (pp. 40–48). Graz: FH Joanneum.
Richter, K. (2017). Researching tertiary EMI and pronunciation. A case study from Vienna. In J. Valcke and R. Wilkinson (eds) *Integrating Content and Language in*

Higher Education. Perspectives on Professional Practice (pp. 117–134). Frankfurt: Peter Lang.

Rigg, P. (2013) English as the Lingua Franca of Higher Education. *University World News*. See http://www.universityworldnews.com/article.php?story=20131121152245865 (accessed 15 May 2015).

Riney, T.J. and Flege, J.E. (1998) Changes over time in global foreign accent and liquid identifiability and accuracy. *Studies in Second Language Acquisition* 20, 213–244.

Roach, P. (1991) *English Phonetics and Phonology*. Cambridge: Cambridge University Press.

Roach, P. (2004) Illustrations of the IPA. British English: Received Pronunciation. *Journals of the International Phonetic Association* 34, 239–245.

Rockhill, K. (1993) Gender, language, and the politics of literacy. In B. Street (ed.) *Cross-Cultural Approaches to Literacy* (pp. 156–175). Cambridge: Cambridge University Press.

Rogier, D. (2012) The effects of English-medium instruction on language proficiency of students enrolled in higher education in the UAE. PhD thesis, University of Exeter.

Romova, Z., Smith, J. and Neville-Barton, P. (2008) Can I change the way I speak? – An exploration into pronunciation and fluency after three years of tertiary EAL study. Prospect. *An Australian Journal of TESOL* 23 (3), 12–23.

Rubio, D.F. and Lirola, M.M. (2010) English as a foreign language in the EU. *European Journal of Language Policy* 2 (1), 23–40.

Ruiz de Zarobe, Y. (2008) CLIL and foreign language learning: A longitudinal study in the Basque Country. *International CLIL Research Journal* 1 (1), 60–73.

Ruiz-Garrido, M. and Fortanet-Gómez, I. (2009) Needs analysis in a CLIL context: A transfer from ESP. In D. Marsh, P. Mehisto, D. Wolff, R. Aliaga, T. Asikainen, M. Frigols-Martin, S. Hughes and G. Langé (eds) *CLIL Practice: Perspectives from the Field* (pp. 179–188). Jyväskylä: CLIL Cascade Network (CCN) University of Jyväskylä.

Rumlich, D. (2016) *Evaluating Bilingual Education in Germany: CLIL Students' General English Proficiency, EFL Self-Concept and Interest*. Frankfurt: Peter Lang.

Saito, Y., Garza, T. and Horwitz, E. (1999) Foreign language reading anxiety. *The Modern Language Journal* 83, 202–218.

Saracaloğlu, A.S. (2000) The relation between traniee teachers' attitudes to foreign languages and their academic success. *Eğitim ve Bilim Dergisi* 254 (115), 65–72.

Scherer, G. and Wollmann, A. (1986) *Englische Phonetik und Phonologie*. Berlin: Erich Schmidt.

Schmidt, V. (2009) Sprachvarietäten: Kaffffe oder Kaffeeeh. *Die Presse* online. See http://diepresse.com/home/science/515792/Sprachvarietaeten_Kaffffe-oder-Kaffeeeh (accessed 26 December 2009).

Schneider, E., Burridge, K., Kortmann, B., Mesthrie, R. and Upton, C. (eds) (2004) *A Handbook of Varieties of English. Vol. 1: Phonology*. Berlin: Mouton de Gruyter.

Schouten, A. (2009) The critical period hypothesis: Support, challenge, and reconceptualization. *Colombia University* 9 (1), 1–16.

Schuderer, A. (2002) *Kontrastive Phonetik und Phonologie: suprasegmentale Merkmale*. See http://www.schuderer.net/Prosodies19.pdf (accessed 20 May 2015).

SchuG. Schulunterrichtsgesetz. See https://www.jusline.at/Schulunterrichtsgesetz_(SchUG).html (accessed 14 May 2014).

Schumann, J.H. (1975) Affective factors and the problem of age in second language acquisition. *Language Learning* 25, 205–235.

Schumann, J.H. (1976) Second language acquisition research: Getting a more global look at the learner. In H. Brown (ed.) *Papers in Second Language Acquisition, Language Learning* (pp. 135–1443). Special Issue 4. Ann Arbor, MI: Michigan State University.

Schumann, J.H. (1978) Social and psychological factors in second language acquisition. In J.C. Richards (ed.) *Understanding Second and Foreign Language Learning* (pp. 163–178). Rowley, MA: Newbury House Publishers.

Schumann, J. H. (1986). Research on the acculturation model for second language acquisition. *Journal of Multilingual and Multicultural Development* 7 (5), 379–392.

Schumann, J.H. (1990) Extending the scope of the acculturation/pidginization model to include cognition. *TESOL Quarterly* 24, 667–684.

Schumann, J.H. (1997) *The Neurobiology of Affect in Language. Supplement to Language Learning*. Malden, MA: Blackwell.

Scott, J. and Huskisson, E. (1976) Graphic representation of pain. *Pain* 2, 175–184.

Scovel, T. (1969) Foreign accents, language acquisition, and cerebral dominance. *Language Learning* 19 (3 and 4), 245–253.

Scovel, T. (1978) The effect of affect on foreign language learning: a review of the anxiety research. *Language Learning* 28, 129–142.

Scovel, T. (1988) *A Time to Speak: A Psycholinguistic Inquiry into the Critical Period for Human Speech*. New York: Newbury House/Harper and Row.

Scovel, T. (2000) A critical review of the critical period research. *Annual Review of Applied Linguistics* 20, 213–223.

Segalowitz, N., and Freed, B. (2004) Context, contact, and cognition in oral fluency acquisition: Learning Spanish in at-home and study abroad contexts. *Studies in Second Language Acquisition* 26, 173-200.

Seikkula-Leino, J. (2007) CLIL learning: Achievement levels and affective factors. *Language and Education* 21, 328–341.

Seliger, H., Krashen, S. and Ladefoged, P. (1975) Maturational constraints in the acquisition of second language accent. *Language Sciences* 36, 20–22.

Seliger, H.W. (1978) Implications of a multiple critical periods hypothesis for second language learning. In W. Ritchie (ed.) *Second Language Acquisition Research* (pp. 11–19). New York: Academic Press.

Selinker, L. (1969) Language transfer. *General Linguistics* 9 (2), 67–92.

Selinker, L. (1972) Interlanguage. *IRAL – International Review of Applied Linguistics in Language Teaching* 10 (3), 209–231.

Selinker, L. and Lakshmanan, U. (1992) Language transfer and fossilization: The multiple effects principle. In S. Gass and L. Selinker (eds) *Language Transfer in Language Learning* (pp. 197–216). Rowley, MA: Newbury House.

Selinker, L., Swain, M. and Dumas, G. (1975) The interlanguage hypothesis extended to children. *Language Learning* 25 (1), 139–152.

Serrano Lopez, S. (2009) Learning languages in study abroad and at home contexts: A critical review of comparative studies. *Porta Linguarum* 13 (2010), 149–163.

Shams, A.N. (2005) The use of computerized pronunciation practice in the reduction of foreign language classroom anxiety (Doctoral dissertation, Florida State University).

Shams, A.N. (2006) The use of computerized pronunciation practice in the reduction of foreign language classroom anxiety. PhD thesis, Florida State University College of Arts and Sciences.

Shehadeh, A. (1991) Comprehension and performance in second language acquisition: A study of second language learners' production of modified comprehensible output. PhD thesis, University of Durham.

Shumin, K. (1997) Factors to consider: Developing adult EFL students' speaking abilities. *Forum Online* 25 (3), 8–18.

Silva-Corvalan, C. (2001) *Sociolingüística y pragmática*. Washington, DC: Georgetown University Press.

Simpson, A.P. (1998) Phonetische Datenbanken des Deutschen in der empirischen Sprachforschung und der phonologischen Theoriebildung. *Arbeitsberichte des Instituts für Phonetik und digitale Sprachverarbeitung der Universität Kiel* (AIPUK) 33.

Simpson, A. (2003) Possible articulatory reasons for sex-specific differences in vowel duration. *Proceedings of the 6th International Seminar on Speech Production*, Sydney. See http://www.personal.uni-jena.de/~x1siad/papers/issp03proc.pdf (accessed 16 April 2015).

Simpson, A. and Ericsdotter, C. (2003) Sex-specific durational differences in English and Swedish. *Proceedings of XVth IVPhS* (pp. 1111–1116). Barcelona 39 August.

Singleton, D. (1981) *Age as a Factor in Second Language Acquisition: A Review of Some Recent Research* (CLCS Occasional Paper 3). Dublin: Trinity College, Centre for Language and Communciation Studies. See https://files.eric.ed.gov/fulltext/ED217712.pdf (accessed 20 May 2016).

Singleton, D. (1989) *Language Acquisition: The Age Factor*. Clevedon: Multilingual Matters.

Singleton, D. (2001) Age and second language acquisition. *Annual Review of Applied Linguistics* 21, 77–91.

Singleton, D. (2005) The critical period hypothesis: A coat of many colours. *International Review of Applied Linguistics* 43, 269–285.

Singleton, D. and Ryan, L. (2004) *Language Acquisition: The Age Factor*. Clevedon: Multilingual Matters.

Skutnabb-Kangas, T. (2001) The globalization of (educational) language rights. *International Review of Education* 47 (3–4), 201–219.

Slevc, L.R. and Miyake, A. (2006) Individual differences in second language proficiency: Does music ability matter? *Psychological Science* 17, 675–681.

Smit, U. (2002) The interaction of motivation and achievement in advanced EFL pronunciation learners. *IRAL International Review of Applied Linguistics for Language Teaching* 40 (2), 89–115.

Smit, U. (2003) English as lingua franca (ELF) as medium of learning in a hotel management educational program: An applied linguistic approach. *VIEWS Vienna English Working Papers* 12 (2), 40–74.

Smit, U. (2010) *English as a Lingua Franca in Higher Education: A Longitudinal Study of Classroom Discourse*. Berlin/New York: De Gruyter Mouton.

Smit, U. and Dalton-Puffer, C. (2000) Motivational patterns in advanced EFL pronunciation learners. *IRAL International Review of Applied Linguistics for Language Teaching* 38 (3–4), 229–246.

Smit, U. and Dafouz, E. (eds) (2012) Integrating content and language in higher education: An introduction to English-medium policies, conceptual issues and research practices across Europe. *AILA Review* 25, 1–12.

Smith, R. (2005) The role of fine phonetic detail in word segmentation. PhD thesis, University of Cambridge.

Snow, C.E. (1992) Perspectives on second-language development: Implications for bilingual education. *Educational Researcher* 21 (2), 16–19.

Snow, C.E. and Hoefnagel-Hohle, M. (1977) Age differences in the pronunciation of foreign sounds. *Language and Speech* 20, 357–365.

Southwood, M. and Flege, J. (1999) Scaling foreign accent: Direct magnitude versus interval scaling. *Clinical Linguistics & Phonetics* 13, 335–349.

Spolsky, B. (1989) *Conditions for Second Language Learning. Introduction to a General Theory*. Oxford: Oxford University Press.

Spolsky, B. (2000) Language motivation revisited. *Applied Linguistics* 21 (2), 157–169.

Stephenson Wilson, J. (2006) Anxiety in learning English as a foreign language: Its associations with student variables, with overall proficiency, and with performance on an oral test. PhD thesis, Universidad de Granada.

Stern, H.H. (1983) *Fundamental Concepts of Language Teaching*. Oxford: Oxford University Press.

Stokes, J. (2001) Factors in the acquisition of Spanish pronunciation. *International Review of Applied Linguistics* 131–132, 63–68.

Sundqvist, P. (2009) Extramural English matters: Out-of-school English and its impact on Swedish ninth graders' oral proficiency and vocabulary. PhD dissertation, Karlstad University. See https://www.skolverket.se/skolutveckling/forskning/amnen-omraden/it-i-skolan/elevers-anvandning/extramural-english-1.141614 (accessed 6 June 2016).

Suter, R.W. (1976) Predictors of pronunciation accuracy in second language learning. *Language Learning* 26, 233–253.

Suter, R.W. and Purcell, E.T. (1980) Predictors of pronunciation accuracy: A re-examination. *Language Learning* 30, 271–287.

Swain, M. (1985) Communicative competence: Some roles of comprehensible input and comprehensible output in its development. In S.M. Gass and C. Madden (eds) *Input in Second Language Acquisition* (pp. 235–253). Rowley, MA: Newbury House.

Swain, M. (1993) The output hypothesis: Just speaking and writing aren't enough. *The Canadian Modern Language Review* 50, 158–164.

Swain, M. (1995) Three functions of output in second language learning. In G. Cook and B. Seidlhofer (eds) *For H.G. Widdowson: Principles and Practice in the Study of Language* (pp. 125–144). Oxford: Oxford University Press.

Swain, M. (1996) Discovering successful second language teaching strategies and teaching strategies and practices: From program evaluation to classroom experimentation. *Journal of Multilingual and Multicultural Development* 17, 89–104.

Swain, M. and Lapkin, S. (1995) Problems in output and the cognitive processes they generate: A step towards second language learning. *Applied Linguistics* 16 (3), 371–391.

Swales, J. (1997) English as Tyrannosaurus rex. *World Englishes* 16 (3), 373–382.

Swan, M. and Smith, B. (eds) (2001) *Learner English: A Teacher's Guide to Interference and Other Problems* (9th edn). Cambridge: Cambridge University Press.

Sylvén, L. (2004) Teaching in English or English teaching? On the effects of content and language integrated learning on Swedish learners' incidental vocabulary acquisition. PhD thesis, Göteborg University.

Szyszka, M. (2011) Foreign language anxiety and self-perceived English pronunciation competence. *Studies in Second Language Learning and Teaching* 1 (2), 283–300.

Taft, R. (2015) Are international internships on the rise? Go overseas. See http://www.gooverseas.com/blog/are-international-internships-on-the-rise(accessed 24 February 2016).

Tahta, S., Wood, M. and Loewenthal, K. (1981a) Foreign accents: Factors relating to transfer of accent from the first language to the second language. *Language and Speech* 24, 265–272.

Tahta, S., Wood, M. and Loewenthal, K. (1981b) Age changes in the ability to replicate foreign pronunciation and intonation. *Language and Speech* 24, 363–372.

Tarone, E. (1984) The role of the syllable in interlanguage phonology. In S. Eliasson (ed.) *Studies in Descriptive Linguistics: Theoretical Issues in Contrastive Phonology* (pp. 63–72). Heidelberg: Julius Groos Verlag.

Tarone, E. and Swain, M. (1995) A sociolinguistic perspective on second-language use in immersion classrooms. *Modern Language Journal* 79, 166–178.

Tatzl, D. (2011) English-medium masters' programmes at an Austrian university of applied sciences: attitudes, experiences and challenges. *Journal of English for Academic Purposes* 10 (4), 252–270.

Tatzl, D. (2012) Pronunciation Problems in Aeronautical Engineering Students' Presentations. *ICT for language learning*. 5th edition. Accessed 26 June 2013. https://conference.pixel-online.net/conferences/ICT4LL2012/common/download/Paper_pdf/178-LSP07-FP-Tatzl-ICT2012.pdf

Thompson, I. (1991) Foreign accents revisited: The English pronunciation of Russian immigrants. *Language Learning* 41, 177–204.

Tillmann, B., Janata, P. and Bharucha, J. (2003) Activation of the inferior frontal cortex in musical priming. *Cognitive Brain Research* 16, 145–161.

Todeva, E. (1992) On fossilization in SLA theory. *Papers in Applied Linguistics* 7, 216–254.

Trubetzkoy, N.S. (1969) *Principles of Phonology*. Berkeley, CA: University of California Press.
Trudgill, P. (1974) *The Social Differentiation of English in Norwich*. Cambridge: Cambridge University Press.
Unterberger, B. (2014) English-medium degree programmes in Austrian tertiary business studies: Policies and programme design. PhD thesis, University of Vienna.
Unterberger, B. and Wilhelmer, N. (2011) English-medium education in economics and business studies: Capturing the status quo at Austrian universities. *ITL – International Journal of Applied Linguistics* 161, 90–110.
Ushioda, E. (1993) *Acculturation Theory and Linguistic Fossilization: A Comparative Case Study* (CLCS Occasional Paper No. 37). Dublin: Centre for Language and Communication Studies.
Uskoski, O. (2011) Playing video games: A waste of time... or not? Exploring the connection between playing video games and English grades. PhD thesis, University of Helsinki, Department of Modern Languages.
Valcke, J. and Pavon, V. (2015) A comparative study on the use of pronunciation strategies for highlighting information in university lectures. In R. Wilkinson and M. Walsh (eds) *Integrating Content and Language in Higher Education: From Theory to Practice Selected Papers from the 2013 ICLHE Conference* (pp. 323–341). Frankfurt: Peter Lang.
Valcke, J. and Wilkinson, R. (eds) (2017) *Integrating Content and Language in Higher Education. Perspectives on Professional Practice*. Frankfurt: Peter Lang.
van Leeuwen, C. (2007) Preface. In R. Wilkinson and V. Zegers (eds) *Researching Content and Language Integration in Higher Education* (pp. 7–9). Nijmegen: Valkhof Pers.
VanPatten, B. and Glass, W. (1999) Grammar learning as a source of language anxiety: A discussion. In D.J. Young (ed.) *Affect in Foreign Language and Second Language Learning* (pp. 89–105). New York: McGraw Hill.
Varchmin, B. (2008) Effects of Content and Language Integrated Learning (CLIL) on final devoicing and the pronunciation of dental fricatives. MA thesis, Goldsmiths College–University of London.
Varonis, E.M. and Gass, S. (1981) The comprehensibility of non-native speech. *Studies in Second Language Acquisition* 4, 114–136.
Vigil, N.A. and Oller, J.W. (1976) Rule fossilization: A tentative model. *Language Learning* 26 (2), 281–295.
Vygotsky, L.S. (1978) *Mind in Society: The Development of Higher Psychological Processes*. Cambridge, MA: Harvard University Press.
Wächter, B. and Maiworm, F. (2008) *English-Taught Programmes in European Higher Education: The Picture in 2007* (ACA Papers on International Cooperation in Education). Bonn: Lemmens.
Wächter, B. and Maiworm, F. (eds) (2014) *English-Taught Programmes in European Higher Education: The State of Play in 2014*. Bonn: Lemmens.
Walker, R. (2010) *Teaching the Pronunciation of English as a Lingua Franca*. Oxford: Oxford University Press.
Watt, D. and Allen, W. (2003) Illustrations of the IPA. Tynside English. *Journal of the International Phonetic Association* 33, 267–271.
Wei, X. (2008) Implication of IL fossilization in second language acquisition. *English Language Teaching* 1 (1), 127–131.
Weiss, L. (1970) Auditory discrimination and pronunciation of French vowel phonemes. PhD thesis, Stanford University.
Wells, J.C. (1982) *Accents of English-Beyond the British Isles*. Cambridge: Cambridge University Press.
Whiteside, S. (1995) Temporal-based speaker sex differences in read speech: A sociophonetic approach. In K. Elenius and P. Braderud (eds) *Proceedings of the XIIIth*

International Congress of Phonetic Sciences ICPhS 95 (pp. 516–519). Stockholm: Congress organisers at KTH and Stockholm University.
Whiteside, S. (1996) Temporal-based acoustic-phonetic patterns in read speech: Some evidence for speaker sex differences. *Journal of the International Phonetic Association* 26 (1), 23–40.
Widdowson, H. (1990) *Aspects of Language Teaching*. Oxford: Oxford University Press.
Widdowson, H. (1994) The ownership of English. *TESOL Quarterly* 28 (2), 377–389.
Wieden, W. and Nemser, W. (1991) *The Pronunciation of English in Austria*. Tübingen: Gunter Narr Verlag.
Wiesinger, P. (2000) Nation und Sprache in Österreich. In A. Gard (ed.) *Nation und Sprache. Die Diskussion ihres Verhältnisses in Geschichte und Gegenwart* (pp. 525–562). Berlin/New York: de Gruyter.
Wilkinson, R. (2008a) English-taught study courses: Principles and practice. In C. Gnutzmann (ed.) *English in Academia. Catalyst or Barrier?* (pp. 169–182). Tübingen: Gunter Narr Verlag.
Wilkinson, R. (2011) If all business education were in English, would it matter? *ITL – International Journal of Applied Linguistics* 161, 111–123.
Wilkinson, R. and Walsh, M. (eds) (2015) *Integrating Content and Language in Higher Education from Theory to Practice Selected Papers from the 2013 ICLHE Conference*. Frankfurt am Main: Peter Lang.
Williams, M., Burden, L. and Lanvers, U. (2002) French is the language of love and stuff: Students' perceptions of issues related to motivation in learning a foreign language. *British Educational Research Journal* 28, 503–528.
Woodrow, L. (2006) Anxiety and speaking English as a second language. *Regional Language Centre (RELC) Journal* 37, 308–328.
Wrembel, M. (2010) L2-accented speech in L3 production. *International Journal of Multilingualism* 7 (1), 75–90.
Wright, M. (1999) Influences on learner attitude towards foreign language and culture. *Educational Research* 41 (2), 197–208.
Wu, M. (2008) Beliefs about language learning of Chinese ESL learners undertaking vocational education in Hong Kong. *New Horizons in Education* 56 (2), 1–17.
Xi, X. and Mollaun, P. (2011) Using raters from India to score a large-scale speaking test. *Language Learning* 61 (4), 1222–1255.
Young, D.J. (1991) Creating a low-anxiety classroom environment: What does the language anxiety research suggest? *Modern Language Journal* 75, 425–439.
Young-Scholten, M. (1995) The negative effects of 'positive' evidence on L2 phonology. In L. Eubank, L. Selinker and M. Smith (eds) *The Current State of Interlanguage: Studies in Honor of William E. Rutherford* (pp. 107–123). Amsterdam: John Benjamins.
Yu, H. (2005) Recognizing sloppy speech. PhD thesis, Carnegie Mellon University.
Zafar, M. (2009) Monitoring the monitor. A critique of Krashen's five hypotheses. *The Dhaka University Journal of Linguistics* 2 (4), 139–146.
Zhang, Y. and Wang, Y. (2007) Neural plasticity in speech acquisition and learning. *Bilingualism: Language and Cognition* 10 (2), 147–160.
Zheng, Y. (2010) Chinese university students' motivation, anxiety, global awareness, linguistic confidence, and English test performance. PhD thesis, Queen's University, Canada.
Zydatiß, W. (2007a) Bilingualer Fachunterricht in Deutschland: eine Bilanz. *Fremdsprachen Lehren und Lernen* 36, 8–25.
Zydatiß, W. (2007b) *Deutsch-Englische Züge in Berlin (DEZIBEL)*. Frankfurt am Main: Peter Lang.

Index

Achievement 12, 30, 44, 54, 76, 86–90, 93, 96, 102, 104, 109
Adjunct ESP 16
Affective Filter Hypothesis 31, 32
Affordances 60
Age effects 6, 41–60, 101
Age of onset of learning (AOL) 25, 86, 100, 105, 120, 121
Aptitude 41, 45, 48, 65, 83, 102, 103, 104
Approximation 37, 57, 139
Assimilation 38, 41, 51, 52, 54, 90, 91
Attainment 12, 44, 48, 49, 54, 56, 58, 70, 74, 75, 82, 84, 86, 97, 106, 107
Attitude 7, 13, 41, 82, 84–86, 90, 99, 100, 109, 110, 111, 113, 114, 115, 117, 118, 121, 122, 154, 160
Austrian accent in English 7, 10–13, 70–71, 130–159

Bilingual programme 2, 3, 4, 5, 17, 23, 25, 26, 47, 72, 73, 75, 81, 90, 124, 126–129, 154, 160–161
Bologna Declaration 18, 20, 21

Content-based learning (CBL) 14
Content and Language Integrated Learning (CLIL) 5, 14–16, 19, 28–32, 39, 61, 62–64, 74, 75, 122
Communicative strategies 34, 106
Comparative Analysis Hypothesis (CAH) 41, 43, 54–59
Comprehensibility 9, 12, 35, 37, 63, 66, 81, 158
Comprehensible input 29–35, 39–40, 104
Contrastive Analysis Hypothesis 41, 54, 149

Consonants 42, 51–52, 57, 100–101, 131–153
Critical Period Hypothesis 4, 6, 41, 43–54
Curriculum 4, 5, 17, 18, 24, 25, 140, 157, 160

Degree of foreign accent 65–81, 82, 108, 111, 154, 156
Development 1, 2, 4, 5, 6, 10, 11, 12, 13, 18, 22, 27, 28, 30, 32, 35, 36, 37, 38, 41, 43, 45, 60, 62, 65, 66, 67, 70, 73, 74, 76, 77, 78, 80, 81, 83, 84, 90, 101, 104, 106, 109, 110, 111, 112, 113, 117, 121, 127, 129, 130–153, 154, 155, 156, 158, 160
Dialects 66
Dynamic systems theory 112

English for Academic Purposes (EAP) 14, 16, 17, 95
English for Specific Purposes (ESP) 2, 14, 16, 17, 24, 25, 72, 80, 154, 160
Educational linguistics 2, 12
EFL classroom 11, 13, 35, 153, 159
English as a Lingua Franca (ELF) 11, 14, 20, 158
Lecturers 17, 19, 24–25, 40, 62, 71, 72, 151, 156, 160
EMI programme 1, 6, 8, 14, 20–21, 26, 61, 160
English for Specific Purposes (ESP) 2, 14, 15–17, 24, 72, 80, 154, 160
European Union 2, 12, 107
Exchange semester 6, 81, 110–114, 117, 119, 123, 124, 125, 127, 128, 129, 158

Exposure 5, 17, 25, 28, 30, 32, 39, 41, 44, 45, 47, 48, 52, 60–64, 70, 75, 81, 82, 104–19, 110, 111, 113, 116–130, 140, 154–155, 158–160
Extramural English 108

Fluency 5, 7, 10, 30, 41, 45, 61, 62, 63, 64, 68, 70, 71, 97, 98, 106, 107, 108, 115, 118, 119, 120
Foreign accent 6, 10, 11–13, 27, 42–59, 65–81, 82, 86, 98, 105, 108, 111–112, 134, 154, 155–160
Formal pronunciation instruction 29, 41, 96–99
Fossilisation 58–59
Fricatives 64, 12, 133, 134, 136, 147

Gender 99–102, 30, 41, 68, 73, 82, 91, 92, 110, 111, 120, 146
General American 131, 155, 159
Globalization 19, 21, 89, 106, 128
Grammar 10, 41, 56, 58, 62, 63, 94, 115, 118, 119, 120

High achiever 112–117, 120
Higher education 3–7, 12, 14–26, 60, 62, 103, 158, 161

Integrating Content and Language in Higher Education (ICLHE) 4, 14, 16, 17
Identity 84–86, 88, 89, 90, 91, 136, 156
Immersion 33, 39, 105
Incidental learning 1, 5, 16, 25, 60
Input Hypothesis 27, 28–32, 34
Instrumental motivation 87, 88, 89. 99
Integrative motivation 87, 89–91
Intelligibility 12, 41, 63, 68, 81, 103, 158
Interaction 8, 27, 28, 31, 32–36, 37, 38, 40, 54, 60, 66, 87, 95, 104, 109, 111, 112, 116, 117, 156
Interaction Hypothesis IH 27, 28, 32, 34–36
Interlanguage 41, 43, 55, 56, 58–60
Interlanguage Hypothesis 41, 43, 58–60
Internationalization 1, 3, 11, 12, 18–21, 106, 128
Internship 6, 7, 8, 25, 81, 110, 111, 114, 116, 117, 119, 120, 121, 123, 124–126, 127, 128, 129, 152, 158, 160
Intonation 9, 42, 54, 70 96, 131, 134, 135, 137, 139, 140, 141

Labour market 2, 3
Language Acquisition Device LAD 30, 31
Language learning 1, 6, 10, 11, 13, 15, 16, 17, 25—81–87, 89, 92, 93, 94, 99, 107–108, 116, 117, 122, 154–157
Language Learning Anxiety 13, 31, 32, 34, 82, 90, 92–96, 111, 113, 119, 122, 129, 154, 155, 159
Language policy 2, 9, 106
Learning styles 83
Linking 131, 133, 135, 144, 145, 152, 153, 155, 160
Length of Residence (LOR) 41, 86
Low achiever 112, 117–120

Markedness Differential Hypothesis 57
Media exposure 105, 107, 108, 111, 113, 120, 123, 126–131, 158
Monitor Hypothesis 29, 30
Motivation 2, 5, 9, 13, 32, 41, 47, 48, 58, 59, 61, 75, 82, 83, 86–92, 93, 99, 100, 106, 110, 111, 113, 117, 121, 122, 129, 154, 155, 159, 160
Motivational Self System Model 88
Musicality 82, 102–104, 110, 111, 113, 121, 122, 129

Native Language Magnet Theory 42
Native speakers (NS) 3, 7, 11, 25, 32, 44, 46, 47, 50, 51, 52, 54, 57, 58, 59, 62, 63, 65, 69, 70, 71, 73, 75, 85, 99, 114, 119, 147, 154, 158
Natural Order Hypothesis 30
Negotiating meaning 32, 33, 34, 35, 36, 40, 81
Neural plasticity 44, 46, 48
Norm 11, 12, 42, 57, 136

Output Hypothesis 32, 33–34

Perception 7, 12, 33, 42, 46–54, 79–83, 90, 92, 95, 98, 102, 107, 114, 115, 120, 135, 137, 149, 153, 156

Perceptual assimilation model (PAM) 41, 49–53
Phonemes 29, 49, 51, 52, 54, 55, 97, 103, 132–134, 140–160
Phonological gains 62–65, 75, 108, 160
Picture story 66, 73, 113, 118, 145, 154
Pitch 42, 70, 103
Plosives 133, 136
Proficiency 5, 9–10, 24, 32, 34, 37, 43–48, 57, 61, 63, 75, 77, 80, 87, 90, 93, 96, 98, 101–103, 108–109, 117
Prominence 20, 140, 141
Pronunciation skills 1, 2, 4, 5, 10, 27, 31, 64–117, 154–158
Prosody 42, 97, 103, 139

Quality of input 5, 45, 47, 48, 64, 99
Quantity of input 5, 64

Rater 67–69, 70–77, 144, 146, 156, 157
Rating scale 67, 70
Received pronunciation (RP) 66, 97, 131–134
Respondents 72, 94, 110, 126, 131, 146, 151

Second language acquisition (SLA) 28, 29, 32, 35, 38, 56, 82
Secondary school (education) 1, 4, 5, 7, 15, 40, 61, 63, 64, 74, 75, 113, 118, 122, 131
Segmentals 42, 45, 56, 49, 55, 70, 90, 96, 97, 131–134, 136–137, 140, 142–145, 147–152, 155, 161
Self-assessment 78, 115–118, 119, 120–122
Schwa 100, 140, 143, 145
Singing 103, 104, 113, 116, 118
Socio-Cultural Theory SCT 27, 36–40
Speech learning model 41, 149
Stress pattern 56, 139, 141

Study-abroad (SA) 106, 123–124, 127–128, 160

Talent 2, 65, 75, 101, 103, 118, 129, 155
Target language 5, 7, 28, 29, 30, 32, 35, 39, 42, 43, 47, 54–56, 58, 70, 82, 94, 104, 106, 108, 110, 111, 122, 127, 128, 130, 133, 140, 148, 156, 158
Tertiary education (Higher education) 1, 4, 6, 7, 14–26, 60–61, 98, 116, 156, 158
The North Wind and the Sun 66, 68, 73, 75, 143, 145, 152, 154
Typological markedness 57

Ultimate attainment 12, 48–49, 56, 58, 70, 74, 75, 82, 86, 97
University of Applied Sciences (UAS) 1–8, 13, 17, 23–26, 65–81, 104, 109–129, 144–153, 154, 156–160

Variables 2, 10, 13, 29, 30, 38 ,40, 41, 71, 82, 83, 84–110, 111, 112, 113, 121, 122, 123, 127, 129, 130, 160
Variation 10, 30, 41, 49, 57, 58, 82, 103, 109, 136
Visual Analogue Scale (VAS) 68
Vocabulary 5, 34, 41, 45, 46, 61, 63, 67, 103, 106, 108, 115, 118–120, 131
Vowels 42, 47–53, 100–101, 131–138, 140–148, 153

Weak forms 131, 134–135, 141, 145, 152, 153, 155
Word stress 56, 131, 134, 137, 139, 140, 145, 152

Zone of Proximal Development (ZDP) 36–37

For Product Safety Concerns and Information please contact our EU Authorised Representative:

Easy Access System Europe

Mustamäe tee 50

10621 Tallinn

Estonia

gpsr.requests@easproject.com